Modern marketing

Modern Marketing

Frank Jefkins
BSc(Econ), BA(Hons), MCAM, FIPR, FAIE, FLCC
ABC, MCIM

Second Edition

THE M & E HANDBOOK SERIES

Pitman Publishing
128 Long Acre, London WC2E 9AN

A Division of Longman Group UK Limited

First published 1983
Second edition 1989
Reprinted 1989, 1990
Reprinted in this format 1991 (twice)

© Frank Jefkins 1983, 1989

British Library Cataloguing in Publication Data
Jefkins, Frank
  Modern marketing. – 2nd ed.
  1. Marketing
  I. Title
  658.8

ISBN 0 7121 1023 2

Founding Editor: P.W.D. Redmond

Printed and bound in Singapore

Contents

Preface to the second edition   ix

1 Marketing defined   1
Development of marketing; Definition of marketing; Aspects of
marketing; Marketing in developing countries

2 Customer behaviour   15
What makes people buy?; Other influences; How, when, why and
where; Consumer sovereignty; Re-purchase and new products;
Shopping characteristics

3 The marketing mix   33
Introduction; Twenty-element marketing mix

4 Marketing research   66
Introduction; Forms and methods of research; Social grades and
socio-economic   groups;   Marketing   research   techniques;
Questionnaires

5 Packaging   85
Introduction; Essentials of packaging; Materials; Forms of packaging

6 Naming and branding   94
Origins of names; Different types of name; Creating a new name
today

7   Pricing   104

The economics of pricing; Four basic kinds of price; Price in relation to delivery; Other pricing considerations; Researching prices; Price and promotion; Legal aspects of pricing

8   Distribution   121

Aims of distribution; Modern developments in distribution methods; Other forms of distribution

9   Direct response marketing   132

Shopping without shops; The modern form of mail order; New users of direct response marketing; Reasons for trading and buying direct; Methods and media

10   The after-market   141

Introduction; After-market techniques

11   Point-of-sale material, sales promotion and dealer relations   149

Introduction and definition; Point-of-sale material; Sales promotion schemes; Encouraging dealers to stock up and sell

12   Advertising and the marketing mix   170

The role of advertising; The advertiser; The advertising agent; The media owner; Self-regulatory control of advertising

13   Creativity and media   191

Introduction; Creative skills; Above-the-line media; Below-the-line media; Media research

14   Public relations   214

Scope and importance; Definitions; Six-point PR planning model; PR and the marketing mix; PR department or PR consultancy?

15   Introduction to codes of practice and law   228

Codes of practice; Law; Law of contract; Defamation; Copyright; Competitions; Trade descriptions

16   Industrial marketing   240
Products and customers; Sales staff; Marketing and product
research; Advertising; Public relations; Channels of distribution

17   Overseas marketing   249
Introduction; Developing an overseas market; Government and
other aid to exporters

18   The computer in marketing   260
Introduction; Some typical applications; Problems with computers

Appendices   270
1 Addresses of societies and educational organisations; 2 Marketing, advertising and public relations services; 3 Further reading; 4
Syllabus for the London Chamber of Commerce Higher Certificate
examination in marketing; 5 Examination technique;   6 Specimen
paper

Index   287

To
my daughter Valerie, my son-in-law Grant and my grandchildren,
Rebecca and Adam.

Preface to second edition

Modern marketing has been subject to many changes in recent years, both in the UK and overseas. These changes are reflected in the syllabuses and examination questions of international examining bodies such as the Chartered Institute of Marketing, The Communication, Advertising and Marketing Education Foundation, the London Chamber of Commerce and Industry and the Royal Society of Arts. Students, teachers and examiners have to be aware of these changes which range from new cross-frontier media like satellite television to bar coding of products and electronic devices used by cashiers in shops.

This *Handbook* is a new edition which discusses many of these developments. It also looks at marketing in a practical sense, trying to draw a balance between the practice of marketing in the Old and the New Worlds—the North and the South—recognising that what may work in Europe or North America may not necessarily work in Africa, the Middle East or Asia.

The avalanche of theories which fill so many marketing textbooks is avoided in favour of what actually happens in the marketing of goods and services to achieve the two complementary objectives, customer satisfaction and profitability. In relation to the marketing mix, public relations is shown as part of the whole strategy, and not merely as 'publicity' as suggested in the rather out-dated 4Ps formula. With the growth of 'marketing communications', this is a logical approach.

In the North, marketing has enjoyed the benefits of new technology. During the late 80s the media scene changed with the exodus from Fleet Street, the success of new newspapers like *The Independent*, the introduction of better quality typesetting and printing and colour into popular newspapers, the launch of more weekend magazines, and the emergence of Saturday as an important publishing and advertising day. With revolutionary government proposals for television and radio in the 90s, and the arrival of Sky and BSB in 1989, marketing has new media to consider. Meanwhile, direct response marketing has galloped ahead and new legislation such as the Financial Services Act has made the world of financial services a great user of 'selling without shops' techniques.

In the High Street, numerous speciality shops have arrived, serving various market segments and age groups, and the trend towards traffic-free shopping areas, plazas and malls has brought to Britain many forms of retailing found in the USA and other countries.

The developing or industrialising world has not been slow to borrow marketing ideas from the industrial countries, but the situation remains very different from that of the more prosperous North. It is not enough to use grand titles like marketing director for sales director when marketing is virtually unknown. Marketing requires facilities for marketing research (which are often absent), good distribution (which may be difficult due to distance, climate or poor transportation), the ability to advertise (which depends on both availability of media and ability to buy, read or receive media), and a substantial cash economy.

In many parts of the developing world 50 per cent of the population are too young to be in the market and have no purchasing power. The population triangle is so different from that in the North that conventional marketing is impossible. Yet, it is necessary for marketing techniques to be adapted to these countries, especially where there are enterprising indigenous industries and the selling of goods is not limited to the street market.

This *Handbook* tries to show marketing as an exciting and practical concept based on assessing the wants and needs of potential customers and then satisfying them profitably. Marketing techniques are brought together as they apply in different parts of the world, many of which the author has visited.

It is also hoped that this *Handbook* will encourage readers to observe and understand the marketing tactics which take place all around them in the media and the shops. As a customer, the reader is as much a part of the marketing scene as those who market the products and services he or she buys.

F.J.
1989

1
Marketing defined

Development of marketing

1. Selling. Before there were large urban populations, connecting transport systems, and mass-producing industries, *marketing*, in the sense of producing and selling at a profit what the market will buy, did not exist. Marketing is a comparatively modern concept. Until its adoption there was only *selling*, i.e. selling goods and services without first finding out what people really wanted to buy.

Goods, whether raw materials, fresh produce or made-up goods, were offered to likely buyers. They may have been brought from the countryside to the nearest town, or carried long distances by overland caravan or ship. For example, British wool, and later woollen cloth, were shipped to Europe and sold in the famous 'marts' in the Low Countries, now known as Belgium and the Netherlands. Similarly, grain was brought to these market centres from north-eastern Europe. The wealth of the East — spices and silks — was brought to Europe by caravan. In the Third World this process has hardly changed. As seen in the streets of Lagos or Kano, the market stall is a common shop. Before calendars became common in Nigeria, the days of the week were named after market days.

While some things have always been made to customers' requirements, the practice of finding markets for goods rather than producing goods for markets persisted until about fifty years ago. People caught fish, grew vegetables, made cloth and even built railways, hoping afterwards to find buyers or customers. Usually, there was a seller's market in which demand was greater than the ability to supply. The customer had little or no choice and the supplier could sell all his stock.

2. Arrival of marketing. The big change came with the greater choice and introduction of competition provided by modern production, transportation and distribution. It became economically necessary to produce or supply what people were most likely to buy, provided that could be done at a profit. This was very different from selling at a profit what people had to buy because there was no other choice. The modern business became marketing-oriented instead of sales-oriented.

This did not happen overnight, of course. In the early years of the twentieth century Henry Ford had introduced mass production, but he also made his famous sales offer of any colour motor car provided it was black.

Marketing, together with market research, was first developed in the USA, and American research companies such as A.C. Nielsen and Gallup came to Britain in the late 1930s. The Second World War intervened, however, and although marketing and market research progressed in the USA it was not until controls and rationing ended in the early 1950s that marketing techniques became widely adopted in Britain. By then there were many new things to market, e.g. plastics, detergents and holidays abroad, to name but a few. There was full employment and with money to spend people created a buyer's market to which suppliers had to respond with goods that satisfied demand. Motor cars were offered in a range of colours and a black one became a rarity.

Definition of marketing

3. Chartered Institute of Marketing definition. The Chartered Institute of Marketing defines marketing as: 'the management process responsible for identifying, anticipating and satisfying customer requirements profitably'. This definition is analysed in **4–7** below.

4. Marketing as a management process. Emphasis is placed on the *management* aspect of marketing, i.e. the responsibility of business management 'for identifying, anticipating and satisfying customer requirements profitably'.

The Chartered Institute of Marketing (CIM) has criticised British management for not being sufficiently marketing-oriented, for relying on existing products instead of discovering what the market wants or may need. Failure to satisfy the market led to the successful marketing of imported Japanese cars which had been unknown in Britain before 1969. It was not until the 1980s that BL's Metro and subsequent models showed what could happen when there was a combination of modern production and marketing-oriented management. The *marketing concept*, as crystallised in the IM definition, has not always entered into management philosophy. The quality of the product and the provision of after-sales services are essential requirements of successful marketing. They have been recognised by both German and Japanese management to the detriment of British home and export sales.

5. Professional marketing management. It follows that professional marketing management makes itself responsible for finding out precisely what the market needs or wants (which may be a product or service currently absent from the market but which people would buy if it was available). There is, however, a difference in marketing terminology (as distinct from lay usage) between a 'need' and a 'want', and this will be explained later (*see* 8).

Marketing management has developed from sales management, and one has to be careful to distinguish between the two. It has become fashionable to call selling (e.g. selling advertising media) 'marketing' although no marketing is involved (by law, a British commercial television company is forbidden to produce a pro–gramme solely to satisfy advertisers). Remember that marketing aims to satisfy wants and needs profitably, while salesmanship sells what there is to sell. It is interesting to note that the Chartered Institute of Marketing was originally the Institute of Sales Management, and that a more recent development has been the creation of a private Institute of Sales Management and Marketing with emphasis on salesmanship.

6. The marketing function. The three key words in the IM definition are *identifying, anticipating* and *satisfying.*

(*a*) *Identifying.* Various forms of marketing research, as described in **4**, can be used to find out what people want. It may be that they want something quite different from what is on the market at the present time. Manufacturers can assume that people want drinks in glass bottles only to find that they prefer them in plastic bottles or cans. Coca-Cola, for instance, had to move with the times and adopt cans and lightweight two-litre bottles although this meant losing the identification of the famous pinch-sided bottle. Too easily, a manufacturer can use a form of packaging which suits his convenience rather than that of the customer. A good example of this was a proposal by a motor car manufacturer to dispense with the spare wheel, but motorists did not accept the idea. In contrast, manufacturers in the poorer developing countries (such as Bangladesh) make it marketing policy to pack goods in containers which have a secondary after-use.

(*b*) *Anticipating.* Many 'new products' are in fact innovations, i.e. improvements on or adaptations of former products, and there are few original inventions. Very often, product changes or improvements .anticipate a need, such as cartons of fruit juice, standby air fares, foil pouches for tobacco, and higher interest rate schemes offered by building societies. The need for as yet unknown products is a different matter. The idea may look good to the design team, but the likely volume of take-up by the buying public may be difficult to assess. Great confidence may be needed in anticipating needs and in seeking to satisfy them with new products, especially when one considers that the vast majority of new products fail. Until the arrival of the compact camcorder, video cameras were slow to take off.

(*c*) *Satisfying.* Satisfying customer requirements involves design, testing, manufacturing, naming, pricing, packaging, distribution, performance and enjoyment. Satisfaction may go further and include a money-back or exchange guarantee, a guarantee of performance, availability of spare parts and their cost, servicing, accessories and all the post-sales responsibilities of what is known collectively as the 'after-market'. Satisfaction may embrace pleasure and pride, vanity and status as well as practical or rational factors such as value for money or good performance.

7. Profitability. Finally, the CIM definition refers to 'satisfying customer requirements *profitably*'. A business or trading organ-isation has to make a profit if it is to survive. Even a non-profitmaking charity or subsidised public service has to market its products or services and could be measured by its success in fulfilling its commitments.

An organisation operating on a business basis cannot afford to produce or supply goods or services unless there is a profit (either immediate or forecast) over costs. These costs may include interest on borrowed money, raw materials, labour (which may be as high as 70 per cent of the selling price), production and distribution (which embraces transport, trade discounts and advertising). Gross profit may be a small percentage of the return, and it will have to pay taxes, provide interest for shareholders, and permit reinvestment.

The above is true of industrialised nations where wages and salaries are high. The situation is different in other parts of the world where labour and raw material costs may be low and profits high. However, it should be remembered that without high incomes people in the North could not buy the vast range of goods and services available. It is also important to note that a small unit profit on a large volume of sales can be enormous, so that volume of sales will be a key to profitability (*see also* 12).

Aspects of marketing

8. Needs and Wants. *Needs* are the essentials of life, i.e. the staple economic requirements of food, clothes and shelter, however simple or sophisticated. These needs will vary from one society, class or climate to another. A tent may satisfy a nomad, and urban-dwellers will need flats and houses, but a king will need a palace. In cold climates there will be a demand for heating fuels and central heating systems, but in hot climates the demand will be for air-conditioning. In recent decades, former luxuries such as central heating and air-conditioning have been transformed into needs. The demand for needs will depend on life-styles and living standards, and the market will grow as prosperity increases. It is said that the expansion of the brewing industry in Nigeria was a reflection of that country's growing prosperity in spite of the vagaries of the oil industry.

With the majority of people, including quite young people, coming within the cash economy, that is, with money to spend, there will be a demand for a huge volume of goods and wide choice between competing brands of similar goods. In less developed countries this will be less so. The population triangle (*see* 15) will be different in the South from that in the North. The North has an ageing population, whereas in developing countries perhaps 80 per cent of the people will be rural dwellers, and 50 per cent will be under fifteen years of age and have no purchasing money, not even pocket-money given them by their parents.

Consequently, needs will be different country by country. In the USA electrical domestic goods, e.g. refrigerators, were common much sooner than they were in Britain. Goods that were once luxuries have become necessities, as in the examples above of central heating and air-conditioning. Fifty years ago in Britain few houses were built with garages, so that in older urban areas today the streets at night are full of parked cars. A garage is a normal part of private housing (including flats) built today, and there may even be a double garage, or the owner may add a carport. The 'town house' has been developed, the house being built on top of a garage. Thus, a garage has become a modern need.

Wants are goods and services for which demand can be created only after they have been put on the market, like compact discs or home computers. People did not want to fly the Atlantic until pioneers like Alcock and Brown, Lindbergh and Amelia Earhart showed that it could be done. There had been some limited Atlantic air transportation such as the Graf Zeppelin flights to South America, while Lufthansa had catapulted mail planes from German ships approaching New York. It was, however, the flying of American bombers to Britain during the Second World War which showed the feasibility of transatlantic air travel and led to the development of commercial passenger flights after the war. In more recent years it has become possible for package tour operators to use their enterprise to satisfy substantial international air travel needs.

As the examples of central heating, air-conditioning, CDs, computers and air travel show, much of modern marketing is therefore to do with anticipating *wants*, i.e. 'customer requirements', as the CIM definition states, and converting them into *needs*.

9. Market theory. The terms *marketing concept* — which has been discussed so far — and *market theory* are often confused, but they describe two entirely different aspects of marketing. The first refers to the activity of marketing and the second to the place or market where goods are sold.

Market theory is about producing goods where it is most economic to do so. This may be determined by factors such as available expertise and finance which could be more important than, say, the proximity of raw materials. Japan has no raw materials, yet does have the skills and finance to be an industrial country and a major exporter able to maintain high living standards at home. Newsprint (paper made from wood-pulp) is produced in Scandinavia and North America, and even Russia buys American wheat; Asia excels in cotton goods; and Britain leads in banking, insurance and other financial services. The classic example of the market theory in operation is the American aircraft industry which enjoys a large home as well as overseas market, an advantage not enjoyed by British aircraft firms in spite of their pioneer achievements.

Therefore, market theory bears strongly on decisions to produce and market. Disasters have occurred because things have been made in the wrong place, such as the siting of part of the British motor industry in Scotland. Circumstances have changed, too, and while in the past it paid to locate industries close to the source of the heaviest raw materials it now pays to locate them near the sea if raw materials have to be imported. This has happened with steel in many parts of the world, with new steelworks being located on the coast.

10. Linkage. This term is used to describe the locating of industry so that it is conveniently supplied with materials and parts. This should not be confused with market theory (*see* 9) where it may be economic to produce things because of the existence of a domestic market, as in the case of the American aircraft industry. Simple examples of linkage are the existence of legal stationers close to law offices, or suppliers of materials and components in the vicinity of furniture makers.

11. Market centrality. This is similar to linkage but is concerned with retail sellers to the public. Shops of a kind, or sellers of goods of a kind, are located close together to form a common market where it is easy for people not only to find what they want to buy but also to compare competitive offers. Certain streets, towns or even countries have become known as specialised sources of supply, such as Hatton Garden in London for jewellery, Amsterdam for diamonds, and Switzerland for watches.

12. Marketing and profits. Profitability is a key part of the CIM definition of marketing, and it has been pointed out already in 7 above that profit may represent only a very small percentage of the return received in the form of the selling price. A company may adopt one of two philosophies regarding profit.

(*a*) *Maximising profits.* This concept calls for the rigorous trimming of costs, and can be brought about by using cheaper materials (e.g. plastics instead of metals), reducing labour costs (e.g. by introducing robotics), cutting out frills and generally economising. However, if this practice is taken to the extreme it can prove to be antisocial and therefore undesirable, leading to inferior products, unemployment and environmental damage. The more cheaply made product may be less durable, industrial relations may be impaired, and there can be disposal problems as, for example, with indestructible plastic containers. The company which seeks to maximise profits at the expense of society will court criticism, and its sales could suffer in the long run. Nevertheless, a lean and efficient company could be a social asset if an ailing industry is made profitable.

(*b*) *Satisficing.* In contrast to maximising profits there is the more humane and less greedy decision-making concept of *satisficing*, introduced by the American psychologist H.A. Simon. This suggests that a company might aim for satisfactory and likely results or achievements. The company would still make a profit, but it would not make drastic attempts to squeeze out the last drop of profit: it could instead choose to give the customer a more refined product or to be located in pleasant surroundings, even if more profit could be made by eliminating something or if it would be more economic to be sited elsewhere.

Some companies recognise that goodwill and a good reputation — in other words, good public relations — result from consideration for the customer rather than from cold-blooded profit-taking. Compare, for example, those international airlines which offer exceptional cabin service, good meals, free drinks and free headphones with those which do not bother to do so.

Marketing in developing countries

13. North and South. The world today is divided between the industrial societies of the West (or North as it is now known), which include not only those in Europe and North America but also Australia, New Zealand, Japan and South Africa, and the developing and underdeveloped countries of the Third World (now known as the South or the Group of Seventy–Seven). In between we have the newly industrialised countries (the NICs) such as Korea and Taiwan. Hong Kong and Singapore have considerable industry and wealth, while Nigeria — a large country containing a quarter of black Africa's population — has made great advances in spite of its relying too much on income from oil.

14. Marketing students. There are many students of marketing in the South, especially in such countries as Hong Kong, Indonesia, Kenya, Malaysia, Nigeria, Singapore, Trinidad and Zimbabwe. They may be perplexed by marketing theories and techniques which may seem remote from their experience and their country's requirements. Let us look at this dilemma more closely and consider some of the conditions which affect the application of marketing techniques.

15. Population triangles. A population triangle is seldom a true 'triangle' but a shape representing the number of people in each age group. In industrialised and urbanised countries of the North, where the extended family (all ages living together) has given way to the nuclear family (husband, wife and their children only), the number of children is less than in countries of the South. At the same time improved dietary and health conditions have extended life and there is an ageing population. The population triangle in the North therefore tends to show more people at the top of the triangle and less at the bottom, while in contrast the population triangle in the South shows more people (children) at the bottom (*see* Fig. 1.1).

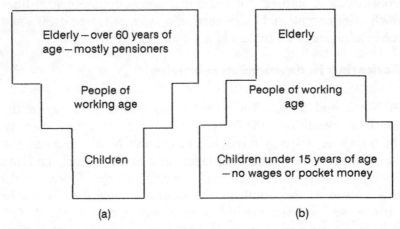

(a)   (b)

Figure 1.1 *Population triangles: (a) industrialised country of the North; (b) developing country of the South.*

As already stated in **8**, half the people in most developing countries are under fifteen years of age, earn no money, and are outside the sphere of marketing. Thus, a marketing problem in such countries is that the consumer market is far smaller than in an industrialised country where children have considerable pocket-money. In addition to this, in the poorer countries producing mostly primary (agricultural, extractive and fishery) products, a large number of people may be at subsistence level, providing mainly for themselves and having little or nothing to sell. They cannot buy, except perhaps very basic goods such as seed which they need to maintain their meagre production.

16. The cash economy. It may be that only 20 per cent of the population in a developing country, the educated urban élite plus those who work in industry, are in the market for consumer goods (foods, drinks, toiletries, pharmaceuticals, clothes and household goods) and consumer durables (domestic appliances, radios, televisions and motor cars). To a smaller degree, rural people who sell their produce will buy some of these goods but less frequently or in smaller quantities than do people in the North. There is no mass market, and mass production and competitive marketing will not exist, or at least will be on a much smaller scale than in the North. In fact, many of the consumer and consumer durable goods will be imported because it is uneconomic to produce locally for a limited market.

17. Does marketing exist in the South? It may be worth while to ask whether marketing exists in some developing countries, and whether for 'marketing' one should read 'selling'. Has it become fashionable to borrow the word marketing for operations and managerial titles when this is not justified?

(*a*) Gordon Draper of the University of the West Indies in Trinidad, has pointed out that in the Caribbean marketing does not exist, only selling and advertising.

(*b*) In his excellent book, *Modern Marketing for Nigeria* (Macmillan, 1981), Nonyelu G. Nwokoye of the Institute of Management and Technology, Enugu, discusses 'the reluctance of [Nigerian] merchants and other businessmen to enter manu-facturing'. Why? As Nwokoye explains: 'The Nigerian businessman operates on relatively short time horizons and wants quick profits to accrue from his business dealings, as in importation, supply contracting and transportation. In short, he has to learn the patient cultivation of profits.' In fact, he has yet to adopt marketing which requires research, development and investment in future profits.

The potential for progress from selling to marketing lies in the fact that few if any of the imported products were ever conceived for the overseas markets in which they are sold. There have been a few miracles of acceptability such as the reliable Peugeot, the ubiquitous Coke, and, surprisingly, Guinness. In contrast the Chinese *have* to produce themselves a typewriter to cope with hundreds of characters, but then the Chinese have been producing things for 5,000 years compared to Europe's mere 500.

(*c*) Marketing does not exist when the market is easily satisfied and will take up any goods which are sold to it, or when no effort is made to identify and anticipate customer requirements. In developing countries real marketing comes about only when the requirements of the market are investigated before goods are produced. This is very different from selling people goods which they think they need either because the goods are successful in their places of origin, or because people wish to emulate the living standards and life-styles of foreigners. These tastes may have been acquired by living abroad, perhaps as students.

(*d*) True marketing is also denied when lack of regulations makes it possible to dump products which would be illegal in their places of origin. Into this category come cigarettes with high tar content (which are cheaper to produce than those with low tar content), medicines which are regarded as dangerous (as banned in Bangladesh), and even some fairly harmless food products which British firms advertise abroad in terms which at home would be offences against the British Code of Advertising Practice. Some of the world's greatest names in the tobacco, pharmaceutical, food and other industries are guilty of these unethical practices. No one can pretend that such products are sold as a result of identifying, anticipating and satisfying customer requirements. They are merely sold profitably to overseas distributors who have no scruples about selling to ignorant or gullible buyers. They represent contradictions between marketing theory and practice.

18. Conditions necessary for marketing. There is, however, a definite place in developing countries for marketing, as defined here and described in succeeding chapters, when the following conditions permit.

(*a*) When goods are manufactured, or services are offered, by indigenous companies which do seek to find out what prospective customers want, and then endeavour to supply them profitably; or when goods are imported *after* the same principles have been applied. A camera, for example, is universally satisfying, even to the extent in some cases of carrying a world-wide guarantee. A motor car without air-conditioning rarely is.

(*b*) As marketing research methods become more common,

depending on the availability of reliable statistical and other information ranging from census figures to voters' lists.

(c) As the prosperity of the country improves and more people have purchasing power.

(d) As education becomes more universal and the population becomes more literate. This must also include the development of adult literacy classes, and discouragement of lost literacy among rural school–leavers.

(e) With the growth of media to carry advertisements to a wider public, which may also depend on literacy and purchasing power or electricity for television.

(f) With improved distribution as roads are built or improved and railway systems are made efficient.

(g) With improved communications, e.g. postal and telephone services.

19. Marketing situation today. The conditions listed in **18**, which are found in the most developed of the seventy–seven countries of the South today, are roughly those existing in Britain a hundred years ago. The important difference is that the products and services being offered belong to the present day! In these countries marketing has to leapfrog a century of evolution experienced more leisurely in Europe and North America, and this leap is required at a time when the more advanced countries of the North are already discarding the industrial age for the technologies of the microprocessor age. Perhaps the South can avoid some of the catching–up process by joining the rest of the world in its use of computers, satellites, quartz, information technology and other wonders of recent years. After all, the satellite has given Indonesians national television.

In many developing countries where multinationals are present the expatriate organisation may be restricted to production while distribution is handled by a national 'marketing' company. Marketing may be an optimistic word if the company is merely trading or selling and perhaps operating in a seller's market (*see* **1**). However, it is these trading companies which need to adopt marketing techniques as the conditions outlined in **18** become increasingly prevalent. If such companies are only 'supplying' or 'selling' they are a long way from marketing, and this applies even when foreign products such as motor cars are assembled in local plants.

Progress test 1

1. What is the difference between selling and marketing? **(1, 2)**
2. What is the Chartered Institute of Marketing definition of marketing? **(3)**
3. Explain the difference between a *need* and a *want*.. **(8)**
4. Explain what is meant by *market theory*. **(9)**
5. What is the difference between *maximising profits* and *satisficing*? **(12)**
6. What is a population triangle? **(15)**
7. What is the main difference between the population triangles of countries of the North and those of countries of the South? **(15)**
8. To what extent, if at all, does modern marketing exist in developing countries? **(17)**
9. What conditions are necessary for marketing to succeed in developing countries? **(18)**

2
Customer behaviour

What makes people buy?

1. Introduction. The buying process is not as simple as it may seem. People do not merely go to a shop and buy what they want. Motives, choices and decisions are involved, and they will be different for each individual (psychologically) and for each group (sociologically).

First, there must be *incentive* to buy. Second, the buyer must have the ability to buy, that is, have *purchasing power*. Third, the goods or services must be *available*.

(*a*) *Incentive* involves not only desire but also knowledge of the existence of the possible purchase. A person may suffer a pain but not know what to buy to relieve it, or wish to travel somewhere but not know how to get there. Marketing techniques, such as advertising, can provide the bridge between desire and satisfaction.

(*b*) *Purchasing power* will depend on income, credit facilities and decisions on what to buy with the money one has. This requires choices between alternatives, concentrating on essentials, making sacrifices for luxuries and even mortgaging future purchasing power by buying on credit by means of hire purchase or credit card.

(*c*) *Availability* implies knowledge about the distribution of goods or services, and again advertising can be a means of bringing the customer to the place of purchase.

The above is a simple analysis of what makes people buy but much depends on the individual motivation.

2. Role-playing. An important factor is the role the buyer is playing. In the course of a short time such as a day, or at various stages in his life, a person will play many roles, and buy according to the particular role he is playing at the time.

During a single day a man may be husband, father, commuter to and from work, employee, and voluntary worker in his spare time. Similarly, a woman may be wife, mother, housekeeper, cook and nurse, and perhaps commuter, employee and social worker too. The employee could himself be an employer if he engaged staff. Many roles will be played by a person in a lifetime and at different stages of that lifetime, such as student, trainee, parent, member of the Armed Forces, holder of an elected office, pensioner and perhaps invalid. In all these numerous positions and situations, all with varying needs, wants and responsibilities, he or she will be a customer required to make different buying decisions.

This should be remembered when thinking about satisfying customers, for in reality they are the seller's customers for only a portion of the time. They are multi-customers with many motives and forms of purchasing power, and varying knowledge of what and where things are available. The man who strikes a hard bargain in business may also refuse his child's demands yet squander money on his wife, mistress, home or person.

3. Effect of different circumstances. There can be subtle changes of buying behaviour without any distinct role-playing. A person may buy quite differently in different circumstances. He may, for example, eat different foods when away from home, whether on a shopping trip, on a business journey or on holiday, perhaps indulging in treats and fancies. There may be other purchases which are made, not because the customer is playing a different role but simply because the opportunity is presented. At home the same person may never ride in a taxi, buy an ice cream in the street, smoke a cigar, eat oysters, go to a theatre or visit an art gallery.

This chameleon-like nature of the customer, this liberal rather than conservative buying behaviour, is important to the marketing

strategy of some products and services, for example, transportation, hotels, catering and entertainments. Away from home,
customers are liable to buy unconventionally, more indulgently and
more extravagantly. They may be playing the role of holidaymaker
or business traveller, but they could be just temporarily enjoying
circumstances which permit different buying behaviour because
there is greater freedom of choice and the temptation to do
something different for a change.

Other influences

4. The Maslow hierarchy. American sociologists have reduced to a
handful the list of instincts originally introduced by the British
psychologist William McDougall (*see* 5) and applied them to
customer behaviour. In his *Motivation and Personality* (Harper and
Row, New York, 1954), A.M. Maslow first set out his own well-
known hierarchy of human needs. Maslow says there are two
essential and therefore primary needs and three secondary ones.
They are as follows:

   (*a*) *Primary:*
   (*i*)   basic physiological needs (relating to conditions affecting
the human body, e.g. hunger, sleep, temperature);
   (*ii*)   safety needs (self-protection against present and future
dangers);
   (*b*) *Secondary*
   (*i*)   the need for recognition, for love and belonging;
   (*ii*)   ego-satisfying needs (desire for self-esteem, self-
respect);
   (*iii*)   self-fulfilment needs (realisation of complete self, creativity). This need is felt and satisfied by relatively few.

NOTE: If the reader is confused by American and British writers
giving different meanings to the same words he should
understand the following. (1) Psychologists and sociologists both
invent words and give familiar words special meanings. It even
happens that psychologists and sociologists give different
meanings to the same word. So beware of the jargon of social
scientists. (2) American-English is not the same as the English

used in Britain. Different words, meanings, spellings and pronunciations occur on each side of the Atlantic. For example, an American housewife goes *marketing*, but a British housewife goes *shopping*. Americans refer to cookies, not biscuits; candies, not sweets; trash, not rubbish; truck, not lorry; and subway, not underground railway. (3) American books on marketing are often written in the ivory towers of universities and supported by philanthropic grants from industry. British books on marketing are usually written on the basis of practical experience, and they are written in the authors' spare time without any advance financial encouragement. Not surprisingly, American textbooks may contain theories which may be unrelated to reality, or to circumstances in other parts of the world including Europe.

5. McDougall's list of instincts and emotions. Let us then consider the original instincts and emotions as set out in William McDougall's much reprinted book, *Social Psychology* (first published in 1908).

INSTINCT	EMOTION
Flight	Fear
Repulsion	Disgust
Curiosity	Wonder
Pugnacity	Anger
Self–abasement	Subjection (shame)
Self–assertion	Elation (vanity)
Parental	Tender

In addition, McDougall defined sexual (or reproductive), gregarious, acquisitive and constructive instincts. In Britain, McDougall's inherent causes of behaviour have been related mainly to advertising in the sense of copy themes for advertisements. They do form basic customer behaviour, and McDougall's instincts and emotions are more searching than Maslow's later analysis of primary and secondary needs.

For example, the security benefits of banking, insurance and building societies satisfy the instinct of *flight* and the emotion of *fear*. Hygiene products– soaps, detergents and deodorants– satisfy the instinct of *repulsion* and the emotion of *disgust*. Many things, e.g. tourism, books and entertainments, may satisfy the instinct of *curiosity* and the emotion of *wonder*. We may assert ourselves and seek *elation* through purchase of various things ranging from training for professional examinations to fashion goods, jewellery and cosmetics. The *parental* instinct and *tender* emotion concern not only the purchase of babies' and children's goods but also support for charities such as Dr Barnardo's and the Save the Children Fund. The *gregarious* instinct is active in the appeal of the crowd at a sports gathering or of the audience in a theatre. We obey the *acquisitive* instinct when we collect things like books, cassettes, paintings, postage stamps, coins or antiques.

6. Threefold analysis of needs. Borrowing from the contributions of the sciences, it can be said that there are three sorts of fundamental wants or needs, these being:

(*a*) physical needs necessary to survival, namely food, clothes and shelter and the benefits of modern society such as medicines;

(*b*) psychological needs and wants which satisfy pleasure, e.g. a new hair-style, perfume, entertainment, holidays or a video cassette recorder;

(*c*) sociological needs and wants to do with our relations with other people, e.g. affection for others or the satisfaction of our own esteem, vanity and pride.

7. Perceived advantages and preferences. These have a connection with role-playing (*see* 2). The value of a product or service may differ according to individual attitudes and tastes (which may relate to environmental background), and here we see the place of role-playing again. It is easy to over-simplify the buying motives of the so-called mass market (with advertising in the mass media) and talk glibly about the 'ad-mass' when it consists of millions of individuals with a multitude of reasons for buying even such commonplace products as beer or bread.

How, when, why and where

8. Introduction. The London Chamber of Commerce Marketing syllabus requires students to understand how, when, why and where people buy. Since this examination is sat throughout the world the examiners will accept that the answers to such questions will reflect a variety of local conditions. However, some of the reasons are universal, for people are people wherever they may live.

9. How do people buy? Buying and selling is an exchange system, both sides making a surrender of something of value to them. A planned parenthood adviser tried to persuade a Kenyan farmer of the value of family planning, but he retorted that the idea was nonsense since he could sell daughters for beer. This was actually a real-life sequence in a prize-winning film on family planning!

(a) *Forms of payment.* In different parts of the world many things can be exchanged for goods. Cattle may be kept for this purpose, and in Africa and some Pacific countries the cowrie shell was used as a medium of exchange. Nowadays the most common forms of money are paper money such as private notes, bank notes and cheques, and most recently plastic money in the shape of credit cards. Labour has also been a form of payment from the days of serfdom to indentured labour and share cropping.

(b) *Sources of money.* Money is distributed and gained in a surprisingly large number of ways, e.g. wages, salaries, commissions, bonuses, pocket-money, housekeeping money, loans, credit, subsidies, annuities, public assistance allowances, unemployment benefit, private allowances, dividends, profits and pensions. When planning a marketing campaign it could be important to know where purchasing monies are coming from and whether people have the ability to pay. For instance, one might need to be reluctant about accepting an order from a country with a bad external balance of payments which might make the country's central bank refuse or hold up export of funds. Or, as a bedding manufacturer discovered in the Caribbean, there was a big market for his products when there was a large increase in weddings following the carnival season.

(c) *Making payment easy.* There may be certain times of the year when purchases are more easily made, or there may be certain groups of people who are better able to spend. Bank marketing, for instance, has very cleverly sought out the university student who

is in receipt of grants. Building societies have pointed out to
people with credit balances at their banks that this money could
earn interest if it were temporarily placed in a building society
account. Direct response firms illustrate credit cards in their
advertisements to show how easily payment can be made, and to
seek business with those holding credit cards. Hotels will accept
credit cards when they will not accept cheques. Local evening
newspapers carry most advertising at the end of the week when
wages have been paid. These examples show the importance in
marketing of the question 'how, will, or can, customers pay?'
Making payment easy, making sure of payment and seeking out
those who are able to pay are essential to successful marketing.

10. When do people buy? The how and the when may be
interwoven as we have seen above, but there can be special times
or seasons when people buy, and the frequency of their purchases
may vary. Season and frequency will dictate when and how
promotion must have its impact. The following are some examples.

(a) *Products suitable for gifts* are likely to be bought at
Christmas, Easter and other festival times, or they may be sold at
holiday resorts where gifts may be bought for friends or at airports
where returning travellers may seek gifts to take home. The
marketing tactic is to tap as many gift-buying markets as possible.
This has been developed into the premium gift market with
products being bought commercially and used as incentives, prizes
and company gifts.

(b) *Household purchases such as furniture and carpets* are
bought perhaps only two or three times in a lifetime, for example,
when setting up house for the first time, when moving to another
house or when refurnishing.

(c) *Necessities such as food and drink* are bought on one or
more days a week depending on whether they are perishable and
whether they can be refrigerated or deep-frozen. Milk and bread
may be bought daily.

(d) *A motor car* may be bought every two or more years, and
peak buying times are usually in the spring and summer.

(e) *Summer holidays* are usually planned and booked in January
or February, but business travel is constant throughout the year,

and other holidays such as winter sports or winter breaks will be booked in the summer. The holiday and travel business has to try to find customers throughout the year.

From these five examples of very different products and services it will be seen that the marketing strategy has to contend with some very rigid consumer behaviour patterns. It may be necessary to change them if a factory is to run at full or even economic capacity throughout the year. For instance, there was a time when ice-cream was sold only in the summer and even this fluctuated if the weather was not hot, but ice-cream has now been converted into an all-year-round food.

11. Why do people buy? Knowing the reasons why people buy is important because this can affect elements of the marketing strategy such as price, packaging, retail or other means of distribution and selling, and particularly the advertising approach. Buying motives are related to:

(*a*) for whom the purchases are being made (*see* **12**); and
(*b*) influences or stimuli such as reputation, price and packaging (*see* **13**).

12. For whom are customers buying? The following are the main areas of purchasing.

(*a*) *For themselves.* Buyers may be satisfying their basic day-to-day needs, or they may be satisfying their greed, fears, pleasure or vanity. They may be obeying the acquisitive instinct, or the instinct of flight and the emotion of fear by taking out insurance for protection, or indulging the desire for pleasure, or bolstering their self-esteem (*see* **5**). Dr Ernst Dichter, exponent of motivation research (*see* **4.25**), has pointed out that people often buy to reward themselves for hard work or tedious lives, and with this reasoning he has justified the purchase of seemingly trivial things. This has been translated by astute advertisers into reasons for buying beer and chocolate. 'Give yourself a treat–you've earned it' is a familiar advertising ploy.

(*b*) *For their families.* Many of these purchases will be primary ones for the welfare of the family and will consist of the mass consumer goods to be found in the street market, supermarket or neighbourhood shop. Foods, drinks, toiletries, household goods and clothes will dominate such family purchases, although there will also be holidays and perhaps a 'family car'. Buying decisions in this area will concern several members of the family.

(c) *For others*. Some purchases will be for friends and relations, usually gifts and cards bought at Easter and Christmas or for weddings, birthdays, anniversaries and other special occasions.

(d) *For an employer*. Here, the buyer may buy on behalf of their organisation, either as a normal part of his or her duties or as a specialist buyer (as in a department store), or as a purchasing officer responsible for authorising company purchases.

In all four cases we see the role-playing status of the buyer (*see* **2**). The same person could fulfil all four roles at different times. He or she could buy a packet of cigarettes, a bag of groceries, a bunch of flowers and a suite of office furniture, all in the same day. In each case the buyer is subject to different motives and stimuli.

13. What stimuli influence purchases? The following are some examples.

(a) *Reputation*. The name of a manufacturer or supplier with a good corporate image may be sufficient to impress the buyer. If the name is unknown the buyer may be suspicious, or if the organisation has a poor reputation he will be careful. The criticism is often made that the price of a particular item is high because buyers are 'paying for the name'. However, a lot of customer satisfaction lies in paying for a reliable product. Unknown and lesser–known products (which *may* be just as good or better) have to earn their good name. Much effort and investment may be put into deserving a good reputation. That investment may, for instance, involve the cost of research, quality control, guarantees and after-sales service. Does the cheaper, less well-known product give the same satisfaction? It is generally true that we get what we pay for.

(b) *Recommendation*. Fortunate is the company whose products or services sell because they are recommended by customers and clients. This is better than advertising because the stimulus is independent. One of Britain's most successful companies has derived much of its success from the fact that 60 per cent of its business has come from recommendations. People are very willing to grumble and criticize, or to be proud of wise purchases. A company which is jealous of its reputation, and takes pains to earn recommendations, has learned the lesson that good marketing requires good public relations.

(c) *The package.* The dominant design or the practical convenience of the package may well induce purchase. This is particularly true in the supermarket where the excellence of the package can help sell the product off the shelf, or even encourage impulse buying. The latter may result from some sales promotion scheme such as a premium offer or a flash pack with a price-cut offer, or it could simply be a familiar pack which is easily spotted among the rival brands.

(d) *Price.* Even when price varies from shop to shop, goods may be placed in a particular price bracket as with pens, perfume or motor cars, and the stimulus may be that it is a bargain price, a modest price or an expensive one. Price is often one of the most compelling stimuli, for various reasons. Customers may want the most they can get for their money, judge value by price, or wish to impress because the cost has been high. One has only to look at advertisements and shop windows to see that price has a major sales appeal.

(e) *Promotion.* Advertising in all its forms, in the media and at the point-of-sale, stimulates sales by providing information and by being competitive. If there were no advertising, customers would be unaware of the existence or availability of the goods or services offered, nor would their interest be sustained and repeat purchases made. For fast-moving consumer goods (FMCGs) — mostly small unit ones — it is necessary to promote regular sales and to foster consumer or brand loyalty (*see also* 19).

A factory can sell its output economically and profitably only if sales continue at a target volume, and the price level will depend on this. The argument that prices could be reduced if less was spent on advertising is a fallacy. It is necessary to continue stimulating people to buy products, however well known or long established they may be. The customer's memory is short, and there are competitors to entice him to buy something else. All forms of promotion are therefore essential stimuli.

(f) *Place of purchase.* The supplier may also be an important stimulus. Goods may be bought because they are sold by certain stores, their reputation having a halo effect since the customer may have faith in the store's ability to choose and buy the best merchandise. The 'best' may be interpreted in terms of quality, price, reliability or range of choice. The place of purchase could be somewhere exciting such as a street market, like those of Lagos or in the old city of Kano, a floating market like that of Bangkok, or an oriental or Arab bazaar where wares are shouted, prices are haggled over and bargains struck. A cattle market, an auction at Sotheby's or the floor of a Stock Exchange are much the same. There can be an excitement in such buying, stimulating all manner of instinctive buying impulses.

14. Where people buy. Inevitably, in 13(f) we have touched on the stimulus of the place where sales and purchases are made; the *why* and the *where* often go together. The period since the Second World War has seen some important changes in the nature of distributive outlets. The street market, the shop, the department store and even the supermarket are giving way to variations and totally different means of buying, such as:

(a) traffic-free shopping precincts;
(b) shopping malls or plazas;
(c) discount stores;
(d) hypermarkets;
(e) cash-and-carry warehouses;
(f) direct response marketing;
(g) telemarketing;
(h) home selling and party selling;
(i) vending machines.

These and other developments are discussed in detail in 8.6 –18. They have created new consumer behaviour patterns with appeals to different stimuli such as convenience and time-saving. It can be a pleasure to shop at leisure, not having to struggle home loaded with heavy shopping, not having to go out in bad weather or wait for the infrequent bus, and not even requiring a purse full of money. A long time ago the American Gordon Selfridge opened up his store in London's Oxford Street and stimulated buyers to visit his store as a day's outing, putting pleasure into shopping. Life-styles have changed and now it is easier to enjoy shopping at home with a catalogue, the post, a television set and the telephone (*see also* **25** below and **18.9** and **10**).

Consumer sovereignty

15. The customer is king. Very relevant to 'satisfying customer requirements' (*see* **1, 3**) is the critical attitude of articulate customers whose views can influence the production, presentation and distribution of goods and services. This is represented by:

(*a*) *consumerism* (expressed through societies such as the Consumers' Association with its *Which?* reports which take up consumer interests);

(*b*) *hot line columns* in newspapers which report and perhaps investigate consumer complaints, and also television programmes such as Esther Rantzen's *That's Life* and *World in Action* reports.

(*c*) *consumer protection*, in the form of legislation to enforce production and sale of safe products, ensures that goods are correctly described and that they perform satisfactorily, and protects customers against unfair warranties and guarantees.

(*d*) *codes of practice*, such as the British Code of Practice as administered by the Advertising Standards Authority. Complaints about misleading advertisements are invited from the public, investigated and acted upon as necessary. This is an 'industry' code which has a double purpose: to protect the public from misleading advertising and to protect the good name of advertising.

There is considerable consumer protection legislation, plus the Office of Fair Trading, which has investigated unfair trading practices, and the Monopolies and Mergers Commission, which has studied and reported on alleged monopolies in production and marketing of items as varied as sparking plugs, pest control and contraceptives.

16. Naderism. In the USA Ralph Nader has created 'Naderism' which has produced some dramatic and effective investigations and criticisms of unsatisfactory products, such as unsafe American motor cars. Variously known as 'the crusading lawyer' and 'the citizen's champion', Nader's achievements include the Auto Safety Act, the Wholesome Meat Act, the Coal Mine Safety Act and the Air Pollution Act. His criticism of the poor welding of the Chevrolet Corvair caused a 93 per cent fall in sales and abandonment of the car. His attacks have continued into many other fields, e.g. potentially dangerous toys.

In 1989 Nader attacked the British legal system and its lack of juries in civil cases, and campaigned for changes to bring levels of compensation for victims of personal injury and accidents in line with American practice.

17. Environmental and international issues. War On Want, the magazine *New Internationalist*, Friends of the Earth and Greenpeace have also campaigned against antisocial marketing. Friends of the Earth demonstrated their criticism of pollution as a result of non-returnable plastic bottles by dumping a load outside the premises of Schweppes. The intention to put milk into plastic bottles was demolished by the assertion that in a year there would be enough discarded plastic milk bottles to reach the moon.

Re-purchase and new products

18. Habit buying. Reference was made in 13(e) to the use of promotional methods to maintain regular sales and brand loyalty. This is an aspect of customer behaviour that is worth separate consideration. It is almost a contradiction of freedom of choice, and yet it is essential for a business to have a hard core of regular customers. There will always be losses by wastage as a result of death, unemployment, loss of income, and different tastes at different ages; there will always be different or potential customers as new ones enter the market; but some products will be bought regularly for a lifetime.

Customer behaviour can sometimes be difficult to control. For instance, newspapers may be bought on the way to work, but how much more regular and permanent is the sale if the newspaper is delivered at home. A newspaper needs regular readers. The casual reader may not necessarily buy a rival newspaper; he may not buy one at all. Various devices, from free insurance to Bingo, have been used to encourage the placing of regular orders. The crossword has been one of the most persistent attractions.

Sales promotion schemes have been used to maintain brand loyalty for teas, coffees, breakfast cereals and cigarettes. Such schemes include cash tokens, premium offer items such as tableware, picture cards and gift coupons (*see* 10, **8 –22**).

Most of these methods are expensive, and counter-effective if there is intense competition. In the end, habit buying is best achieved through the excellence and popularity of the product. It is customer satisfaction that is the ultimate reason for habit buying, even if this has to be nurtured by reminder advertising.

Even more difficult is the maintenance of customer satisfaction and loyalty when the product is bought infrequently. When a product, such as a domestic appliance, is beginning to age and needs replacement, the satisfaction may be lessened by poorer performance and there may be the temptation to try something different next time. Consumer behaviour can be fickle; the customer may be seduced into buying another make. Part of the marketing strategy must be to maintain customer interest, and encourage re–purchase (*see also* **9**).

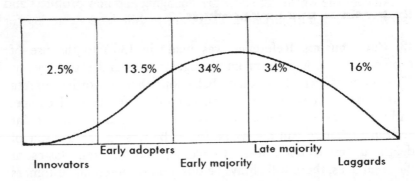

Figure 2.1 *Innovator or dispersion theory*

19. Innovator or dispersion theory. This theory is best demonstrated by the five-step dispersion model shown in Fig.2..1 There are some products which will not sell if promotion is aimed at the broad market. Acceptance depends on an enterprising person acting as an *innovator*. His confidence is then extended to others who copy him and so become *early adopters*. Their example is then followed by the *early majority adopters* after which come the *late majority adopters*. Eventually, the most conservative-minded adopt the idea or product and these late-comers are called the *laggards*.

This is a well-known theory which has been applied for more than a century to the introduction of new methods to farmers, whether it be McCormick's ploughs and combine harvesters in America's Midwest in the 1860s, a blackcurrant picker in Essex in the 1960s, or power farming in Nigeria in the 1980s (*see also* 12, 24(*i*)).

20. Changing life-styles. People tend to be conservative, clinging to the safety of the familiar, although the novelty of some products will attract the curious, and there are always the bold innovators who will experiment. Nevertheless, revolutions in buying behaviour do take place. There was a time when few people in developing countries would have set foot in an aeroplane, when Singaporeans would not have worn jeans, when Hausas would not have drunk beer or Hong Kong Chinese would not have travelled underground by train.

All over the world life-styles are changing and new products and services are being marketed. There are mobile banks catering for people who are learning that mattresses and savings can catch fire. Energy in the form of liquid gas is changing the cooking habits of villagers. Inland fish farms are changing diets. The Green Revolution is becoming a reality in African countries where urbanisation has broken down old systems of peasant farming.

21. Home-produced products. A problem when marketing home-produced goods in a developing country which has been used to imported goods is the suspicion local buyers may have that the home-produced product is inferior to the original imported one. This lack of faith, pride or credibility is common throughout developing countries, and it is a kind of inferiority complex which is not always justified. An example is the Barbados company Towels which produces excellent products, has achieved sufficient production to be able to export 80 per cent of its products to other Caribbean countries, yet still encounters this frustrating attitude.

22. Cognitive dissonance. We owe something to the foresight of the American psychologist Leon Festinger and his theory of *cognitive dissonance.* Beliefs can be rationalised and the new can replace the old because once a customer is converted to a new idea the new becomes traditional and the former belief is renounced. This is an interesting theory which finds reality in marketing. A person will swear he will never change a habit but, having changed it, will regard the old habit with distaste. People who said they would never ride in a train, motor car or aeroplane; take a holiday abroad or eat foreign food; buy a colour television set or a video cassette recorder; replace cassettes with compact discs; or buy a Japanese car or a British wine, have in fact been converted to doing so, and have been satisfied. More than that, they have become critical of what they used to prefer.

Cognitive dissonance is of relevance to the marketing of wants rather than needs and to the changing of customer behaviour. The latter process is known as *dissonance reduction*, or the removal of inconsistencies between human attitudes and behaviour. Consonance is achieved when satisfaction results from acceptance of the new idea or product, and the old idea or product is rejected as the weaker or inferior one.

Shopping characteristics

23. Types of goods. There are three principal types of goods found in shops, namely shopping goods, convenience goods and speciality goods.

(a) Shopping goods are those where the customer 'shops around', comparing items, prices and values in different shops. A person who hunts for price-cuts and special offers is known as a 'cherry-picker'.

(b) Convenience goods are those which are bought frequently, the staple goods which require little choice. They are also known as fast-moving consumer goods (FMCGs), and consist of the numerous popular brands found in supermarkets, as well as fresh fruit, vegetables, fish, milk and so on. The degree of satisfaction is not very high.

(c) *Speciality or durable goods* are ones which are bought only occasionally, and with great care so that the degree of satisfaction is high. The price is usually considerably higher than that of either shopping goods or convenience goods. Examples are furniture and furnishings, motor cars, jewellery, hi-fi, televisions, video cassette recorders and CD players, cameras, domestic appliances and garden equipment.

24. Location of shops. In general, people tend to buy food fairly locally, while durables may be bought at a town shopping centre and clothes at a city shopping centre. However, these facilities may not all be available and all purchases could be made either at an out-of-town shopping centre or in a city, and some might be obtained by direct response. Where there is a city shopping precinct it is often found that the furniture and clothing shops will be large premises in the centre while food shops such as bakers and butchers will occupy small premises on the perimeter.

There is also a tendency for shops of a kind to congregate in what are known as *congeries* or colonies of shops some of which, like London's Hatton Garden (jewellery) or Oxford Street (department stores), are world famous.

25. Hotelling's theory. There is, however, an interesting theory about the locational interdependence of competitive shops introduced by Harold Hotelling. This states that given an evenly distributed population (or number of shoppers) along a linear market (such as a street), and where transport costs per unit of distance are equal, two competing firms with identical products selling at the same price can position themselves to share the market. Hotelling's theory states that ultimately both firms will gravitate towards the centre of the market and will locate side by side. However, stability could also be achieved if they each located at an equal distance from the centre of the market, as in Fig.2.2. The theory can be very well demonstrated with two mobile salesmen such as ice-cream vendors, but it could be applied similarly to newsagents or chemists' shops.

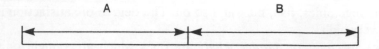

Figure 2.2 *Hotelling theory of stability in competition and locational interdependence. A and B are equal distance from centre of market.*

Progress test 2

1. What roles may an average person play in the course of a day? **(2)**
2. Describe the Maslow hierarchy. **(4)**
3. How do McDougall's flight, curiosity, parental, gregarious and acquisitive instincts affect customer behaviour towards certain products or services? **(5)**
4. What are physical needs? **(6)**
5. What are psychological needs? **(6)**
6. What are sociological needs? **(6)**
7. What is meant by the expression 'buying and selling is an exchange system'? **(9)**
8. How do special times and seasons affect the purchase of goods? **(10)**
9. For whom may customers buy? **(12)**
10. List some of the stimuli which encourage purchase. **(13)**
11. What are some of the recent developments in distribution methods? **(14)**
12. What is meant by 'consumer sovereignty'? **(15)**
13. Give an example of 'Naderism'. **(16)**
14. Explain the innovator theory. **(19)**
15. What is cognitive dissonance? **(22)**
16. How do convenience goods differ from speciality goods? **(23)**
17. What is a congerie? **(24)**
18. Explain the Hotelling theory of shop location. **(25)**

3

The marketing mix

Introduction

1. Definition. The *marketing mix*, or the marketing strategy, is the combination of elements necessary to the planning and execution of the total marketing operation. It should not be confused with the *product mix* which is the range of products or services a company may market, such as a range of blends of tea, or brands of cigarette, all produced by the same company (*see* 13).

2. Scope. The idea of the marketing mix was originally conceived by Professor Neil Borden of the Harvard Business School, but it was one that was limited to a small number of elements, e.g. the product, price, distribution, selling, advertising, promotion and market research. This was subsequently rationalised by E. Jerome McCarthy into the 'Four Ps': Product, Place, Price and Promotion. However, the 'Four Ps' is an unhappy oversimplification which loses sight of the chronological sequence (from conception of product to the after-market) which a proper understanding of the marketing mix requires. Moreover, the 'Four Ps', as developed by Philip Kotler, confuses publicity with promotion when he ignores public relations and does not realise or accept that public relations is not a form of advertising. We shall return to this in 13.

In this chapter an extended marketing mix will be described. The implications here are that PR is not a separate element in the marketing mix (like advertising) but is involved in most if not all of the elements because:

(*a*) they are forms of communication;
(*b*) they can provoke either goodwill or ill-will; and
(*c*) both marketing and PR are about human relations.

Consequently, a good marketing manager should be PR-minded throughout the whole strategy and operation, and not regard PR as an optional extra which he may or may not use.

Without stressing the PR aspect unduly, the extended marketing mix will now be analysed from the point of view of planning the total marketing programme from the creation of the product or service to the after-market. It should be remembered that in a large company with a diversity, or large range, of products or services many 'mixes' will be operating simultaneously and at different stages.

Twenty-element marketing mix

3. **The twenty elements.** In rough chronological order, although some may be considered simultaneously, these elements are:

(*a*) conception, invention, innovation or modification of product or service;
(*b*) the product life cycle;
(*c*) marketing research;
(*d*) naming and branding;
(*e*) product image;
(*f*) market segment;
(*g*) pricing;
(*h*) product mix, rationalisation and standardisation;
(*i*) packaging;
(*j*) distribution;
(*k*) sales force;
(*l*) market education;
(*m*) corporate and financial PR;
(*n*) industrial relations;
(*o*) test-marketing;
(*p*) advertising;
(*q*) advertising research;
(*r*) sales promotion;

(s) the after-market; and

(t) maintaining customer interest and loyalty.

4. Conception, invention, innovation, modification (3)(*a*)). Some products are totally new ideas, but many are improvements upon former products. By products we mean both the natural produce of the land and the sea, and manufactured goods. Thus we include both vegetables and the saucepans or pots to cook them in. By services we mean banking, insurance, travel, hotels, laundries, restaurants, hairdressing and professional services (which may, however, have certain limits on how or whether they may be promoted).

Associated with the introduction of new or modified products is *research and development* (R & D), and many companies will have laboratories, design offices and test houses where new products, including uses of new materials, will be subject to a continuous process of research and testing. Products such as pharmaceuticals are often expensive because the cost of years of research has to be recovered in the price in addition to the normal costs of production and distribution.

As we shall see in **5(*d*)**, some products obey a product life cycle process and have to be replaced at intervals. Their popularity may wane, or they may become outmoded by new developments. New models have to be created and made ready for production before the previous model loses sales altogether. Motor cars are a typical example; new models are ready to go into production before old models are withdrawn.

5. The product life cycle (3(*b*)). There are in fact a number of different product life cycles (PLCs), as follows:

(*a*) *The traditional or standard product life cycle* is shown in Fig. 3.1. The model describes six stages in the life of a product which may be extended over any time-scale, e.g. a few months for a fashion good or several years for a motor car. Following *development* of the product, it is launched in the *introduction* stage and then, as it gains acceptance and succeeds through the *growth* stage, the fourth stage of *maturity* is reached. Sales top out at the *saturation* point and then *decline* sets in.

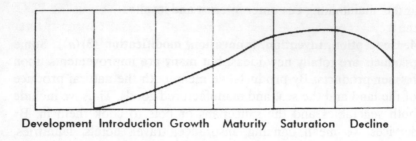

Development Introduction Growth Maturity Saturation Decline

Figure 3.1 *Standard product life cycle*

b) In contrast to (*a*), there are products which survive for decades and even centuries, suffering their ups and downs but never declining utterly and perhaps having an overall growth.

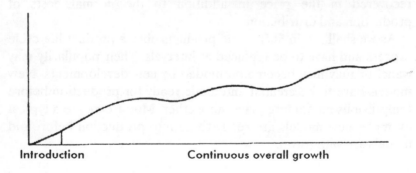

Introduction   Continuous overall growth

Figure 3.2 *Continuous product life cycle*

Figure 3.2 illustrates the model of the continuous product life cycle. Until the world runs out of coal this is the PLC of coal, spanning 2,000 years, while that of copper is even longer with an upsurge this century. On a shorter time-scale and less erratically, such a life cycle applies also to Guinness.

(*c*) There are also well-known products which have survived a long time because they have been rejuvenated by improved formulae, additives or merely the face-lift of a more modern package. These include toothpastes, remedies, coffees, detergents and confectionery. For these we have another version of the PLC, the *recycled product life cycle* (*see* Fig. 3.3). The chart suggests final decline, but the curve could continue on a switchback course if other improvements, for example sales promotion offers, were introduced. A number of fast-moving consumer goods behave like this under competitive conditions.

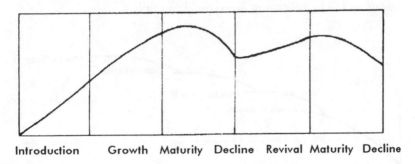

Introduction   Growth   Maturity   Decline   Revival   Maturity   Decline

Figure 3.3   *Recycled product life cycle*

(*d*) Yet another form of PLC is the *leapfrog effect product life cycle*. As explained in 4, these are consumer durable goods which have a history or life cycle of replacement models, and the chart looks like Fig. 3.4.

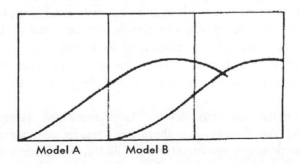

Model A   Model B

Figure 3.4   *Leapfrog effect product life cycle*

(*e*) Finally, there is perhaps the most interesting PLC, the *staircase effect product life cycle* (*see* Fig. 3.5) which fits the growth company or the one which diversifies to suit the times. It is another continuous one, but one which reflects great marketing ingenuity and resourcefulness. Here we have a product or service which never declines because new uses are introduced which propel the business from one cycle to another. In some cases one cycle may eliminate an earlier one, but all the market uses could be concurrent. The following are typical examples.

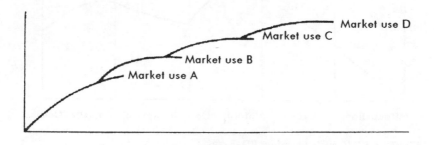

Figure 3.5 *Staircase effect product life cycle*

(*i*) *Nylon.* This is the most quoted example and since its first application we have seen nylon used for products as diverse as hosiery, textiles, carpets, parachutes, fishing nets, rope, tooth-brushes and motor-cycle wheels.

(*ii*) *Shipping and shipping lines.* In this case there has been diversification to meet new ideas and circumstances. Shipping lines have moved from sailing ships to paddle steamers and oil-burning steamers, liners have been converted to cruise ships, and new vessels such as car ferries, roll-on-roll-off ships, bulk carriers, cellular container ships, hovercraft and hydrofoils have been developed.

(*iii*) *Razors and razor blades.* Ever since the safety razor replaced the 'cut-throat' razor there has been intense competition between the principal manufacturers, Gillette, Wilkinson and more recently Schick. Various types of razors and blades have resulted, from safety razors with stroppers to twin-blades, ejector packs and throw-away razors.

(*iv*) *Financial services.* As a result of changes in financial and building society laws the staircase effect has occurred within financial services such as banks, insurance companies and building societies which now offer many new services such as unit trusts, pensions and estate agency ownership.

6. Marketing research (3(*c*)). This is the intelligence system of the marketing strategy and Chapter 4 is reserved for its fuller discussion. Marketing research should be regarded as a form of insurance against making blunders. It will, on the whole, indicate *tendencies* rather than produce *facts*, and its results should be interpreted according to the kind of survey conducted, the size and kind of sample used, and the kind of questions asked. It is possible for entirely different answers to result from a study using a different survey technique, a different kind of sample, and a different (or even the same) set of questions. In the main there are three types of enquiry:

(*a*) to discover *opinions, attitudes* or *awareness*, and to record shifts or changes over time;
(*b*) to discover *preferences*; and
(*c*) to discover *motives*.

The three use entirely different techniques and are not to be confused; for instance, an opinion poll cannot discover buying motives.

7. Naming and branding (3(*d*)). (*See also* 6.) Three types of name are to be considered here, although these expressions are sometimes loosely used:

(*a*) *company names*, e.g. Nicholas Laboratories or Cadbury Schweppes, which are registered under the Companies Acts (*see* 8);
(*b*) *brand names*, which may be company names, e.g. Guinness or Dunlop, may be incorporated in registered trade marks (*see* 9), and may also be registered names;
(*c*) *trade names* or *generic names* which are unregistered, e.g.

aspirin or hoover (the Oxford Dictionary now defines the latter as 'to clean (a carpet, etc.) with a vacuum cleaner').

Generic names such as instant coffee, hovercraft, ball-point pen, soft drink or word processor have become common. Companies with registered names such as Coke or Pop make special efforts to protect the correct use of their names with an initial capital letter. This registration is often pointed out in advertisements, and every quarter the *UK Press Gazette* publishes a supplement which lists registered names for the benefit of journalists who might otherwise refer to them as common instead of proper nouns.

8. Company names. The choice of a company name is important because it should distinguish an organisation and make it easy to remember. Ideally, it should characterise the business, like First Bank of Nigeria, a name which is historically true (*see* 6, **12**). In the past, company names were derived from that of the founder, e.g. Cadbury, Ford and Woolworth, or from the place of origin, e.g. Halifax Building Society. Today a good new name needs to be more imaginative. Nationwide Building Society being a good example.

9. Brand names. Product names need to be easy to pronounce, remember and recognise, and the use of vowels helps to give them rhythm, e.g. Bisto, Kodak, Lego and Oxo. As in these examples, short words are easy to say, recall and display on packs and in advertising (*see* **10 –16**).

The apt choice of name is basic marketing communication. Branding also makes possible the advertising of a product. Brands acquire a character or brand image which is a valuable property as demonstrated by Van den Bergh who continued to advertise Stork margarine throughout the Second World War. The product was unobtainable because wartime food rationing allowed only one 'standard' margarine, but the company was anxious that so well established a product should not be forgotten.

Associated with this are 'own-label' or 'own-brand' products such as those found in chain stores and supermarkets, for example Marks & Spencer, Debenhams, Woolworth, Sainsbury's and Tesco. They are produced under contract by regular manufacturers, usually to a special specification, and are labelled with the name of the retailer. They may be sold at a price lower than the nationally advertised brands of the manufacturers concerned, giving the retailer the opportunity to offer competitively priced goods. There are two ways in which this can happen: in the case of a chain or department store the retailer may monopolise production, while in the case of the supermarket the manufacturer may be willing to increase production to supply special own-label goods.

Branding is not confined to the name and its representation in some special form (like the Coca-Cola script), but is often further distinguished by a colour scheme or house colour (which may be part of a corporate identity scheme), and again by a specially designed mark or label. The simplest forms are the stamp JAFFA or OUTSPAN on citrus fruit, and the oval label on the banana, originated by Fyffes. The brown Guinness, the yellow Kodak and the blue Optrex labels are typical. The container itself may have a characteristic colour scheme such as the familiar yellow Swan Vestas matchbox, the gold Gold Block tobacco tin or pouch, and the blue Cadbury's and red Bournville wrappers. This is known legally as the 'get-up', and anyone trying to trick people into buying a product which appears to be in the package of a well-known brand is guilty of 'passing off' and a successful court action may be taken if it can be shown that trade has been lost because of the deception (see 14, 19–20).

10. Product image (3(e)). Branding and packaging may help to establish the product image but more important is the individual design, class and performance of the product. The image could be inexpensive like that of a Bic pen or expensive like a Parker; champagne has a different image from port or vermouth; and a Rolls-Royce has a different image from an Audi or a Metro.

The image may also be contrived as a result of design, formulation or recipe, while in other cases it will develop as a result of usage and familiarity. A certain chocolate may be especially 'smooth', a particular paint may be more enduring, a beer may be dark and have a head, and a motor car may have certain safety features. Such characteristics help to create a product image and they can be stressed and exploited as selling points in advertising.

11. Market segment (3(f)). The product image can be linked to the market segment since products with particular characteristics are likely to appeal to distinct sections of the market, groups of customers or social grades. The segment is often defined by price, but it may be part of the marketing strategy to seek to satisfy a segment of the market which is not already satisfied by a suitable product or service. Some products may satisfy all segments but others, e.g. newspapers like the *Financial Times* and the *Sun*, satisfy particular ones. It is important, therefore, to define the segment or segments to which the product or service is likely to appeal.

(*a*) *A company may expand its business* by selling the same product to a new segment. An example of this has been the Cornhill Insurance Company which, while by no means a small company, used not to be as widely known as it is today. This was because its policies were mostly sold by brokers. However, the company was aware that there was a larger market of people in lower social grades who possessed household and personal goods such as hi-fi and cameras which should be insured. In other words, there was another segment of potential business lower down the market. The technique used to familiarise a large public with the existence of Cornhill was to enter into a five-year agreement with the cricket authorities to sponsor test cricket. Within the first year of sponsorship there was a dramatic improvement in awareness of Cornhill and new business was substantial. In succeeding years the objectives of Cornhill's public relations and advertising programmes have been well satisfied and the sponsorship has been renewed.

(*b*) *Alternatively, a company may extend its range of products or services* by finding new segments to serve. The airline business does this with different classes of fare which are often necessary to sell the enormous capacity of modern jet or 'jumbo jet' wide-bodied aircraft. Except on an extremely busy route, it is doubtful whether all the seats could be sold at the regular price. Devices such as the following have therefore been used to sell seats to segments of the market which would not normally pay the full fare.

(*i*)   Excursion or Apex tickets, bought a month in advance, provided the period of stay is of a certain length.

(*ii*)   Clubs for members to buy tickets in order to visit friends or relatives in the country of a national airline.

(*iii*)   Special fare arrangements with package tour operators.

(*iv*)   Party rates for groups of visitors, conference delegates and so on.

(*v*)   Standby fares for people who are prepared to take a chance on spare seats being available after check-in has elapsed.

(*vi*)   Shuttle services whereby passengers pay on board rather like a bus service.

(*vii*)   Special grades of pricing such as first-class, executive or club, and tourist, with privileges for those who will pay more than the basic but less than the first-class fare.

(*viii*)   Special cheap-rate sales of tickets through travel agents or 'bucket' shops which specialise in selling tickets at bargain prices (although the legality of the supply has been challenged).

Thus an airline can satisfy many segments of the market and increase the proportion of seats filled on large aircraft by providing passengers with a variety of possible fares.

(*c*) *Department stores* are also ingenious at increasing store traffic, and their sales, by attracting various segments, even though the character of the store may seem to draw a certain class of trade. There may be a bargain basement or selling events such as sales, while many stores now carry out direct response or mail-order business through press advertising, direct mail and catalogues. It is not beneath the dignity of Harrods, for example, to have a January sale and to promote it through popular media such as independent local radio.

(*d*) *Motor car manufacturers* are astute at seeking to satisfy the various segments of the motoring market. A single manufacturer may produce baby cars, hatchbacks, family saloons, estates, sports cars, and executive and prestige models. The family saloon may also be aimed at fleet owners, and baby cars may be sold as mini-cabs, while larger cars have special markets as police cars, taxis and hire cars. The segmentation of a motor-car manufacturer's range of models is a prime example of this type of marketing. It can be extended to commercial vehicles and special ones such as ambulances, buses and coaches, fire appliances, campers and 'iron horse' power units for trailers.

Much marketing skill thus lies in finding ways to satisfy isolated market needs by creating the necessary supply, perhaps doing this better than rival companies or even monopolising the situation. If no one is satisfying particular segments the enterprising company can score by filling the gap. Some businesses have been created solely because there was an unfilled gap in the market. This often occurs in the hotel and catering industry. For example, self-catering holidays have been developed in recent years, while local-brew pubs have become popular.

12. Pricing (3(g)). Pricing policy and market segments go together, products and services being supplied to satisfy a particular price bracket. Obviously, a baby car and a Rolls-Royce or a Cadillac appeal to people with different buying power.

Generally speaking, the price should be one which will recover costs and show profit. However, if the costs are so high that the price is prohibitive, the goods will be priced out of the market. It is therefore market forces, i.e. supply and demand, which tend to govern prices. This, however, may be too much of a generalisation because increased costs which are imposed, such as import duty, taxes (as on petroleum, beer, wines and spirits, and tobacco), rates on property and value added tax, all push up prices and customers may be obliged to pay the higher prices. Moreover, government price controls can be impractical if they fail to recognise the causes of price increases, which may include the price of energy or higher costs of labour. The inflationary spiral is a result of prices chasing higher costs.

Nevertheless, prices do not unnecessarily follow a simple market forces pattern, and this has been shown by the failure of too narrowly applied monetarist policies. Other influences, policies and decisions determine prices, and these are fully discussed in Chapter 7.

Another form of pricing also concerns the marketing strategy and this involves the discounted price or the trade terms which the manufacturer or supplier is prepared to allow different types of distributor. Nowadays, chain stores and supermarkets are able to negotiate virtually wholesale prices for bulk purchases. While distribution costs by way of commissions and discounts have to be recovered in the retail selling price, the tail can wag the dog if the retailer both cuts his selling price and demands a keen buying price. It was intense competition over the sale of bread, especially cut loaves, which forced Spillers to close its plant bakeries, costs being increased by industrial action, making it uneconomic all round.

13. The product mix (3(h)). Not to be confused with the marketing mix, the product mix is the range of goods or services which a firm decides to produce and offer for sale. Crucial decisions include:

(a) the range of models;
(b) the range of sizes;
(c) the range of colours, flavours, designs and so on; and
(d) the range of prices.

14. Examples. It will be realised that the product range may be related to the market segment, but not always. Let us consider some examples.

(a) *A confectionery manufacturer* may have a range of brands like Mars, Galaxy and Milky Way. Over the years Cadbury, Rowntree and Mackintosh have maintained the sales of certain brands, e.g. Dairy Milk, Black Magic and Quality Street. On the other hand, certain lines have been withdrawn and new ones like Wisp have been introduced. The product life cycles have varied enormously: some have gone on for generations while others have been of shorter duration. In this industry the question may be asked whether it is more profitable to concentrate on the triangular bar of Toblerone and the familiar Mars, or to speculate on competitive new lines. Which stimulates profitable sales, familiarity or variety?

(b) *Tea companies* tend to maintain brands, e.g. Typhoo, Brooke Bond PG Tips and Lyons Quick Brew, the only changes being the introduction of tea bags, and there may be associated brands.

(c) *Soup companies* tend to be more innovative with tinned, packeted and instant soups, and they offer a changing or increasing variety of flavours or recipes.

(*d*) *Motor car manufacturers* are different. They either have a range of vehicles which satisfy market segments, or they specialise in vehicles which satisfy a particular segment whether they be sports cars or commercial vehicles.

(*e*) *Package tours* will be organised to satisfy different market segments, and the tour operator has to concentrate on particular groups if sufficient bookings of the same kind are to be secured. The price is often the distinguishing feature and this will depend on whether the destinations are highly popular and charter aircraft can be filled, on length of tour and distances involved, and on whether transportation is by road, rail, sea or air or, possibly, a combination. All these have to be planned very carefully to supply what is wanted within certain price brackets. It is unlikely that a tour of China would be offered in the same brochure as inexpensive holidays in Majorca or coach tours of Europe.

15. Proliferation, rationalisation and standardisation. Three other aspects of the product mix can now be considered.

(*a*) *Proliferation* occurs when there exists a great variety of brands in the same market. It may be because variety induces purchase (especially impulse buying), because the market demands many choices (as with colours of paints), because it is a means of competing with rival firms (as with confectionery), or because it creates individuality (as with the menus of different restaurants).

Proliferation can be wasteful and unpopular. For instance, a supermarket (in spite of its size) has to limit shelf space to the products that sell best, which may be those that are most heavily advertised, or have achieved habit purchase. There can be some contradictions here. A firm with a small range of products may sell only if there is a big demand for them, e.g. McDougalls flour, whereas another firm may sell because of its range, e.g. Heinz with their many 'varieties', or because it is more convenient for a retailer to buy from one source which can supply a large range rather than from several firms with short ranges. However, a solution to the problem of distributing a manufacturer's short or speciality range is for him to use a wholesaler, as with stationery lines, pharmaceuticals and, of course, groceries.

(b) *Rationalisation* means reducing to the essential minimum. To some extent, it is a policy of maximising profits. If the absolutely inessential are cut out, greater profit is possible. It is a hard policy, good for business, but probably bad for the customer. The customer may prefer to have a bigger choice but he is obliged to accept what he is given.

Thus the choice between the half pint, pint and quart gave way to the solitary pint and eventually the litre. With some products the rationalisation has gone upwards to larger quantities such as two or five litres obliging the customer to buy more in the 'economy' size. Some of this has been necessary as the costs of filling and packaging have increased. These forms of rationalisation have been seen in liquids such as milk, beer, soft drinks, wines, cooking oil and engine oil.

With expensive products such as garden insecticides and proprietary medicines the move has been to smaller sizes which tend to suggest a more acceptable price. The economies of production and marketing are evident in rationalisation.

(c) *Standardisation*, however, tends to benefit the customer as when goods are made in standard sizes so that they are interchangeable (e.g. wheels and tyres), fit various products (e.g. dry batteries or electric light bulbs), conform to measurements that can be worked with (e.g. nuts and spanners) or are sold in standard sizes (e.g. bottled goods). The fact that printers' typefaces conform to standard point system sizes has defied metrication! Standardisation is a means of simplifying goods, and has proved a good marketing aid. In a sense, it is a kind of rationalisation which has reduced proliferation.

16. Economical products. The product mix, market segmentation, pricing and other elements of the marketing mix all influence *product planning*. An important aspect of product planning which should be mentioned here is the development of economical products, i.e. those which can be produced:

(a) with existing resources and so do not require additional production capacity (and investment), labour, sales force and distribution network; or

(*b*) with economical use of fresh investment in production, extra labour, and more salesmen, but distributing through the same outlets if possible.

The first might be a new biscuit made with existing facilities, while the second might be a new dairy product requiring an additional creamery. It will be noticed that emphasis is made on using the same distribution network which includes depots, delivery vehicles and the existing goodwill of the trade. It could be uneconomical if the company diversified to the extent that a new distribution pattern was necessary for a new product, and a new section of the retail trade had to be approached which was unfamiliar with the manufacturer. This happened with a company which normally sold its products through chemists and hardware shops and then produced a floor polish which needed the support of the big supermarket chains. It failed.

17. Packaging (3(*i*)). This is one of the most vital aspects of the marketing mix and is discussed separately in 5. It shares importance with the *naming* and *branding* which will appear on the package. By package is meant the container, label and any further wrapping such as a carton holding, say, a bottle. It does not, in this context, refer to cartons, crates, pallets, sea-going containers or other means of transporting bulk quantities of goods.

There are two main considerations:

(*a*) The actual containing of the product for its protection, and so that it may be marketed in certain quantities, including the material from which the package is made.

(*b*) The use of the package as a means of identifying and promoting the product. In developing countries (and especially in underdeveloped countries like Bangladesh) the after-use of the container could be important.

18. Distribution (3(*j*)). Once again, one element is linked with others and we have already touched on distribution in previous sections. Methods of distribution are constantly changing, as indicated in 2, **14**, reflecting changes in consumer behaviour. In recent years we have seen the arrival of 'one-stop shopping' and an increase in direct response marketing, and now it is even possible to indulge in telemarketing by calling up shopping information on the television and ordering with an answer-back system (*see* 8,16).

Non-store retailing of various kinds is increasing rapidly. For instance, there has been a remarkable increase in direct response marketing by post, and not only through typical press and direct mail advertising. Charge card companies such as American Express and Diners Club make mail-order offers. The Automobile Association offers its large membership books and a variety of motoring and other goods such as watches and sunglasses by mail order. Many charities raise funds through gift catalogues, and retail stores have been quick to develop postal sales, although this is not new.

The industrial societies have succeeded not merely because production was mechanised and mass production became possible, but because of their ability to distribute efficiently to a mass market which was largely urbanised. In many developing countries it is not difficult to produce, but it may be difficult to distribute and the population is mostly rural. For more than a hundred years distribution has been relatively simple in the North because of road, rail and canal transportation, large areas of population with numerous shops and popular media in which to advertise. The channels of distribution are shown in Fig. 3.6. Within this framework a complex system of distribution exists which will be dealt with more fully in Chapter 8.

Figure 3.6   *Channels of distribution*

The retailer may be a multiple, chain, department store, independent shop, a shop owned by the manufacturer or a direct response marketer. The wholesaler may include agents, factors or cash–and–carry warehouses. Direct sales from manufacturer to consumer may be made by a visiting salesman or roundsman or by mail order.

19. The sales force (3(k)). Every company will organise its sales force according to its size, the industry it is in, and the channels of distribution adopted. A retail establishment will have its shop assistants, a manufacturer will have field salespeople calling on wholesalers and/or retailers, an insurance company will sell through brokers or representatives, and a newspaper may sell space through either sales representatives or telephone sales staff.

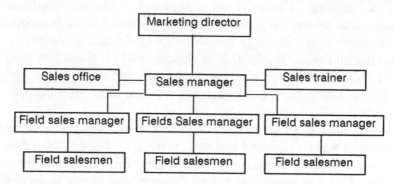

Figure 3.7 *The sales organisation*

(a) *A typical sales organisation* is illustrated in Fig. 3.7. There may be different kinds of salespeople, the industrial company employing technical salespeople, while a food manufacturer may employ van salespeople who sell either to retailers or direct to customers and collect payment as they deliver. It will be noticed that Fig. 3.7 includes a sales office which deals with the paperwork of handling orders and accounts and arranges with the warehouse for delivery. There is also a sales trainer who trains both new recruits and existing salespeople when new products or services are introduced. The sales manager will direct operations, usually by organising sales territories, setting sales targets, communicating sales information to the sales force and receiving sales reports which may be daily or weekly or both.

(b) *Journey cycle.* Salespeople will be allocated territories and will usually cover them by means of a journey cycle system. The journey cycle should not be confused with the *product cycle*, which is the time it takes a product to be made and distributed, or the *product life cycle* already explained in **5**. There are two kinds of journey cycle, as follows:

(i) The *continuous* kind follows a sequential route, each customer or stockist being called upon once in so many days, weeks or months. Thus a four-weekly journey cycle would enable the salesperson to call on each of his clients thirteen times a year.

(ii) The *quadrant* kind usually applies in a large urban area which can be traversed so that some customers can be visited more often than others.

There may also have to be an allowance for additional calls on new prospects, and for *cold calling* when uninvited calls are made on possible clients.

(c) *Remuneration* may be by one of the following methods:

(i)   a straight salary, irrespective of sales achieved;
(ii) a commission on all sales obtained;
(iii) a basic salary plus commission on all sales;
(iv) a bonus on sales beyond the set target, irrespective of other methods of remuneration.

Further *incentives* may be offered such as cash awards, awarding of points or vouchers which can be converted into goods from a catalogue, and sales contest prizes such as holidays for the winner.

(d) *Support material* for salespeople will include the following:

(i) *Sales presenter, portfolio or promoter* in the form of a ring binder to which items can be added or withdrawn from time to time, this is a means of laying before the buyer such things as sales arguments, price lists, photographs of goods, samples and specimens of advertisements and media schedules.

(ii) *Desk-top projectors*. Visual demonstrations can be given using slides, films, film loops or cassettes according to the type of machine. The projector folds into a case and is portable.

(iii) *Point-of-sale material*. Although display material may be supplied direct to the retailer, it can be a service to the retailer, and it will certainly ensure display, if the salesperson has with him supplies of show-cards, window bills, shelf-edging strips, door transfers and other POS material. He may be able to position them himself.

(iv) *Buffer stocks*. If the retailer is out-of-stock it will be very practical if the salesperson has in his vehicle supplies of the product, i.e. buffer stocks, from which he can supply the retailer.

(*e*) *Control of salespeople* is important as already mentioned when describing the sales manager's duties. Some of the methods used are as follows:

(*i*) *Sales manual.* How to demonstrate and sell the product or service can be set out in a sales manual to which the salesperson can refer for instructions.

(*ii*) *Sales meetings.* At regional or national level, sales meetings bring together the sales staff to be briefed on new products or company policies and to meet management. These meetings are essential for good management and staff relations.

(*iii*) *Sales bulletins.* Regular news bulletins with encouragement to sell are an important form of communication between head office and the often rather isolated salesperson in the field. Bulletins can be put on cassette for playing in the salesperson's car.

(*iv*) *Sales reports and salesperson's records.* These provide essential feedback from the field and demonstrate whether or not the expected number of calls are being made, as well as giving the result of the salesperson's efforts. They may take the form of customer record cards kept by the salesperson, daily, weekly and monthly reports, and expenses claims. The preparation of these reports is part of the discipline maintained by the sales manager.

From the above summary of the sales function it will be seen how important this is to the successful execution of the marketing strategy.

20. Market education (3(*l*)). Here we have a major PR facet of the marketing mix. Far too little market education is carried out by those companies which mistakenly believe that the power of advertising is sufficient to create a favourable marketing situation. Advertising may fail—and there have been several expensive instances of this—if potential customers do not understand what is being advertised and have no faith in the product or service. Expensive, technical or new and unknown products usually depend on considerable market education, both before the launch and afterwards. Computers, word processors, video cassette recorders and other products involving new technology have been subject to intensive market education programmes. So, too, have things as diverse as new holiday destinations, foodstuffs, air routes, decorating materials, housing estates, savings schemes and shopping centres.

The techniques employed are discussed in 14. Here, the point is made that part of the marketing strategy may be to time the product launch sufficiently far ahead to allow for market education to prepare the way. Impatience could be costly. This is where the wise marketing manager shows how well he understands PR.

21. Corporate and financial PR (3(m)). It may be asked what this has to do with the marketing department. It is an example of the many aspects of PR which are conducted outside the marketing department and which only go to show that PR (since it concerns the total organisation) should not be positioned within marketing. It also demonstrates that PR which concerns the board of management and the financial director can be of great value and importance to marketing. It can help sell goods.

The effects of the marketing strategy will be enhanced if:

(*a*) both the trade and ultimate consumers have a clear *corporate image* or impression of the company;

(*b*) the visible *corporate identity* scheme (e.g. logo, livery, typography, colour) is recognised; and

(*c*) the financial fortunes (e.g. share quotations on the Stock Exchange) are sound.

Respect, reputation, good-will and credibility are assets resulting from corporate and financial PR. They can all help to reduce sales resistance and ease both the selling-in and selling-out operations.

NOTE: The reader should note the difference between corporate *image* and corporate *identity*, as outlined above.

22. Industrial relations (3(n)). The marketing manager may not be able to influence relations between labour and management; nevertheless, industrial strife or peace will influence customer attitudes and delivery dates. What can the marketing manager do, if anything? It will certainly do no harm, and it would create a sense of involvement, pride and job satisfaction, if employees of all kinds were made more aware of the effect of marketing skills on employment and earnings. A lot of industrial disputes result from frustration and ignorance. This is perhaps inevitable when there is lack of worker participation and a lack of managerial candour.

One way in which the marketing manager can influence industrial relations is by taking advantage of employee/employer communication systems such as staff newspapers, video magazines, notice boards and other internal media. For example, are the staff told when press, radio, TV and poster advertisements are appearing, or do they merely come across them accidentally? Such advertisements are seeking to produce jobs and wages, not only profits, since the cost of labour is often the biggest proportion of the selling price!

23. Test-marketing (3(o)). As a final insurance before launching a new product on the market it can be very sensible to test-market, provided that the test area is a reasonable miniature of the national broad-scale market, and that reasonable time is allowed to achieve a predetermined rate of sales or percentage of the market. The method has resulted in the abandonment of apparently excellent products, although some products have still failed after a promising test-marketing exercise. This should not be confused with product pre-testing which takes place much earlier. Here we are concerned with testing the complete marketing strategy.

The notion is sometimes expressed that test-marketing is unwise because it reveals a company's merits to rival firms who could put their own competitive product on the market. There are two arguments against this.

(a) Without test-marketing a company could lose a fortune but with test-marketing it can either save or make a fortune.

(b) The company undertaking the test has already spent months developing the product and planning the marketing programme, and it is unlikely that a rival would have time to catch up short of producing a copy.

24. Conditions for test-marketing. These must be right, and they may not exist in all parts of the world. The test-market town or area should have the following qualities:

(a) a typical range of retail outlets;
(b) remoteness from other sales areas;
(c) advertising media that are compatible with national media (e.g. regional TV);
(d) a typical demographic breakdown of potential buyers;
(e) available marketing research facilities such as dealer audit.

Of these (c) is the key to whether the test area is suitable. It can be the weakest feature in test-marketing if the local media are unrepresentative of national media or at least the media planned for the national advertising campaign.

Fortunately, in Britain, the right media are available. There are regional TV and local radio which could be networked nationally; some national newspapers will run slip editions, that is, they will insert an extra page in copies sold in a region; and some popular magazines, e.g. *TV Times*, and some Sunday newspaper colour magazines will carry regional advertising in regional editions. Poster advertising can be extended nationally and point-of-sale material, sales promotion schemes and in-store demonstrations can be localised and then used nationally. In some areas there are local exhibitions, and mail drops can be carried out anywhere.

25. Method. To be effective, a target percentage of sales or share of the market should be determined. Then there should be three phases to the test.

(a) First, there should be a *pre-test* to establish a base. This will show the shares of the market held by existing brands when those for the new brand are nil.

(b) Then there should be the *actual test* which should be long enough to record initial or trial purchases (which may be high because of the trial or curiosity nature of first purchases) and repeat purchases.

(c) Finally, there should be a *post test* to see how sales have settled down, although if the product is very popular sales may have risen.

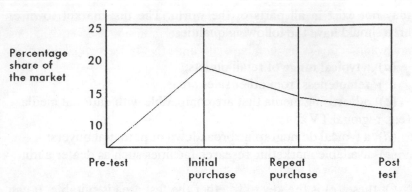

Figure 3.8 *Simulated test-marketing performance*

Figure 3.8 shows how the results of the test might be presented graphically. If the target was $12\frac{1}{2}$ per cent, this graph would represent a very pleasing test result because the target has been exceeded. The length of the test would depend on the average interval between purchases of such a product. A cat or dog food bought weekly could be tested adequately over a month, but a toothpaste would require longer. Buying habits would need to be taken into consideration; different people might buy different sizes or quantities. Allowances would need to be made for seasonal fluctuations and also for whether people stored the product in refrigerators or deep-freezers.

26. Industrial test-marketing. Industrial products may call for different kinds of testing. A product may be tested at a government, trade association or independent research station, and sometimes the laboratory resources of universities may be used. Another method is to place a prototype in industrial situations where it can be tested in practical service (*see* 15, 8).

27. Zoned launches. More forthright test-marketing (or at least initial marketing) occurs when a product is launched in a zoned or regional market before going on sale nationally. If it is a mass consumer product it is easy in Britain to simulate a local campaign of national quality, thanks particularly to the existence of regional TV on the one hand and the presence locally of branches of national supermarket and store chains.

Such a launch may also be convenient if the manufacturer either lacks production capacity to supply the national market, or does not want to invest in such capacity until this is seen to be justified by sales in a selected zone. It is also possible to develop the national market zone by zone.

Only certain products can be launched like this, and it has proved successful with foods and drinks (e.g. Mosaic Cyprus Sherry and St Ivel Gold). It would not apply to, say, motor cars, but could be suitable for furniture which does not require sophisticated production lines.

28. Advertising (3(*p*)). This is such an important element in the marketing mix that Chapters 12 and 13 are devoted to it. It is also the subject of a separate LCC examination. At this point it is sufficient to say that although advertising may at first seem to be very 'expensive' this high cost has to be related to objectives and results. Without advertising it may be impossible to market the product or service. It is like saying that no matter how good the engine a motor car cannot move without petrol. Advertising is the fuel of marketing. It can be the cheapest way of reaching prospective customers. It is the *means of making known in order to sell*, whether the method used is the town crier of years ago or today's television commercial.

However, the extent to which advertising is used will depend on the nature of the product or service. Fast-moving consumer goods are usually heavily advertised because it is necessary to persuade people to buy repeatedly to maintain production capacity. The price of such goods is as low as it is only as long as there are volume sales. Package holidays are relatively cheap because prices are based on volume sales. These sales are produced by advertising.

Industrial goods rely less on media advertising and more on technical salesmen, trade exhibitions and public relations such as market education. Such media advertising as may be used will be in specialised trade and technical magazines, and not in the mass media of the popular press, radio, television or posters (*see* 15).

Advertising media are divided into *above-the-line* (the five traditional media of press, television, radio, outdoor and cinema) and *below-the-line* (direct mail, exhibitions, sponsorship, sales literature, sales promotion and point-of-sale). (*See* 12,11.) Note that public relations is not listed under below-the-line because it is not a form of advertising and plays a quite different role.

29. Advertising research (3(*a*)). This is a special form of marketing research which can be divided into three sections:

    (*a*) copy-testing or re-testing (*see* 30);

    (*b*) media research (*see* 31); and

    (*c*) researching the effectiveness and the cost-effectiveness of advertising (*see* 32).

The first and last forms of research can be undertaken or commissioned by the advertiser or his advertising agency, but media research is conducted either by independent research bodies or by the media owners themselves.

30. Pre-testing advertisements. It is easy for creative people to convince themselves that they have brilliant ideas, whether in design or in writing, but they could be obscure, ambiguous or unappealing to readers, listeners or viewers. David Bernstein, one of Britain's leading advertising creators, tells the story of his experience when serving as a judge of TV commercials at the Cannes Film Festival. He and his fellow judges had decided on the winning commercial and then they found they could not remember the name of the advertiser!

It is sometimes difficult to please customers. British Telecom received a lot of criticism for its TV commercials featuring Buzby, a bird character who sat on the telephone wires and delivered sales messages. According to British Telecom the advertising produced results in spite of the criticism. In this case the criticism was probably a result of characteristic British resistance to advertising, and a confused belief that increased telephone charges were related to the high cost of television advertising. However, the family cameos featuring the comedy actress Maureen Lipman were outstandingly popular.

(*a*) *Press advertisements* can be tested by the folder technique. A number of advertisements for various products, including the one being tested (or several different advertisements for the same product), are placed in a folder with plastic sleeves. Typical customers are asked to study the folder and, after returning it to the interviewer, are asked to recall the contents of the different advertisements. In this way it is possible to discover which headlines, illustrations, slogans, copy themes, selling points, prices, brand and company names are remembered. It is wise to mix the order in which the advertisements appear in the folder because there is a psychological tendency for people to remember best the first and last in a series.

There are variations on this technique. The advertisements could be on slides and projected on to a screen with all the respondents forming an audience. After the presentation, the respondents could either write down what they recalled, or become a discussion group directed by a group leader. The folder technique is perhaps simpler and easier to measure quantitatively with scores for each advertisement.

(b) *Television commercials* can be tested by in-theatre methods such as showing a commercial and measuring response, then screening other film material and showing the commercial again to measure any increase in response. Recall can also be measured in a similar way. Using field survey interviews it is also possible to conduct day-after recall tests to discover what is remembered by people who had watched commercial television the previous day. Two different commercials can be shown on different channels, and results can be compared to see which of the two commercials achieved the highest recall. This can be done very effectively in regions where there are two transmitters.

31. Media research. This takes two forms:

(a) the publication by the Audit Bureau of Circulations of audited net sales figures known as *circulation*, that is, the average number of copies sold;

(b) research into *readership* or *audiences* and the characteristics of readers, listeners and viewers.

The latter is conducted by the Joint Industry Committee for National Readership Surveys (JICNARS), the Joint Industry Committee for Radio Audience Research (JICRAR) and the

Broadcasting Audience Research Board (BARB). (*See also* 12, 33– 36.)

32. Effectiveness of advertising. Reading and noting tests can be conducted to measure the percentage of men and women who saw an advertisement and who remembered the contents. This soft of research can reveal good and bad recall of headlines, slogans, pictures, copy and selling points. (The reading and noting method can be used for copy-testing purposes, the advertisement being inserted in a newspaper, tested and amended as a result of faults being revealed during this dummy run.)

Ordinary field surveys can be carried out with interviewers using questionnaires and calling on a representative sample of householders to check whether they saw the advertisement and what they remembered of it. As described in 30(*b*) above, day-after recall tests can be held to check the effectiveness of TV commercials. The discussion group technique can also be used, a representative group of people being assembled to discuss the advertising which has appeared.

Tracking studies go beyond simple day-after recall tests and record how advertising works over long time-periods. This type of post research can reveal, for example, the rate at which a campaign decays over time, or whether the advertising is so effective that it defies decay. Effective advertising increases the value of the advertising budget, and the 'share of voice' enjoyed by the advertising. This is clearly a more practical evaluation of advertising than testing the ability of people to remember a new advertisement.

Dealer audit research can be used to see how the goods have actually sold and to measure the impact of the advertising in terms of market share. Dealer audit research regularly checks the sales of most kinds of consumer products, not merely the ones advertised, and so it is possible to measure the comparative sales performances of all the brands in the advertiser's group (*see also* 4, 24).

Another method is to measure direct response to advertisements especially if they are mail-order goods, or an offer is made with or without a coupon. The results to be measured may be direct sales or applications for whatever is offered, such as a free sample, premium offer, leaflet or catalogue. These replies can then be calculated against the cost of the space to produce a cost-per-reply (and also perhaps the cost-per-conversion into sales). This cost analysis will reveal which are the most economical media, and also which day of the week or which size space is most productive.

33. Sales promotion (3(r)). (*See also* 10.) It is necessary to understand this term clearly. In Britain it refers to short-term promotional exercises such as premium offers, prize competitions, money-off offers and so on which used to be called merchandising. In the USA sales promotion consists of below-the-line advertising. Consequently, students taking British examinations should ignore the American meaning.

(*a*) *Definition*: The Institute of Sales Promotion defines sales promotion as 'the function of marketing which seeks to achieve given objectives by the adding of extrinsic, tangible value to a product or service (*see* 10, **2**).

(*b*) *Reasons for organising sales promotion schemes* are to:
- (*i*)   bringing the manufacturer closer to the customer;
- (*ii*)   launch a new product;
- (*iii*) revive falling sales;
- (*iv*)   challenge competition;
- (*v*)   encourage retailers to stock the product;
- (*vi*)   induce impulse buying;
- (*vii*) boost sales when there are seasonal opportunities (e.g. Christmas);
- (*viii*) encourage habit buying.

34. The after-market (3(s)). (*See also* 10.) Sales may depend on what the manufacturer has to offer to continue to satisfy the customer after the purchase has been made. A big problem in developing countries has been the inability of customers to enjoy this essential satisfaction. For example, batteries for radios are too expensive, restrictions on imports make spare parts scarce, resulting in black marketing, and there may be few trained service engineers. Consequently, sophisticated products break down, are junked and there is waste; or, as in Nigeria, people are afraid to drive long distances in case of a breakdown, and the domestic air services are overbooked. Ill-will builds up for manufacturers and distributors when there is an unsatisfactory after-market.

Methods of satisfying the after-market include the following.

(a) *Instructions*. These may be on the package, in the form of a 'stuffer' (as with films), or supplied separately in a booklet or manual. If the product is exported the instructions should be repeated in a variety of languages, or special language versions should be printed if the foreign market is big enough. If the required languages are too many, if there are unwritten languages, or if customers are likely to be illiterate, pictures, drawings or cartoons should be used.

(b) *Spare parts*. Few things will help to 'clinch the sale' more than the promise that spare parts are easily obtainable. However, it may go beyond this: one motor car manufacturer's parts may be inexpensive while those of, say, a foreign manufacturer may be expensive, while yet another make may be so reliable that spares are rarely required. The manner in which spares are supplied is another factor: is there a good distribution of parts; can they be obtained by post; are they delivered in good protective packages; can they be obtained for obsolete models? When an aircraft is phased out, the manufacturers usually guarantee that spares will remain available.

The company's policy on spares and replacements could be crucial to the maintenance of goodwill through customer satisfaction. When a customer returns with a defective product only to find that it is now regarded as obsolete and parts are no longer available, he is apt to feel angry. However, it may be uneconomic for a manufacturer to continue supplying parts after a certain time. A solution with some products is to construct them with interchangeable modules as with solid-state electronic products.

(c) *Servicing*. This should be done by trained technicians, and the wise manufacturer will operate a training school for service staff and retailers. Market education may include training distributors (which may include works visits or the provision of video cassettes or video discs). A number of products have failed to sell because the shop assistant has been so ignorant about the product that he has been unable to secure the customer's confidence. Thus servicing can precede as well as follow the sale. Some firms, e.g. lawnmower manufacturers and opticians, have follow-up systems of reminding customers that periodic servicing is advised if the product is to continue to perform efficiently.

(*d*) *Advice bureau*. Although information centres may be principally for the purpose of creating sales, they can also be an excellent form of after-sales service when, for example, the customer wants to ask questions.

(*e*) *Guarantees and promises*. Customer confidence can be inspired by written guarantees, and many products carry a guarantee for a certain period of time. Better still is the simple *promise* that a product will perform, as introduced by Corning Glass in respect of ovenware and coffee pots. It is not only technical products which should be guaranteed. Fast-moving consumer goods often contain a reference number and address to which complaints may be made. Even if the customer is perfectly satisfied, the ability to complain is reassuring.

(*f*) *Cash refunds or exchange of goods*. Once again we see the implicit public relations nature of after-sales service when the dissatisfied customer enjoys the right to claim, without a fuss or embarrassment, a refund, a credit or an exchange of goods.

(*g*) *Accessories*. An interesting form of after-sales service is the provision of accessories which can be added to the basic product, thus extending interest in and use of the product. A typical example is the Olympus camera which has a well-organised system of additional lenses, filters and attachments. It may also be an advantage if there is standardisation and other products are compatible, as with films for cameras.

35. Maintaining customer interest and loyalty (3(*t*)). Quite apart from after-sales services there is the question of how the marketing manager retains and develops customer interest and loyalty in the product. This is an often neglected area.

(*a*) *Objectives*. By the use of some of the PR techniques described in Chapter 14 it is possible to:

   (*i*)   foster goodwill towards the company, its products and its services;

(*ii*)   help the customer to enjoy the benefits of the product or service, as when a food manufacturer publishes a cookery book or recipe leaflets or runs cookery competitions;

(*iii*)   encourage satisfied customers to make recommendations to other buyers; and

(*iv*)   stimulate customers' loyalty so that they continue as regular customers, or eventually replace the product with the same make.

(*b*) *Methods*. These include the following.

(*i*)   Customer clubs which bring, say, motor car owners together in joint activities.

(*ii*)   External house magazines addressed to customers or users, and containing articles on how to enjoy the product, and telling them about new products or accessories.

(*iii*)   Sponsorships of events, sports, personalities, the arts and so on which maintain customer awareness.

(*iv*)   Regular presence in the media via news releases, feature articles and pictures which also maintain customer awareness.

(*v*)   Participation in exhibitions so that customers can see new products and product developments.

(*vi*)   Invitations to attend showings of documentary videos. This has been carried out very well by the Midland Bank, with local managers inviting customers to attend a social evening and the showing of a video on a bank service.

(*vii*)   The supply of video cassettes for showing on domestic VCRs.

(*viii*)   Other demand information systems such as Oracle, Ceefax and Prestel which will enable customers to seek product information through call-up 'pages' on their TV set.

36. Conclusion. In this chapter the marketing mix has been analysed. Some elements will apply to certain products or services more than others, and each will have its particular mix. They are interlinked and the strength of the marketing strategy will depend on the attention which is given to each. As the saying goes, a chain is as strong as its weakest link, and failure to perfect each element could destroy the whole scheme. Lack of marketing research, a poor brand name, bad packaging, weak advertising, frustrating after-sales service and, above all, failure to realise that PR is an integral part of the whole mix, could mean financial disaster. In succeeding chapters we shall return to some of these topics in greater detail, repeating important points where necessary.

Progress test 3

1. What is the marketing mix? **(1, 3)**
2. Chart and describe the variations on the standard PLC. **(5)**
3. Explain the difference between company, brand and trade names. **(7)**
4. In addition to the name, what else is involved in branding? **(9)**
5. What is the 'get-up'? **(9)**
6. What is the product image? **(10)**
7. What is a market segment? **(11)**
8. What are the four basic kinds of price? **(12)**
9. What four decisions are crucial to the product mix? **(13)**
10. What is meant by:
    (*a*) rationalisation;
    (*b*) standardisation;
    (*c*) proliferation? **(15)**
11. What are the two main considerations regarding packaging? **(17)**
12. What are the main channels of distribution? **(18)**
13. Describe some forms of non-store retailing. **(18)**
14. What is the journey cycle? **(19)**
15. How are salesmen remunerated? **(19)**
16. What are buffer stocks? **(19)**
17. What are the means of controlling salesmen's activities? **(19)**
18. How can the marketing manager contribute to good industrial relations? **(22)**
19. What qualities are required of a test-market town? **(24)**
20. What are the three stages of a test-marketing exercise? **(25)**
21. How can advertisements be pre-tested? **(30)**
22. What is BARB? **(31)**
23. What are tracking studies? **(30)**
24. What is a reading and noting test? **(32)**

4
Marketing research

Introduction

1. Definitions. It is important for the reader to distinguish between the terms 'market research' and 'marketing research', which are sometimes wrongly used to mean the same thing. Strictly speaking, market research is concerned with studies of the market, while marketing research embraces studies of anything to do with marketing. The latter, broader term covers special studies such as packaging research and media research into readership and audiences.

(*a*) The (British) Market Research Society defines *market research* as 'a branch of social science which uses scientific methods to collect information about markets for goods or services'.

(*b*) The author's definition of *marketing research* is 'the systematic study of data, including the use of scientific methods, to obtain information relevant to the marketing of products or services'.

2. Need for research. In the days when there was selling and not marketing, the seller had to make assumptions about potential buyers and their preferences and buying motives. In most cases he or she may have made the right assumptions because the choice of goods was fairly limited. However, the modern market is complex and buyers have numerous choices. In such circumstances no assumptions are possible and marketing research is necessary.

3. Objectives. The three main objectives of marketing research are therefore to:

(a) assess opinions, awareness and attitudes;
(b) discover preferences; and
(c) discover motives.

In other words, what people want, what they prefer and why they buy.

Forms and methods of research

4. Primary and secondary research. There are two forms of marketing research, primary and secondary.

(a) *Primary research* is original research, the study being made for the first time and using one of the many techniques described in this chapter.

(b) *Secondary research* means the study of existing information, including research surveys carried out by other people for other purposes which may make it unnecessary to carry out a completely new survey. This is known as *desk research*.

The information obtained is known as *primary data* or *secondary data* as the case may be.

5. Ad hoc and continuous research. Primary research is of two kinds, as follows.

(a) *Ad hoc research* consists of single surveys which conclude the study. For instance, a survey may be conducted to find out what percentage of different types of people buy beverages such as tea and coffee, and where and how often they buy them. This would then produce a report on national beverage drinking habits.

(b) *Continuous research* is conducted periodically in order to produce regular reports on trends against time. If applied to beverages it would reveal whether there were any changes, including perhaps seasonal changes, in the habits of buyers of these drinks. Such a report may show that younger or older people prefer certain drinks, or that they are drunk with particular meals.

6. Need for specialist researchers. To be reliable, marketing research must be conducted by people who are specially trained to do it. The construction of the sample, and the questionnaire, the questioning of respondents, the collation of answers and their interpretation in a report calls for a blend of psychology, sociology and statistics. It is therefore very unwise for ordinary company personnel to attempt to undertake research, and surveys should certainly not be conducted by salesmen because they would be too biased. Marketing research surveys should be *independent* scientific studies carried out by specialist research units.

7. Types of research unit. Marketing surveys may be carried out by the following kinds of research unit.

(*a*) A special research unit within a very large company. (The unit's services may be commissioned by other companies if there is capacity for other work).
(*b*) A research unit which is a subsidiary company of an advertising agency.
(*c*) A completely independent research company. Such a company is likely to specialise in a certain kind of study, e.g. Nielsen in dealer audits, Gallup in reading and noting research and National Opinion Polls (NOP) in opinion polls.

Some large companies, and the larger advertising agencies, employ a research officer who conducts desk research, subscribes to continuous survey reports, and commissions surveys from the various research firms as appropriate. Thus, an advertising agency can advise on marketing research and organise surveys, as part of the service for clients. For example, a responsible agency may refuse to undertake an advertising campaign unless it is allowed to copy-test advertisements in order to arrive at the most effective creative appeal. This is in the interests of both sides.

8. Terminology. Inevitably, words have been introduced already which may seem familiar but which have special meanings in the world of research. Some explanations will be useful. The student should be sure he understands the meanings of these words when they occur in examination questions.

(*a*)   *Population or universe*. Both words mean the total number of people relevant to a particular survey; for instance, all motorists, teachers, housewives or tennis players. It does not mean the total population of a town or country.

(*b*)   *Respondent or interviewee*. A person questioned during a survey.

(*c*)   *Sample*. This means a little of the whole (as in tea tasting or when taking a handful of grain from a sack to examine its quality) and is not to be confused with a 'free sample'. In marketing research a sample is a number of people sufficient to represent the population relevant to the survey.

(*d*)   *Sampling frame*. This is a specification of the kinds of people who will form the sample of respondents, and their *characteristics*.

(*e*)   *Characteristics*. These are the distinctions between different kinds of people such as those who smoke cigarettes, cigars or pipes.

(*f*)   *Quota sample*. This kind of sample is made up of numbers or percentages of people of the kinds relevant to the survey and in proportion to their existence in the census population. For example, a simple sample of men and women might consist of 49 men and 51 women (and multiples of this) if that was the breakdown of men and women in the census population. More often it is based on sex, age and social grade (*see* 9 –11).

(*g*)   *Random sample*. Perhaps more accurately called an *interval* or *probability* sample, this kind of sample is not in fact one in which respondents are chosen 'at random'. It requires a list of names and addresses from which respondents can be selected at regular *intervals*, say every tenth or hundredth name, according to the size of the required sample. The total number of people making up the sample will depend on the money available and the degree of accuracy desired.

The probability is that this 'randomly' selected sample will be a cross-section of the universe. It is best used when everyone in the universe could be relevant, and so applies to subjects which are universal such as most popular consumer goods, as well as politics. Interviewers are given actual people to interview, and are not responsible for finding them as with a quota sample. Moreover, it is usual to expect the interviewer to make at least three attempts to find a given person before a replacement is permitted.

Thus, the random sample is more accurate than a quota sample, but it is likely to be three times more expensive because of the interviewer time involved. The respondent is also asked to give demographic details so that the results can be quantified according to the kinds of people who have given certain answers. As an indication of sample sizes, in an opinion poll 450 people might be interviewed but for the same purpose a random survey is likely to require about 1,500. The size of the random sample is determined mathematically by application of the standard error formula:

$$S = \sqrt{\frac{p\,(100) - p}{n}}$$

where p is the percentage estimate and n is the sample size.

Academics tend to adopt a 'you, you and you' interpretation of random sampling, and in one book on marketing it was even suggested that numbers can be written on slips of paper, shuffled and then drawn until the sample size has been obtained! Ivory tower academics write some peculiar things about marketing! However, the reader should also be aware of the system of *random numbers*, using tables of mixed-up numbers printed in columns; such tables are not used for marketing studies.

(*h*) *Cluster or area sampling.* Still using the random technique, cluster or area sampling occurs when the survey is not conducted nationally but is limited to a group of relevant areas, or to a specific area.

(*i*) *Multi-stage sampling.* This is another method of reducing the scatter of the respondents. Interviews take place in a minimum number of places (*sampling points*) by breaking down the country into counties, states or provinces, and then into smaller areas, interviews being allotted in proportion to the population in each area. Similarly, election polling districts can be used, these being sampled to produce a number of districts in which interviews take place.

(*j*)   *Stratified random sample.* This form of the random sample takes into consideration the demographic make-up of the census population such as the ratio of males to females, and the social grades, so that a random sample may be taken of certain sections of the general population or of specific classes of industry and commerce.

(*k*)   *Random walk or location.* When lists of addresses do not exist, as may occur in a developing country, the random sample technique can be applied to streets, and houses can be selected at regular intervals. This can be done in urban areas, but it does mean that research has to be limited to such areas and may have to ignore the majority of people who live in the rural areas. However, in developing countries a random walk sample will be both more practical and less expensive than a quota sample if quotas are less easy to find.

(*l*)   *Structured interview.* This is an interview conducted *with* a prepared questionnaire.

(*m*)   *Depth interview.* In this case the interview is conducted *without* a prepared questionnaire, the interviewer asking open-ended questions (*see* **29(f)**) and writing down verbatim replies or a summary of longer ones. This type of qualitative sample, using a fairly lengthy interview, is a research method frequently used in developing countries where most of the techniques described above are, save for the random walk, impracticable.

(*n*)   *Special problems which occur in some developing countries.* Statistics such as census figures may not exist. There may be few published lists of people. It may be difficult to recruit reliable interviewers. Those interviewed are likely to be unfamiliar with marketing research, and reluctant to answer questions, fearing how the information may be used against them. There may be religious or tribal taboos about interviewing women or counting children.

Social grades and socio-economic groups

9. Social grades in Britain. In industrial countries *socio-economic groups* (based on income) have given way to *social grades* (based on occupation), but in developing countries gradings based on income, class or education often apply.

British marketing research uses the social grades established for the readership surveys known as JICNARS (*see* 12, 34). These are shown in Table 4A. It will be seen from this that nearly three-quarters of the British population lie in the C^1, C^2 and D groups, forming the mass market for fast-moving consumer goods, and providing the readership of the multi-million circulation popular press, and the bulk of the prime time mid-evening television audience. Table 4B shows how this class breakdown relates to the sale of newspapers.

Table 4A. Social grades in Britain

	Grade	Members	Percentage of Population
A	Upper middle class	Top businessmen, other leaders	3
B	Middle class	Senior executives, managers	15
C^1	Lower middle class	White-collar, white-blouse office workers	23
C^2	Skilled working class	Blue-collar factory workers	28
D	Working class	Semi-and unskilled manual workers	18
E	Lowest level of subsistence	Poor pensioners, disabled, casual workers	14

Table 4B. Class readership of British press

	Social grade	Newspaper
A	Upper middle class	*The Times, Financial Times*
B	Middle class	*Daily Telegraph, Guardian, Independent*
C^1	Lower middle class	*Daily Express, Daily Mail, Today*
C^2,D	Working class	*Sun, Daily Mirror, Daily Star*

10. Developing countries: socio-economic groups. As has been shown in the discussion of population triangles (*see* 1, 15), in

developing countries purchasing power may lie with only 50 per
cent of the population because 50 per cent are below fifteen years
of age and therefore not working and without income. In many
predominantly agricultural countries the urban elite may consist of
no more than 20 per cent of the population. The majority (unlike
the British example) will be so poor that they do not represent the
main market for consumer goods. Consequently the socio–
economic system of grading by income is more appropriate, and a
typical social breakdown will be as shown in Table 4C.

Table 4C. Typical socio–economic groups in developing countries

Socio–economic group	Members	Percentage of population
A Upper class	Royal and well-to-do families	2
B Middle class	Educated people in business, education and health services, civil service, professions, officers in Armed Forces	23
C Lower class	The majority, mostly farmers, factory workers	70
D Subsistence level	Beggars, disabled, unemployed	5

In the even poorer underdeveloped countries the class distinctions
may be much sharper, rather like those shown in Table 4D, based
on a scale of education. One of the tragedies in some rural
countries where many children do go to school is that when they
leave school there is no work requiring literacy, and on going back
to the land they lapse into *lost literacy*.

11. Marketing research in the South. The discussion above on
social grading highlights the difficulty facing marketing and market
research in the South. Perhaps it is significant that in a book as
painstaking as Nwokoye's *Modern Marketing for Nigeria*
(Macmillan, 1981) there is no mention of social grades, socio-
economic groups, or social classes, and that sample selection is

related to 'households'. In other words, the author applies marketing and market research to the broad generality of the elitist urban minority only. The rest are beyond the pale of marketing.

Table 4D. Social classes in very poor countries

Social class	Level of education	Members	Percentage of population
A	University graduate	Teachers, lawyers, doctors, etc.	1
B	Secondary school	Office workers	5
C	Partly literate	Unskilled workers	14
D	Illiterate	Farmers, miners fisherman	80

However, in Kenya surveys have extended into the rural areas, and it is interesting that a national survey into readership of newspapers and magazines produced the category of those who 'listened to newspapers', that is, had them read to them by a literate member of the family.

Meanwhile, the story is told of the British tea company which carried out a survey in Trinidad to find out whether there was a market for tea. It was a very successful study for the majority of Trinidadians expressed their liking for tea. The researchers returned to London and reported confidently that the marketing prospects were excellent. Unfortunately, no one had told them that in Trinidad everything—tea, coffee, cocoa, chocolate and local drinks—are called 'tea'!

Marketing research techniques

12. Introduction. There are many marketing research techniques but most of them are special ways of securing particular information, rather as there are different doctors who specialise in treating certain illnesses, diseases or injuries. Some research firms offer a range of techniques, others specialise in one. The user of such services needs to be careful that they know precisely what kind of information they require, and is able to commission the most suitable technique. Otherwise they would be like a sick person walking down Harley Street and not knowing whether they need a neurologist or a gynaecologist. The principal forms of marketing research available are outlined in 13–27 below.

13. Desk research. This consists of the study of existing or secondary data, which may include:

(*a*) internal records such as production, sales and annual results figures, and salesmen's and other internal reports;

(*b*) government statistics such as censuses of population, production and distribution, statistics resulting from taxes, licence fees and import duties, official social surveys and other figures available from the Central Statistical Office and government departments;

(*c*) privately published statistics and survey reports.

The Central Statistical Office, which is part of the Cabinet Office, co–ordinates the work of the statistics divisions of all major government departments plus the two big data collecting agencies, the Business Statistics Office and the Office of Population Censuses and Surveys (which also includes the registration division of the Registrar General's Office). A very useful free pamphlet, *Government Statistics*, is published annually, and this catalogues the numerous government statistical publications which are on sale at HMSO bookshops, through HMSO local sales agents (e.g. large booksellers) or by post.

An excellent little compendium which demonstrates the wealth of statistics available in the UK is the annual *Marketing Pocket Book* published by the Advertising Association.

14. Opinion, attitude or shift surveys. Structured questionnaires are used in such surveys to discover the percentages of people selected for the sampling frame who express 'Yes', 'No' or 'Don't know' answers. In the public mind this type of survey is usually associated with political issues, especially at election times when a variety of opinion polls are commissioned by newspapers and television stations.

However, opinion surveys are frequently commissioned from

well-known firms such as Social Surveys (Gallup Poll), National Opinion Polls and Harris for commercial purposes. In this case, they are usually used as a form of continuous research, a series of polls recording the shift of opinion or awareness. It is a form of research which is useful for the measurement of public relations campaigns. For example, it could be used to measure the increase in awareness of a company or product as a result of sponsorship or a special advertising campaign (*see* Fig. 4.1). On the other hand, a single opinion poll could be conducted to research possible names for a new product.

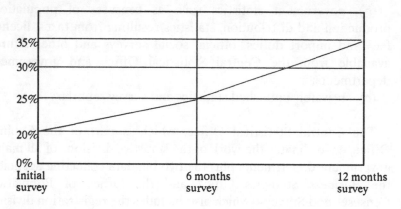

Figure 4.1 *Graphical presentation of the results of a shift survey*

15. Image studies. Such studies seek to discover a company's image by comparing it with that of rival organisations.

Assuming that prior to the advertising, PR or marketing campaign there was 20 per cent awareness of the product, a survey at six months shows that awareness has improved to 25 per cent, and a further survey at twelve months shows that 35 per cent awareness has been achieved.

Questionnaires are prepared to learn how the sample rates a number of companies on a series of common issues such as quality, delivery, price, service, research, after-sales service and so on. These are then recorded on a graph as in Fig. 4.2, the curves for each topic indicating how good or bad each company is regarded issue by issue.

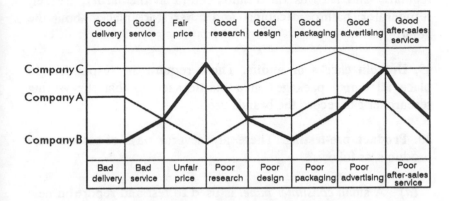

Good delivery	Good service	Fair price	Good research	Good design	Good packaging	Good advertising	Good after-sales service
Company C							
Company A							
Company B							
Bad delivery	Bad service	Unfair price	Poor research	Poor design	Poor packaging	Poor advertising	Poor after-sales service

Figure 4.2   *Graphical representation of the results of an image study comparing opinions of the performance of three companies. One of the companies shown is the one commissioning the survey; any number of companies could be compared.*

16. Consumer panels. These are another form of continuous survey, a number of respondents being recruited on a quota sample or random sample basis to serve as a permanent panel. Supplied with a diary, usually with daily pages printed with headings for different kinds of products, the respondent writes down the brands and sizes bought and the place of purchase. The completed diaries are returned by post to the research firm where the information is processed to show what type of customers buy different brands in various sizes or quantities, how often and where. For this service the respondents receive a small payment such as a grocery token. Some panels are nationwide and will contain a few thousand panelists.

17. Omnibus surveys. Panels are again recruited, but the respondents are sent questionnaires containing sets of questions on various subjects inserted by subscribers, this co-operative commissioning being called 'piggy-backing'. For the subscribers, it is an economical way of conducting research. They can subscribe occasionally or regularly.

18. Brand barometer or 'pantry' check surveys. These also use a recruited panel, but in this case a researcher visits the panelists regularly and records the brands found in the larder, freezer, refrigerator, bathroom cabinet and other store places about the home.

19. Dustbin checks or audits. These require the respondent to place all empty packages in a plastic sack so that the visiting researcher can record the brands used.

20. Product pre-testing. There are several ways of testing new products, as follows.

(*a*)   A small *consumer panel* is used to test and report on new products from time to time.

(*b*)   Interviewers call on a *sample of households*, leaving the product for a test period, and then calling again with a questionnaire.

(*c*)   Another method is the *blind-product* test when respondents are asked to state their preferences for goods in plain packages.

(*d*)   Preferences for packages, wrappers or product colours can be measured by the *paired comparison test* method when a choice is offered between A or B, and then this choice is offered with C, thus arriving at the final choice.

(*e*)   The *living laboratory* technique invites respondents to use various products, including a new product under test, in a home setting, and the behaviour and attitudes of the respondents are recorded.

(*f*)   A similar method is the *play laboratory* in which children's reactions to new products are observed, the observational room being fitted with two-way windows and video and audio recording equipment.

21. Telephone questionnaires. This is an economical technique when the sample is small, scattered or consists of busy people unwilling to grant personal interviews. The method is often used in industrial research when a comparatively small number of important people in distant locations have to be interviewed (*see* 16, 7). Telephone enquiries should be arranged by appointment. Unsolicited telephone calls could be irritating and so produce unreliable results.

22. Postal questionnaires. Again, this is an inexpensive way of obtaining information, but the accuracy of the results could be affected if there was a poor return of completed questionnaires. The method is best used when the respondents are so interested in the subject of the study that they are willing to co-operate.

23. Coupon survey. The questionnaire is printed in the press (or house journal) and readers are asked to answer the questions and send in completed questionnaires. The weakness is that results can be based only on those questionnaires which are received, and there could be bias as well as an unrepresentative sample. However, if *any* information is useful, it may be an acceptable method.

24. Dealer, retail, shop audit. The three are different names for the same thing, the shopkeepers being a recruited panel. A representative of the research firm visits the shops regularly (monthly or two-monthly) to check invoices and remaining stocks of every brand, and the information is processed to show the shares of the market held by each brand. As the audits are continuous it is possible for subscribers to observe the performance of their products in comparison with that of rivals. The effect of their own and their rivals' advertising and promotional activities can be seen in the published reports. Dealer audits are not conducted by individual manufacturers, nor by their salespeople, and dealers are not asked about customer attitudes. Some questions may be asked about the dealer's own promotional activities.

A consumer panel (*see* **16**) and a dealer audit could be used together, the one revealing what consumers buy, the other showing how competing brands sell.

25. Motivation research. The doyen of motivation research is Dr Ernst Dichter of the Institute of Motivational Research, New York. He is the author of many books on the subject (e.g. *Handbook of Consumer Motivation*, McGraw Hill, 1964), and his and Louis Cheskin's work is described in Vance Packard's bestseller, *Hidden Persuaders* (Penguin).

The object of such research is to discover the underlying motives for customer behaviour. When answering a normal questionnaire a respondent may quite sincerely state why he or she buys something, but may not be conscious of the genuine reason. By the use of clinical tests such as sentence completion, word association, story completion, thematic apperception and other tests, motivation research studies both the respondent and the respondent's responses.

Such intense testing means that sample sizes have to be small, and this has led to some criticism of the method. On the other hand, the results of motivational studies have been spectacular, according to the books mentioned above. Obviously, if it is possible to detect the real buying motives of customers it is possible to market goods more objectively, and to use advertising appeals which will win response.

There is the classic case of the airline which learned from ordinary field research using questionnaires that business passenger sales were poor because air travel was thought to be unsafe, whereas a motivational study showed that the real problem was that businessmen were concerned about their family responsibilities if they were involved in an air accident. The first survey called for advertising stressing air safety, but the second resulted in advertising addressed to businessmen's wives, telling them that their husbands would be home sooner if they travelled by air.

A modern form of motivation research is *psychodrawing*, a technique which requires respondents to draw stick men, caption cartoons or complete thought–bubbles in drawings. This releases responses.

Associated with all this is the current tendency to create psychographic types such as yuppies (young upwardly mobile professionals), empty nesters (marrieds without children), woopies (well off older people) and the silver market of retired people.

26. Discussion groups. This method might be described as the poor man's motivation research. A representative group is assembled with a leader who poses questions. Using the 'brainstorming' technique, respondents are encouraged to discuss the subject spontaneously so that comments and answers are provoked which may be more revealing than individual answers to straight questions. Again the sample has to be small, and a criticism is that the leader may introduce bias. However, the method has proved to be effective when those present have been representative of the subject, as when people engaged in an industry or profession have discussed aspects of it under study.

27. Quantitative and qualitative research. From the above analysis it will be seen that there is research which produces results in figures or percentages, and this is known as *quantitative* research. However, when the results are expressed in reasons, statements or other descriptive forms this is known as *qualitative* research. Motivation research and discussion groups come into this category, and as mentioned in 8(*n*) it is particularly successful when researching in developing countries.

Questionnaires

28. Style. Extremely important to the success of surveys which use a questionnaire is the way in which the questions are written, and the styles in which they are presented. Monotony has to be avoided, and the respondent must not be deterred by what appears to be a massive document which threatens a lengthy session. This is particularly true if the interview occurs in the street. Some questionnaires may look longer than they are because there may be sets of alternative questions according to the answers given at various stages of the interview. For instance, the respondent may be asked where he took his last holiday, e.g. at home or abroad, and according to that answer there could be alternative sets of follow–up questions.

Questions should be easy to answer and unambiguous. It is surprising how apparently simple questions can produce wrong answers. If a person is asked whether he owns or rents his house he could consider that having a mortgage did not constitute ownership. In the same way, if a person is asked whether he owns a car he might say 'No' if he drove a company car. It would be better to ask 'Do you drive a car?' Questions have to be precise to get correct answers.

29. Types of question. There are different ways of asking questions, and a questionnaire is made more interesting if various types of question are included. The following are different forms of question.

(a)	Do you drive a car	YES	NO
	If YES, do you own a car	YES	NO

(b) Which of the following makes of car do you normally drive?

BL	Renault
Talbot	Citroen
Vauxhall	Fiat
Ford	Alfa Romeo
Datsun	Audi
Toyota	Volkswagen
Mazda	Volvo
Honda	Saab
Daf	Any other

(c) How would you rate the reliability of the car you normally drive?

Very bad   Bad   Poor   Fairly good   Good   Very good

(d) State briefly why you would, or would not, buy the same make of car again ....
....
....

Figure 4.3. *Mock questionnaire to demonstrate (a) dichotomous, (b) multi–choice, (c) semantic differential, and (d) open–ended questions*

(*a*) *Dichotomous* questions require 'Yes' or 'No' answers, although 'Don't know' may also be included.

(b) *Multi-choice* questions list a number of items and the respondent is asked, perhaps, which one he bought last or would buy next, with a final 'any other' opportunity to state an item not listed. An example might be 'Which of the following makes of motor car do you drive?' or 'Which make would you choose when next buying a motor car?'

(c) *Semantic differential* questions invite respondents to rate something in three degrees of good, and three degrees of bad, to which plus or minus points can be made. A typical range might be 'very good, good, fair, poor, very poor, bad'.

(d) *Order of merit* is somewhat similar to (c), except that a number of items or brands are given and the respondent is asked to rank them in order of merit or preference.

(e) *Recall* questions usually involve some device to test ability to remember, or items such as labels, advertisements or mastheads of newspaper titles will be shown to the respondent to assist recall. The last of these are used in readership surveys when asking if and when the publication was last read. This is called *aided recall*.

(f) *Open-ended* questions are those which invite the respondent to speak freely and a note is made, either in full or in summary, of the answer. This enables the respondent to escape from the restrictions of the structured questions and to express ideas or opinions.

The mock questionnaire in Fig. 4.3 indicates how some of the different types of questions may be set out. A real questionnaire would, of course, have many questions covering several sheets.

30. Tabulation and checking. Boxes (or numbers) are inserted for marking by the interviewer so that all the forms can then be tabulated by computer. The identities of respondents will be lost in the final assessment. However, a supervisor will check the forms to see that replies conform to a reasonable pattern, and a number of respondents may be asked whether they actually gave the answers credited to them. This is a means of checking to see that the interviewer did, in fact, obtain the answers, and did not merely fill in the answers at home!

Progress test 4

1. Define marketing research as distinct from market research. (1)

2. What are the three principal forms of information sought by marketing research? (3)

3. Distinguish between primary and secondary research. (4)

4. What sort of organisations conduct research? (7)

5. What is meant by the population, as distinct from the census population, in marketing research? (80)

6. What is a quota sample? (8)

7. What is a random sample? (8)

8. What is a random walk? (8)

9. How do social grades differ from socio-economic groups? (9,10)

10. How does an opinion survey differ from an image study, both in kinds of questions asked and in the presentation of results? (14,15)

11. How does a consumer panel operate? (16)

12. What is 'piggy-backing'? (17)

13. How can a telephone interview be conducted effectively? (21)

14. How is a dealer audit survey conducted? (24)

15. How does the data gained from a consumer panel differ from that of a dealer audit? (24)

16. What is the difference between quantitative and qualitative research? (27)

17. What are multi-choice questions? (29)

5
Packaging

Introduction

1. Importance of packaging to marketing. Packaging has become a major part of marketing strategy. Colour advertising on posters, in the press and on television has made it possible to establish *pack recognition*. This is important with the development of self-service, supermarkets and hypermarkets where the package has to identify the product quickly and act as a silent salesman. It is very much a vital part of competitive marketing when there are many rival brands.

2. Benefits of packaging. Except in a very few instances, goods are no longer sold 'loose', weighed up and put into bags. Foods are sold more hygienically, items of clothing are supplied more cleanly, small items are packed more safely, and many products are packed more helpfully for the customer's convenience. From the shopkeeper's point of view, many goods are packed so that they display more attractively.

3. Cost. It costs money to package goods, not only for the package itself but for filling and packaging machinery. The customer pays for all this in the price. A balance has to be made between the benefits to the manufacturer and those to the customer, and too lavish and costly packaging should be avoided. However, in certain cases the packaging is part of the customer satisfaction, especially when it is a gift like chocolates or perfume. There are some products where the package costs more then the contents, but this may be psychologically justified. For example, a returnable and washable milk bottle is an expensive package compared with a disposable waxed paper carton. However, a glass milk bottle is strong and more acceptable for door-to-door deliveries than a carton, while the carton is more acceptable than a bottle when milk is purchased at a supermarket and is less heavy to carry.

Essentials of packaging

4. Introduction. The six essentials of packaging are outlined in 5–10 below. Not all of them will have the same importance for every product or in every circumstance. For example, it may be sufficient to place a product in a paper wrapping for the British market, while for overseas markets it is necessary to use a can. This is true of products such as butter and margarine.

5. Distinction. The package should distinguish the product so that it is both easy to identify and distinct from rival brands. There should be no doubt whether one is taking a packet of Aspro, Disprin, Phensic or Anadin off the self-service chemist's or supermarket shelf. The product may be distinguished by the colour or shape of the package, or by the kind of container it is packed in. All this is in addition to the brand name.

6. Protection. Different kinds of protection will be necessary for different types of product. A piece of delicate electronic equipment, a camera or tableware – anything likely to be damaged and possibly having to be delivered – will need interior packaging such as specially shaped blocks of expanded polystyrene, foam rubber or plastic chips. Examples of simpler protective packaging include paper lining bags for tea, corrugated paper for biscuits, silver paper for chocolate, foil blister packs for medicinal tablets and pieces of card inside shirts. The outside package may provide sufficient protection in itself as will be evident when packaging forms and materials are discussed below.

7. Convenience. Is the package so designed that it is easy to carry, use or perhaps convert for reuse? Is it convenient for warehousing, transporting and stocking and displaying?

8. Transportation costs. Some containers, e.g. glass and metal ones, are heavy, and so are goods in liquid rather than powder or tablet form. If goods have to be transported long distances, or exported, the carriage costs could be high if the packaging or form of the product was weighty. Today, many goods are air-freighted and packaging becomes a serious cost consideration.

9. Characteristic. The product should, as far as possible, be in a familiar container – one does not expect to find champagne in a beer bottle. It is more a question of appropriateness since originality of container is often a mark of distinction. The familiar pinched shape Coca-Cola bottle gave the product a distinctive character – it was designed so that it was recognisable even in the dark. However, it is no longer the only pack, and there are now Coca-Cola cans and large disposable plastic bottles.

10. Immediate association. It may help if there is a family resemblance between the products of the same company. This may be achieved by use of the same sort of container, the label, colour scheme or a symbol or logotype. Colour coding can be useful, as with the Gillette system of special colours for different razor packs and their particular blades.

Materials

11. Cost considerations. Today there is a great variety of often competing packaging materials for both containers and outer wrappings, and there are firms which specialise in package design and production.

When planning the package a choice may have to be made between several materials which will be judged according to the factors listed in **5–10**, but there remains the question of *cost*. Is it more economical (apart from being lighter) to pack in polythene instead of cardboard, plastic instead of glass, foil instead of tin? Is it necessary to pack jam in glass jars because the colour of the fruit is visible, but acceptable to pack larger, catering sizes in cans (*see* 12(*a*))? It may pay to use a more expensive material because a poorer pack would 'cost' goodwill. Important marketing decisions have to be made.

12. List of materials. The following are some of the materials that may be used.

(a)   *Glass.* The can and the plastic bottle have not replaced glass, and it remains the popular material for packing liquids and items in liquid. Although breakable, glass is strong, and many glass containers are recovered, cleaned and reused. The transparency of glass is a strong point in its favour, lending itself to the effective marketing of food items which are served on the table on succeeding occasions. This cannot be done with a can. However, bulk supplies of the same items to restaurants may be canned.

(b)   *Wood* is less used today except for sending fruit and vegetables or fish to market, and thence to the retailer. It still has a few traditional uses for packing smaller items, e.g. cigar boxes.

(c)   *Paper,* whether plain, waxed or metallic, is a universal packing material, and is light, clean, strong and easily disposable. It is also easy to print on.

(d)   *Metal foil* i.e. 'silver paper' can be used in lightweight form for confectionery, or in a heavier grade for pouches to contain tobacco. It may also be used to decorate the necks of bottles.

(e)   *Cellophane* is light, visible, clean-looking and useful for protective or see-through purposes, or to seal a packet of cigarettes or a box of chocolates.

(f)   *Metal* protects well and has good keeping qualities. Canned foods have been found to be in perfect condition years after they were packed. Fruit canning has made it possible to preserve and market fruit internationally. Cans can be fitted with lids and made airtight to hold biscuits, cakes, coffee or tobacco (*see* **14**(*d*)). They can also be fitted with rip-pull opening devices so that beer, soft drinks, milk, engine oil, anti-freeze and other liquids can be marketed in a convenient form.

(g)   *Plastics,* with their lightness and pliability, lend themselves to containers for liquids as different as ketchup, washing-up liquid and cosmetics. Rigid plastic materials are used for dispensers of razor blades, mounts for pens, containers for lighters, and many boxed items. Plastic shopping bags enable retailers to provide useful reminders and advertisements as well as an immediate service. Plastic materials are among the most versatile, and are often inexpensive.

Forms of packaging

13. Customer goodwill. Even more versatile are the forms of modern packaging, many of the newer kinds excelling in their ability to satisfy the customer. This goodwill element can be one of the ways in which the marketing manager shows his sense of public relations. It calls for thoughtfulness as well as ingenuity. It is one thing to choose a form of packaging which is economical, preserves and presents the product well, and serves as a good advertisement. However, to do that and please the customer as well is masterly.

14. Forms of packaging. Modern packaging falls into the following categories.

(a) *Cardboard boxes* are useful for a number of loose items such as matches, chocolates, sweets, tablets and toys.

(b) *Cardboard cartons*, which may or may not be sealed, are used to contain either the actual product such as a tool or domestic appliance, or products bought by the packet such as tea or breakfast cereals, or to hold an already packed product such as a jar of face cream or a bottle of cough mixture. It may be asked whether it is necessary to place a bottle in a carton. There are four reasons, as follows.

(i) The carton provides extra protection for the breakable bottle.

(ii) It squares up the final product and makes it easier to distribute in bulk.

(iii) It provides a good means of distinguishing and promoting the product.

(iv) It may be necessary to include a loose instruction leaflet (a 'stuffer') or have the area of the carton on which to print instructions.

Waxed cartons are used for milk, fruit juice and other edible liquids. Small unit goods can be supplied to the retailer in cartons which open up and can be used for counter display purposes, as with confectionery. These are known as *display outers*.

(c) *Cardboard tubs or drums* can be used with card, metal or plastic lids for ice cream, cookery items such as peel or cherries, aspirins, yoghurt, pepper and other small unit goods. Similar receptacles may be made of plastic with snap or screw-on lids.

(*d*) *Metal cans* are used mainly for liquid or powder products. In the case of paints a plastic handle (on a large can) is more comfortable for the holder than a metal handle. Cans may be sealed or have airtight lids; it is necessary to consider whether the can will be completely emptied when used (as with a can of fruit), or have contents taken from it from time to time (as with coffee or paint). Pet foods are badly packed in cans which have to be opened with a can-opener so that they cannot be resealed, and yet the contents are unlikely to be used completely at one feeding. Here is a case of economy conflicting with customer usage. Some pet-owners may not have a refrigerator, and so are deterred from buying economical jumbo packs.

(*e*) *Bottles and jars*, often with screw tops, are convenient packs for products used from time to time, and may be reusable for some other storage purpose. They may have distinctive values such as the special shapes used either for different brands of spirits, or for particular wines such as port, sauterne, brandy, claret, burgundy, hock, vermouth, chianti and champagne.

(*f*) *Plastic bottles* may be used for their lightness or cheapness, but also because they can be squeezed to eject or spray the contents such as washing-up liquid or perfume.

(*g*) *Sachets* (usually plastic or metal foil) containing measured quantities are both convenient and easy to use correctly, so that haphazard measurements with container lids or spoons are unnecessary. Typical product uses are hair shampoos, car waxes, garden insecticides and, in larger sizes, packet soups. Individual portions of condiments are packed in sachets for caterers.

(*h*) *Paper packets* are used for garden seeds, custard powders, flour and individual portions of sugar and milk substitute.

(*i*) *Plastic bubble packs* with card backing are used for do-it-yourself and gardening products which are suspended from display stands for self-service. The plastic bubble contains, protects and makes visible items such as screws, cup-hooks or parts for garden hoses. Small toys and music cassettes are also packed like this.

(*j*) *Tubes* are used for products which can be squeezed out, such as toothpaste, adhesive, shaving cream, mustard, paté and other foods. They may be metal or plastic.

(*k*) *Aerosols* are an expensive but popular form of packaging for hair sprays, shaving cream, deodorants, polishes, air fresheners and insecticides. However, because of the damaging effect of fluorocarbons (used in aerosols) some manufacturers of products such as deodorants now use sticks or roll-on packs.

(*l*) *Paper wrappings* are used for cut loaves of bread, confectionery, butter, lard, margarine and other items which require simple but hygienic covering.

(*m*) *Foil wrapping* may be used both to contain items and to make them look attractive, its applications ranging from butter, margarine and cheeses to high quality confectionery such as chocolate liqueurs.

(*n*) *Ejectors and dispensers* are used for aspirins, sweets, saccharine, razor blades, tissues and toilet paper.

(*o*) *Blister packs* are used for many kinds of medicinal tablets which can be pressed free.

(*p*) *Expanded polystyrene trays* with stretch plastic film covering meat, fruit and vegetables are often found in supermarkets.

(*q*) *Carry packs* have been created for a variety of products such as beers sold in sixes, and there are *carry sacks* with handles for pet litter, lawn fertiliser and other weighty items. Some heavy items like electrical appliances are packed in a stout cardboard box with a handle. Clothing such as suits and coats are packed by the retailer in a fold-up plastic bag which has a handle. Again, this ingenious form of packaging protects the product, and helps the customer to carry the goods home safely and comfortably.

15. Choice of package. From the above it will be realised that choice of package can be the means of achieving marketing success. The ordinary traditional package may suffice, but the well-thought-out one adds to the saleability of the product. One of the best instances is the proprietary medicine that was once packed in liquid form in a clumsy bottle but is now available in tablet form in a handy blister pack that can be carried in the pocket, briefcase or handbag. The advent of the freezer has also made possible the packing of large quantities of ice-cream in large reusable plastic boxes, or large quantities of vegetables such as peas in big plastic bags.

16. Methods of extraction. Associated with some of the modern forms of packaging are clever ways of extracting the product, such as the plastic filling nozzle on the litre oil can, the nozzle on the lighter fuel container, the plastic box of soft drink through which a drink straw can be plunged, and the picture corners which are fed out of a slit in the pack in a continuous strip. On the other hand, there are still many people who find it difficult to cut the tip off a carton of fruit juice without spilling the contents, however convenient the pack may be for purchasing and storage.

A very simple to use product is the Cafenol pain reliever. Cafenol is packed in cards of four tablets for two doses, and there are ten cards in one packet. This packaging helps African rural dwellers, no matter what language they speak, to use the product carefully and correctly.

17. Other forms of packaging. There are certain products which cannot be contained or wrapped, being complete in themselves to the extent that the outer appearance of the product, e.g. the design or colour, is a form of packaging in itself. This occurs with mechanical products which have an external casing for protection, utility or good appearance; for example motor cars, sewing machines, vacuum cleaners and tape recorders. Yet another form of packaging is the dust jacket of a book, paperback novels especially.

18. Face-lifts for old packs. To change a pack completely would suggest an entirely new product, and so the identity of an established product would be lost. On the other hand an old-fashioned design could also have an adverse effect. New buyers are continually coming into the market, and different generations have their own ideas on what sort of package appeals to them. Even so, the basic product may remain unchanged or changed very little. To keep pace with the times, old packs are given face-lifts which retain well-known characteristics while achieving a more modern appearance. Some of these changes are so subtle that they are scarcely noticed by old customers, examples being the changes introduced by Coca-Cola, Guinness, Cadbury, Nestlé, Aspro, Three Nuns tobacco, Eno's cough mixture, Ilford films and Swan Vestas matches over the years. Added interest has been given to Swan Vestas boxes by printing premium offers on the reverse side.

Changes also have to be made when a company alters its name or there is an amalgamation of two or more companies. Such changes can be done in stages, two names appearing for a while until the old one is dropped and the new one becomes the accepted one. This was the case some years ago when Selo film became Ilford film; for a time the film was called Selo-Ilford until the Selo was eventually dropped. The same happened with the Rolls-Bentley with Rolls-Royce surviving, while the Standard-Triumph gave way to the Triumph. Here the 'packaging' was in the car badges and other identifying decorations.

Progress test 5

1. What are the six essentials of a package? **(5–10)**
2. How have plastic materials been applied to modern packaging? **(12, 14)**
3. For what reasons are containers placed in an outer wrapping or carton? **(14)**
4. Describe some of the modern packs which either help the customer to use the product more efficiently, or present the product in a more convenient form. **(14)**
5. Why is it necessary to introduce face-lifts with subtlety? **(18)**

6
Naming and branding

Origins of names

1. Family names. It was natural that the earliest companies should be named after their founders, for they were private companies financed by the founder, perhaps with assistance from relatives and friends. Many were family businesses and, like Pilkington and Sainsbury's, they remained so until fairly recently. Consequently, the pioneers of modern businesses bear names such as Lever, Cadbury, Rowntree, Mackintosh, Brooke Bond, Ford, Woolworth, Marks & Spencer, Sainsbury's, Gillette and Whitbread.

2. Made-up names. Incorporated companies, holding companies and those resulting from amalgamations tend to have impersonal or made–up names. Moreover, as private companies have become public (with shares sold on the stock market) or there have been acquisitions or mergers, family names have been reduced to initials. Examples are RHM (Rank, Hovis, McDougall) and GKN (Guest, Keen and Nettlefold) (*see also* 14).

3. Product names. Many products also took their product brand names and trade marks from the company name, to mention only Coca-Cola, Guinness, Cadbury's and Ford. This is all very well with long-established household names, but the situation is different today. A new name emerges among thousands of other names and has to fight for recognition, acceptance and memorability.

4. Different reasons in the South. In the developing countries, different reasons for the origins of names can be identified.

(*a*) *Superstition.* The Chinese, who are clever businessmen operating in many parts of the world, prefer names which suggest good fortune, and 'Lucky' is a popular business name.

(*b*) *Respect for foreign names.* In some African countries there is a tendency to adopt European names because European standards are considered higher and a company which sounds as if it is European is likely to attract more business.

(*c*) *National pride.* On the other hand, national pride is beginning to assert itself and many companies will prefix company names with their country's name; for example, Nigerian Bottlers and Nigerian Aluminium Extrusions. In Zimbabwe companies originally prefixed Rhodesian or Rho have changed to the country's new name.

5. The Japanese example. It is significant that when the Japanese first exported goods they often used names which seemed to be acceptable abroad such as National Panasonic, Pioneer, Colt and Olympus. Some easily pronounced Japanese names, such as Toyota and Datsun, were used and also contractions like Toshiba for Tokyo Shibaura Electrical Company. Now, however, having gained substantial acceptance in foreign markets, some Japanese companies are reverting to Japanese names, while Subaro and Daihatsu have entered the market with normal Japanese names.

The Japanese experience is interesting for they are experts in marketing tactics. In the 1930s Europeans regarded Japanese products such as celluloid toys and fancy goods made of paper as trivialities. Then there was the effect of war and the post–war unpopularity of the Japanese in places like Manila, Jakarta, Hong Kong and Singapore.

Today, the Japanese motor car dominates these markets. The red Nissan taxis are to Hong Kong what red buses are to London. There are Japanese department stores in Hong Kong, such as the well–established Daimaru and Matsuzakaya and the Mitsukoshi store which occupies the ground and three basement floors of the Hennessy Centre in Causeway Bay. The Japanese also top the tourist figures, making up about 20 per cent of the total according to a Hong Kong Tourist Association census. There is world–wide respect for Japanese technical goods of which opticals, watches, motor cars, motor cycles, sewing machines, electronics and typewriters are typical examples. Even in China, many of the buses and taxis are Toyota or Nissan, and outdoor advertising for Japanese products such as Sony vie with those for Gillette, Mackintosh's Quality Street and numerous Chinese products.

The name may be disguised or it may be obvious but it is a marketing success story in which the acceptance of names is important.

In spite of old prejudices and enmities how have the Japanese won acceptance for their company and brand names? While it is true that because of the common use of easily pronounced vowels (e.g. Toyota, Kawasaki, Honda) the names are easily said and remembered (*see* 11), the goods themselves have been of a quality which has won respect and recommendation. This has been partly because of the high degree of mechanisation, automation and robotics which means that each product is identically well–made. It comes back to the old principle of 'paying for the name', meaning that the name is worth paying for.

Different types of name

6. Company name. The company name may or may not be the brand name. Guinness is both the company name and the brand name, although the company name is extended as may be required legally, the British version being Guinness Sons and Company (Park Royal) Ltd. In contrast, there is no such thing as a General Motors motor car although the brands of Chevrolet, Vauxhall and Opel are familiar.

It could be a marketing policy to exploit the company name or to develop separate brand names of little or unknown parentage. The choice of company name, and its easy recall and respected corporate image, will be important if that name is associated with products, brands and services.

Philips is a company name closely associated with products and with the slogan 'Simply years ahead'. On the other hand, neither CPC (Europe) Ltd. nor CPC (United Kingdom) Ltd. is readily associated with Brown and Polson's cornflour, Knorr soups,

Mazola cooking oil, Frank Cooper marmalade, Dextrosol or Hellman's mayonnaise. Yet both Philips and CPC are large multinationals.

In Europe, CPC (Europe) Ltd. tends to stay in the background as the holding company. This was fortunate when a problem occurred over material supplied to a Dutch cattle-food producer, the incident did not reflect on CPC's domestic products because the latter were known in their own right. However, this policy is not followed world-wide, and in Hong Kong Mazola cooking oil is advertised quite openly as being made by Corn Products Co. (Hong Kong) Ltd.

7. Brand name. This is usually shorter than the company name and is often no more than a single word. The single word or short name may be taken from the full company name, as in the example of Guinness above, or be independent of the parent name, as in the case of brands of matches made by Bryant and May, e.g. Swan Vestas.

Brewing is a growing industry in Nigeria. While Guinness have expanded to three breweries and sell nationally there are many local breweries throughout the numerous states. Brand names proliferate, to quote only Champion, Club, Crystal, Double Crown, Harp, Golden Guinea, Power, Rock, Star, Top and Trophy.

Brand names, written in a special way or arranged in an original design or shape, may be protected by registration as a trade mark under the Trade Marks Act.

8. Trade name. In addition to brand names there may be other names which distinguish the individual products in the product mix. There may be named ranges, usually denoting price, quality or particular style, or individual product names. The company or brand name may be linked as with Ford Sierra or Honda Accord, or it may be separate as in the cases of furniture and carpets. Such names are not usually registered.

9. Generic name. Here we have a name which is not registered and is applied broadly to a kind of product. For example, while we have the business name of Nestlé, and the brand name of Nescafé, there is the generic name of instant coffee which is also used by Maxwell House, Bird's and other makers.

Sometimes brand names may pass into everyday usage and be applied to all products of that type, thus becoming a generic name, e.g. hoover, although companies with registered names like Vaseline will go to great lengths to protect and preserve the legal status of such names.

Creating a new name today

10. Marketing strategy. As we have seen many names have owed more to natural self-identification – the 'my company' vanity of the industrial revolution and development of a century or more ago – than to deliberate marketing purpose. Today it is sensible, especially in a world of so many names competing for attention, to invent or adopt names that will strengthen the marketing strategy. This applies equally to new companies, new products and new names required as a result of mergers, etc. (*see* 13).

11. Six essentials for a new name. The following are some of the chief considerations when deciding on a new name, whether of a company or a product.

(*a*)　*Is it distinctive?* Does it stand out from all others, especially if it identifies one of a product group where there is not a lot of difference between rival brands? Stork is still probably the most distinctive name given to a brand of margarine.

(*b*)　*Is it easy to pronounce?* No one should stumble over the pronunciation of a name, nor be uncertain how to pronounce it. How do you pronounce Audi, Peugeot, Guinness, Hine or Arkansas? These are all names which produce different pronunciations in various parts of the world. On the other hand, Elf, Ford and Coca-Cola are pronounced much the same way anywhere.

The most easily pronounced names are those with two or three vowels and syllables such as Kodak, Texaco, Ramada, Canada, Rentokil and Solignum, or even longer names which have a rhythmic flow like Norwich Union. These names trip off the tongue very nicely.

(*c*) *Is it memorable?* Some names are easy to recall, others are easier to forget. Cathay Pacific has a magical touch, and so has Safari Pacific, but can this be said for the names of some other airlines and hotels?

(*d*) *Is it internationally acceptable?* In the past, companies in the industrial world have done no more than export goods sold in the home market with little or no regard for the effect of these names in other countries. Some names like Coca-Cola, Elf, Lipton and Honda have had no problems, but others may have unfortunate or offensive meanings in other countries, or sound like unfortunate words. Sometimes a name has to be changed completely when the product is sold in certain countries, and this could result in a loss of world-wide impact. This marketing problem has become increasingly apparent with the decline of colonialism and the emergence of independent states which have been very articulate about their marketing susceptibilities.

The advent of cross-frontier satellite television and the single European market of 1992 make it essential that Eurobrands are acceptable throughout Europe. The Rolls-Royce Silver Mist and Irish Mist Whisky have already had their problems when 'mist' means 'dung' in German.

The motor car industry is an example of the use of particular names in different parts of the world, the company name being retained but the trade name varying from country to country or continent to continent. This is particularly true when a product is assembled or made under licence in another country where a more appropriate local name may be used.

(*e*) *Does it assist the corporate image?* When the Hong Kong hotel, the Furama, was first opened people asked whether the name represented a mixture of Japanese and Indian interests. A name should not cause such confusion. Black Magic is a name which enhances the corporate image of Rowntree just as Quality Street enhances that of Mackintosh, and because of the 'halo effect' of each product on the other, the total Rowntree Mackintosh image is also enhanced.

Some names may lose their original significance. Scottish Widows Fund is a famous insurance company with a curious name, but how many people know that the 'Widows' were those of Scottish soldiers lost in the Napoleonic wars?

(f)   *Does it lend itself to advertising, display and packaging?* Does it lend itself easily to the design of a distinctive symbol or logotype and to the overall corporate identity visual effects? Short names do this best. They can appear more dominantly than long words, whether on big outdoor signs or on small labels, examples being ITT, Sony, Oxo and Pond's.

An interesting combination of a name in stylish lettering, associated with the symbol of the moufflon, a mountain sheep, and a signature slogan, is used by Cyprus Airways. This was part of the corporate identity scheme introduced by the airline when it introduced the Airbus to its fleet. It has been repeated in numerous visual representations (especially the moufflon) such as in the livery of aircraft and in advertisements.

Figure 6.1

12. Changing names. When a name is chosen its likely permanence should be considered. Most will last a long time, if not for ever, and to have to change a name can be a costly business since recognition, acceptance and goodwill have to be built up all over again.

Some companies have changed names with bewildering frequency, to mention only the Hillman-Rootes-Chrysler-Talbot-Peugeot succession. Banks are usually old-established and there may be problems over a change of name. In Nigeria, the Standard Bank became the First Bank of Nigeria (a happy choice because it was true of the Standard Bank), which was both an easy change and an acknowledgment of national aspirations. Less easy was the change in Trinidad from Barclays to Republic, but after some initial misgivings the transition proved successful.

When a name is changed it must be an improvement and add strength to the marketing strategy. If there is a risk that the new name may suggest something inferior (simply because it is different and people can be very conservative) it will be better to retain the original name. This problem has occurred in ex-colonial countries which, following independence, have indigenised foreign companies and introduced local names for ones which were internationally famous. When, for example in Zambia, Omo was transformed into Daisy, housewives were inclined to be sceptical about the product with the strange name. The fact that Daisy was the name of the chairman's daughter was irrelevant.

13. Amalgamations, mergers and acquisitions. In recent years we have seen some business combinations which have resulted in confusing changes of name. One British motor car manufacturer has had a confusion of former company names which have also been brand names, e.g. Morris, Austin, Riley, Daimler and Jaguar, and muddled company names such as British Motor Corporation, British Leyland, Austin-Rover, and then Rover. As an example of simplicity we have Rentokil, which was actually the name of the smallest in a group of nearly twenty companies.

14. Use of initials. (*See also* **2**.) The advantage of using initials is that they comply with all or most of the requirements set out in **11**. The names IBM and ICL are synonymous with computers, BAT with tobacco, and KLM with Royal Dutch Airlines. It is not always necessary to know what the initials stand for. Over the years some company names and products have been known by initials which customers may never have interpreted; for example, BDV cigarettes (best dark Virginia); PG Tips tea (pre-digested); IPA (India pale ale); HP sauce (Houses of Parliament); MG cars (Morris Garages) and P & O shipping line (Peninsular and Oriental).

A danger with initials is that they can obscure otherwise well-known names (e.g. RHM seems to destroy the familiar names of Rank, Hovis and McDougall), while different meanings can be applied to initials such as AA (Advertising Association,

Automobile Association, Alcoholics Anonymous, American Airlines). On the other hand, initials can disguise an otherwise unacceptable name. In Hong Kong, Mass Transit Railway had connotations of cattle-trucks, unlike the Metros of Paris and other cities. Within a short time the initials MTR became acceptable, and the original criticism of the name disappeared.

Even so, some full names and their abbreviations as initials are confusing. JICTAR was bad enough; did the 'A' stand for 'advertising' or 'audience'? JICNARS (see 13, 34) was even worse since the 'A' stood for nothing save the first 'a' in National. However, people eventually got used to the initials and related them to media research. With the replacement of JICTAR by BARB (see Chapter 13, 35) more confusion was created. Does the first 'B' stand for 'broadcasting' or 'broadcasters'? The resultant acronym is so remote from TV that it poses problems of communication and understanding.

15. Use of acronyms. The conversion of company initials into acronyms, i.e. pronounceable words, is an excellent device. Sometimes the word is so acceptable that it is not always realised that it is concocted from initials. Good examples are Fiat, Sabena, Amoco, Conoco, Caltex and Esso. Long associated with the 'happy motoring' slogan, Esso is certainly a happier way of saying Standard Oil, which is not very satisfactory if reduced to the initials SO, while the new version Exxon is a hard-sounding unfortunate name. Caltex is a clever amalgamation of abbreviated forms of Standard Oil California and Texaco.

16. Researching names. Nowadays, company and brand names are usually subjected to careful marketing research investigation (after first clearing that a proposed name has not been registered already). Gone are the days when the entrepreneur picked a name that pleased him personally, as in the case of Swarfega, the hand cleansing petroleum jelly. 'Swarf', known to most people as the waste metal in an engineering works, means 'clean' in the Derbyshire area of Belper! When Unigate Foods sought a name for their spread which is neither butter nor margarine they tested some 130 names before selecting what may, by hindsight, seem the obvious one of Gold (see also 18, 16).

17. Use of personal names. When industry was first developing it was natural for founders of companies to use their own names, and many of these have been household names for decades or more. Today it is probably better or even necessary to avoid family names because the business is a limited and perhaps a public company. However, in the case of a professional service, e.g. a firm of consultants, the business name can sound more convincing if the names of the practitioners or partners are used to form the name. This sounds more professional and personal than a made-up name.

Progress test 6

1. How does a trade name differ from a business name?   (6, 8)
2. What is a generic name? Give an example.   (9)
3. What are the six essential considerations when creating a new name?   (11)
4. Give an example of a brand name which is internationally acceptable.   (11)
5. What is meant by the 'halo effect' of a name?   (11)
6. What are the advantages of using initials such as IBM or KLM? (14)
7. What is an acronym? Give an example.   (15)
8. In what circumstances might a business adopt a personal name?   (17)

7
Pricing

The economics of pricing

1. What price? Getting the price right may be one of the most critical aspects of the marketing strategy. The normal basis of a price is that it should recover costs and return a profit. To do otherwise would mean going out of business, or requiring a subsidy from other sales or from some outside source such as the government.

However, it is not always as clear cut as that. *Market forces*, i.e. outside influences, may determine the price. For instance, a manufacturer may be able to produce a better product and sell it at a lower price than an imported product which is dearer because it bears an import duty. However, because quality and value for money are often judged by price, buyers may prefer the dearer foreign product to the cheaper home-produced one. A British watchmaker had to give up making watches because it had made the mistake of charging too little, and so giving a false impression of their quality. The company now imports and sells foreign ones.

2. Prices and company growth. It may be that a company will work strictly to the principle of recovering costs, making profits and investing part of the profit to seek growth. Thus, a business develops step by step. Rentokil's original Woodworm and Dry Rot Control servicing company began with a three-man team and an advertisement in the *Daily Telegraph*. Within a few years it was a national company with forty branches.

In contrast, a German motor car company set out to regain or create world markets after the Second World War by selling its products at reduced prices. The strategy was that when replacement sales occurred the normal price could be charged. This is called 'buying one's way into the market'. An investment is made in future sales.

Only a large company with ample financial resources, such as income from other trade, can afford to lose money while introducing a product. St Ivel Gold was introduced at a calculated loss when the price was deliberately pitched below that of butter and above that of margarine.

3. Skimming or creaming. Other pricing policies may be the opposite of the above. It may be decided to recover costs by means of an initial high price, and seek volume sales with a subsequent price reduction or lower-priced version. Here are some examples of what is called 'skimming' or 'creaming'.

(*a*) Production costs of a book may be recovered from the much higher price of a hardback or case-bound edition, volume sales coming from the cheaper paperback version.

(*b*) Similarly, costs will be recovered from the first sales of a product, after which the same product will be sold more cheaply.

(*c*) After the initial tooling-up costs of a motor car have been recovered, a cheaper model with basic equipment is marketed.

4. Price and demand elasticity. To what extent are demand and price related? Does price come down as demand increases and vice versa? Or is price *inelastic*, and not influenced by changes in demand?

As incomes increase the volume of discretionary income increases, and more and more luxury or semi-luxury goods can be bought while the sale of staples such as bread, potatoes, rice or yams remains the same. In a recession the volume of discretionary income declines, but there is not much change in the volume of staples consumed.

Demand becomes more inelastic as a product becomes adopted as a necessity. In the 1930s, when there was a housing boom, few houses were built with garages. The '£100' Ford, the '£120' Morris Minor, and the even cheaper baby Opels, Fiats and Austin 7 were only just capturing a modest market and domestic garages were rare. When building restrictions were removed in the 1950s a house-builder would offer a garage as an optional extra. By the 1960s garages were not only normal but styles of house ranged from integral garages built within the walls of the house to flats and houses with nearby rows of garages, larger houses with double garages, and carport additions in front of single garages. A house without a garage had become a poor selling proposition.

Although inflation and taxation may have vastly expanded both the money supply and retail prices, the underlying principle of supply and demand still applies, however much it may be distorted by price controls and subsidies. One has only to see the array of goods in a hypermarket or superstore to see how diversified demand has become. Wages and prices tend to match the supply and vice versa. While this may be an 'economic' way of looking at prices the word needs to be used cautiously because there is a special meaning to the expression *economic price* which will be explained in the next section (*see* 6).

Four basic kinds of price

5. Introduction. Although we shall analyse pricing decisions in fuller detail later in this chapter there are four basic kinds of price which have a distinct bearing on every other pricing consideration. They are:

(*a*) economic price;
(*b*) market price;
(*c*) psychological price;
(*d*) opportunity price.

6. Economic price. From the manufacturer's or supplier's point of view the economic price is the lowest that can be charged if costs are to be regained and a satisfactory profit is to be made. Costs are those of production and distribution. Everything must be included, both *fixed costs* such as rent, rates (or taxes) and energy, and *variable costs* such as wages, materials, packaging, transport, trade terms and advertising.

If the definition of marketing (*see* 1, 3) is reconsidered here the significance will be seen of the words 'satisfying customer requirements profitably'. This can be done at an economic price.

To achieve an economic price it may be necessary to cost very carefully the use of labour, raw materials and components. It is sometimes said that a product has been designed 'down to a price'. This may be done by producing a basic model at a competitive economic price, and then offering optional extras which the customer may choose to purchase or not.

This can lead to further competitiveness. For instance, when Datsun cars were first launched on the UK market in 1969, the selling and advertising ploy was that the car came fully equipped with items which were optional extras on the current Ford Cortina.

There is a very true expression that some prices are 'what the traffic will bear', that is, the highest people are prepared to pay. Thus we have a possible price swinging between the lowest *economic* price and the highest *market* price.

7. Market price. Following on from the above comparison, the market price is the price people expect to pay, and which it would be silly to exceed unless in a monopoly situation. However, in contradiction to the situation described in 6, there can be times when the market price is considerably higher than the economic price. People may be unwilling to accept a lower price because it is suspect (*see* example in 1). Usually, the market price is the one people have come to accept, and they may grumble at a slightly higher one, appreciate a lower one, but equally reject one that is either too high or too low.

When planning a new product it will be wise to study the market price and ask the following three questions:

(*a*) Can we make a new product and sell it at the market price profitably?

(*b*) Can we make a new product and undercut the market price profitably?

(*c*) Can we make a new product and sell it at a price higher than the market price because this is justified by superior qualities?

These three questions imply that the market price is a very important consideration. However, there may be no comparable market price if the product or service is the pioneer of its kind. There is no market price, as yet, for a trip to the moon and in early 1989 there was great argument about the price of dishes to receive satellite TV, and the cost of installing them.

8. Psychological price. There are two kinds of price which have a special psychological appeal. Neither is an economic price but both could be a market price.

(*a*) The first kind of psychological price is one which is marked to suggest that it is lower than it really is, nine sounding much less than ten, and ninety-nine much less than one hundred. Instead of saying £1 the price is given as 99p, which sounds almost like a bargain! It is not quite a deception, but it is a device commonly used by many traders.

(*b*) The second sort of psychological price is rather different. This is the price that gives satisfaction, especially when the product is a gift and the known price implies value, regard, generosity or even extravagance. Chocolates, perfumes, pens, jewellery, restaurants, champagne, furs, expensive motor cars and other luxurious products come into this field. Some of these products may be justifiably expensive, some may simply be packaged expensively, while others will have their price inflated far beyond an economic price simply to satisfy the market expectations. There are products which sell mainly because they are expensive. Exclusivity can also increase a price, as with a model dress, although now we are beginning to talk about the effect of rarity on price as occurs when a painting is sold at Sotheby's for millions.

9. Opportunity price. Here the buyer has the opportunity to choose this or that product but cannot afford both. We are now in the realm of discretionary income, that is, purchasing power left over after essentials have been bought. Very often the goods or services are expensive, but this problem may be overcome by credit terms, credit or charge cards, budget schemes, loans and overdrafts. Nevertheless, the choice may have to be made between one or more desirable purchases, and the price may determine which desirable purchase has to be sacrificed.

We have to be careful to recognise that discretionary income

will vary between income groups, and will be acute among poorer
people in developing countries where staples really are staples and
the everyday purchases of industrial countries are counted as
luxuries. In spite of deprivations in Poland, people still buy beer,
but this might be out of the question in some African or Asian
communities.

Price in relation to delivery

10. Introduction. With some products there are delivery charges,
or the price may depend on the location of sale. There can be *ex-
factory* prices, or *escalating* prices according to the distance from
the source of supply. The first applies to motor cars, the second is
true of fuels such as petrol and coal. There are five such facets of
pricing policy:

(*a*) non–discriminatory price;
(*b*) uniform delivery price;
(*c*) special price discrimination;
(*d*) basic point pricing;
(*e*) multiple basing point pricing.

11. Non-discriminatory price. A price is non-discriminatory when
the acceptable or even competitive price (which may be either or
both economic and market) is the one used for selling the product,
i.e. it is the 'list' or 'manufacturer's recommended retail price'
(MRRP). The final price will include carriage, delivery or postal
charges. This could apply to a motor car or to direct response
goods. The list price is the same everywhere, but the final price will
differ.

12. Uniform delivery price. In this case the extra costs of
transportation or carriage are averaged out and the price is the
same in a shop next door to the factory or 500 kilometres away.
Most everyday consumer goods have a uniform delivery price, only
the retailer deciding on variations on the MRRP.

13. Special price discrimination. This can be a very annoying form
of discrimination because the customer never knows what the 'real'

price is. Perhaps it is simply the lowest price obtainable, so that it pays the buyer to shop around. Special price discrimination occurs when different shops have different mark-ups, e.g. one will add 25 per cent and another $33\frac{1}{3}$ per cent to the wholesale price. Special prices occur under monopoly conditions as when a caterer has a concession at an exhibition or other public event, petrol is sold at a motorway service station, or drinks are purchased with a meal in a restaurant. The market price is flaunted in these circumstances where there is no competition and one has to pay the exorbitant price or go without, e.g. when a restaurant charges double the normal retail price for wines, that is, corkage.

14. Basic point pricing. In this case the price differs according to the distance or inconvenience of delivery. Petrol may cost less in a town than in the country. The customer may or may not know the price at source. The pit-head price of coal is cheaper than that at a distance from the mine. In a somewhat disproportionate way, books tend to be imported at an advantageous discount and retailed at an inflated retail price.

15. Multiple basing point pricing. Here the price changes, or rather *increases*, as it passes through a chain of distributors, e.g. wholesalers and retailers, until it reaches the final consumer. This is the most common form of pricing. Objections may be expressed about the 'middleman' taking profits, and putting up the prices of goods for which the maker or producer received little. However, the middleman's profits are payment for the job of transferring large volumes of goods to retailers who require smaller quantities in order to supply single items.

The alternative is for the maker or producer to undertake distribution as well. This does happen occasionally, cutting out the middleman, but more often than not the producer-cum-distributor charges the market price and keeps the middleman's profit. This only goes to show that distribution costs still have to be recovered in the price.

Multiple basing point pricing means that the price escalates as it passes through more and more hands. This is not only because middlemen are taking a profit but because costs such as labour, warehousing, office administration, rates and taxes, account collection, electricity and transport have been recovered at each stage. However, some agents and dealers may simply buy and sell on the telephone or at market place or exchange, and have few costly overheads.

Multiple basing point pricing is a complicated business and a final retail price will depend greatly on circumstances. In Hong Kong, for instance, the cost of living for a European will be far greater than that of a Chinese since the European will rely heavily on imported products. The Chinese will enjoy local products, or ones from mainland China, which are cheap. Or, to take another example, an imported can of Guinness will cost about twice the price of locally brewed San Miguel beer.

Other pricing considerations

16. Distorted price. However much the manufacturer may try to calculate a selling price–trying to achieve an economic price, costing carefully to satisfy the market price, and perhaps being competitive–market or other outside forces may falsify the price. In some countries the rather foolish practice of price controls may be adopted in the attempt to please consumers by keeping prices down. The effect of a price control is usually to bring about inferior products on the one hand and a black market on the other (*see also* **25**).

A typical price distortion is value added tax (VAT) or some form of sales tax which makes a product appear more expensive than it really is, to the manufacturer's or retailer's disadvantage since he has to charge an unreal price. Import duties again distort prices. People have long forgotten the real price of a bottle of whisky or a litre of petrol since a large proportion of the price is tax.

17. Price plateau. This resembles the market price except that it represents the limit that buyers are prepared to pay. If the price goes beyond the plateau people abandon the product or service and turn to something else. An unacceptable price has priced the item out of the market.

18. Price stability. There are some goods which manage to keep the same price for years, or increase in price very little, although high rates of inflation nowadays make it extremely difficult to maintain stability. At best, a price may be kept stable for a stated period. 'No price increase while stocks last', or a promise that, once booked, the price of a package holiday will not be increased, are practical examples. Airline managements sometimes refer to air fares and profitability being dependent upon the 'stability of oil prices'.

19. Penetration price. Leaving aside the economic, market and even psychological price, is there a special price which will enable a firm to enter the market? It may be a matter of adding a new competitive line to an existing product group such as beer, cigarettes, toothpastes or detergents. We can requote the example of St Ivel Gold (*see* 2) when a flexible price between those of butter and margarine was chosen.

The penetration price could also be an *introductory price offer*, e.g. subscribers to a new directory are offered a premium pre-publication price if they order in advance of publication, or goods are placed in the shops with a declaration such as on a flash pack that there is a special introductory offer.

20. Competitive price. The policy of undercutting competitors is called competitive pricing. Retailers do this by sending members of their staff ('shoppers') to visit rival stores and report on prices so that these prices may be undercut. A more direct and commendable method is that used by Currys, the household goods and electrical dealers, who challenge customers to find cheaper prices elsewhere, and offer a refund if the customer succeeds in doing so.

21. Divisionary price. This refers to a hidden cost which the customer may or may not anticipate when considering the list or otherwise stated price, for example the cost of fitting a carpet, gas or electrical appliance or even number plates to a motor car. It can be a selling tactic to offer a 'free tyre fitting' or 'free carpet fitting' service, the cost of this being used as a promotional distribution charge.

22. Dumping price. This occurs where, because of the volume of production, products can be sold to distributors at a very low price, usually based on a marginal cost which still allows a profit. It is a method used rather unscrupulously by companies anxious to sell into foreign markets in order to export excess products, penetrate overseas markets or gain foreign credits. The method usually produces protests from home producers who cannot afford to sell their products at such low prices. There have been conflicts between European motor car and textile firms and foreign firms about such imports.

23. Double pricing or price bashing. When there is no control by manufacturers over the minimum price charged by retailers, the list, catalogue or advertised price (MRRP) issued by the manufacturer may be taken to be the *recommended*, suggested or even maximum price. Thus, the retailer may sell at the full price, or at such lower price as he wishes. Double pricing occurs when the manufacturer deliberately sets a high list price so that the retailer is able to appear generous with his offer price.

In actual fact, where such a pricing policy is adopted, the average retail price may be much the same as the fixed price of the resale price maintenance (RPM) era.

In the 1960s the British government abolished RPM as a political gimmick to reduce consumer prices, the idea being that rings of manufacturers were maintaining or fixing unrealistic high prices when consumers should be able to enjoy the benefits of economies effected by retailers. Moreover, the more unscrupulous rings, such as those controlling tyres and radios, held private courts and penalised (by fine or withdrawal of supplies) those who were found guilty of selling below the fixed price. In the 1970s the abolition of RPM led to the abuse of recommended prices as described above. Legislation was introduced in the form of the Price Commission Act 1977, ostensibly to ban recommended prices, although up to the time of writing there has been no test case.

In other parts of the world, where one may be expected to haggle until the 'last price' is reached, it is interesting to see that the 'last price' in the bazaar and the 'fixed price' in the regular shop are the same. This is not unlike the 'recommended' and 'discounted' prices found in Britain.

24. Geographic pricing. This occurs when the price for the same item is different according to the class of shopping area, whether within one town, from region to region, or from country to country. For example, when exchange rates are favourable there can be a big price differential between motor cars made and sold in their European country of origin and in Britain, with the result that some people will go to the trouble of buying a motor car abroad and bringing it into Britain at a saving of thousands of pounds.

Even the prices of simple things like cosmetics and toiletries can vary remarkably between the West End of London and in a London borough ten miles away.

25. Controlled price. This usually applies to staples such as bread or rice, the aim being to protect consumers, and the poorest ones especially. The danger is that it can create a black market as there will always be people who will endeavour to exploit scarcity for their personal profit. We see this even when the distribution of tickets for major sporting events is controlled, yet ticket touts manage to flourish. Airlines may attempt to control fares, but 'bucket shops' do very well and some airlines are quite willing to supply agencies with an allocation of tickets at low rates. Thus, controlled prices tend to be an act of wishful thinking which is defied by market forces.

26. Subsidised price. Here we have a form of controlled price which is more genuine and workable. The price of a staple is kept low by government subsidy (paid out of taxes or borrowings), and this does benefit the poorer consumer. Another method is to encourage the production of certain goods, e.g. potatoes or milk, by paying producers a subsidy. This also helps to control prices.

However, it may depend on the kind of government in power. A socialist or liberal government may raise taxes or borrowings to keep prices down whereas a conservative government may cut taxes and expenditure and allow prices to find their true level. The first policy takes from the rich to give to the poor, the latter deprives the poor in favour of the better off. Politically, prices may be subject to Robin Hood or Robber Baron attitudes.

27. Guaranteed prices. Unlike the straight subsidy on a yield, as in 26, guaranteed prices mean that producers are told what minimum prices they may expect for their products, especially livestock, for the coming year. This is a kind of subsidy, but not so much a means of encouraging a particular production. It is an assurance to a farmer that it will be profitable to grow or rear a whole range of produce and livestock. It may take the form of an annual farm prices review resulting from negotiations between the government and the farmers' organisation, or the EEC farm prices which are set for Europe's 8 million farmers.

28. Methods of pricing analysed. Twenty-one different forms of price have been explained above. It may be found difficult to digest and distinguish so many kinds. In practice only one, two or three of these may apply to a particular business, product or service. Table 7A will therefore help to show which kinds of price are especially related to typical goods, services or circumstances.

Table 7A. Analysis of 21 kinds of price

	Price	*Definition/application*
(1)	Economic price	Recovers costs and returns planned profit
(2)	Market price	The standard expected and accepted price
(3)	Psychological price	This can be either the psychologically inexpensive, or one which implies a high value, luxury or customer satisfaction
(4)	Opportunity price	One which requires choice between two claims on discretionary income
(5)	Non-discriminatory price	Ex-works price before extras are added, e.g. motor cars
(6)	Uniform delivery price	Applies to most fast-moving consumer goods
(7)	Special price discrimination	Monopoly price as charged in restaurants and hotel bars
(8)	Basic point pricing	According to distance from source, e.g. coal and petrol

(9)	Multiple basing point pricing	Exacting prices as goods are handled by a succession of middlemen, e.g. fish, fruit, vegetables
(10)	Distorted price	Inflated by uncontrollable factors, e.g. VAT, sales tax
(11)	Price stability	Holding price constant, e.g. package holiday booked months in advance
(12)	Price plateau	Ceiling price beyond which sales cease
(13)	Penetration price	Competitive price to enter market
(14)	Competitive price	Reduced price to compete with rivals
(15)	Divisionary price	One which is added for fitting
(16)	Dumping price	Minimum price to sell into foreign markets
(17)	Double pricing	Recommended 'list' and discounted retail prices
(18)	Geographic price	Locational price according to class of area
(19)	Controlled price	Maximum price controlled by law or decree
(20)	Subsidised price	Low price resulting from government subsidy to producer
(21)	Guaranteed price	Minimum price promised to producers by the government

Researching prices

29. Researching the best selling price. There is another psychological aspect of price and that is the particular price among an array of prices which will attract most sales.

It is possible to research reactions to prices by offering goods at different prices, and recording and comparing the sales achieved by each price over a given period. This can be done by displaying the same item but at a different price in a number of shops, provided the class of trade is similar in each case. Direct response marketers can mail differently priced offers to see which price produces the best response.

Usually, there will be little difference between the prices so that the trader hardly gains or loses if a higher or lower price proves to be the most popular. For example, if a direct response firm planned to sell a product at around £1 it would be possible to test four prices in separate simultaneous mailings. It is unlikely that prospects would be aware of the price differences because they would be scattered all over the country and unknown to one another. The results could be:

£1.00	15%
£1.10	5%
£0.95	45%
£0.90	40%

This result would recommend that the price likely to produce maximum sales would be 95p since this price had achieved the largest number of orders from the trial mailing. In other words, 95p had the greatest psychological appeal. More people thought the product was worth buying at 95p than at any other price. Had the trader not carried out the test, but assumed that £1 was the right price, the sales could have been very disappointing.

Price and promotion

30. Presentation of price. Whether it be a flash pack money-off offer, a supermarket press advertisement splattered with bargain prices, or haggling in a market or bazaar, price is often the strongest activating element of a sales transaction. There is an exchange situation. Money and goods have to change hands. Unless the buyer is willing to surrender money, whether it be cash, cheque or credit card, there can be no sale. Money is the root of all selling.

An important factor is the way in which the price is presented. Special prices for bulk purchases, or ones taken up by a certain date, discounts, instalment terms or hire purchase, special cash prices, sale prices and so on all help to urge purchase. A product or service may fail or succeed solely on the pricing policy and its presentation.

The facility to purchase also enters into this, ranging from credit terms to acceptance of credit and charge cards. Today, credit cards are often illustrated in direct response advertisements, especially those in colour magazines. This facility to use 'plastic money' has been extended to telemarketing by means of viewdata systems on TV (*see* 18, 10). The customer is encouraged to be an armchair shopper.

Price features in a great deal of advertising from the vague recommended prices of goods to be found in shops, to the positive prices of stores, supermarkets and direct response traders. However, the discreet absence of price – which can be an irritating practice – may suggest exceptional quality which is believed to be a greater attraction than price.

'Free' offers are also a form of price since the item is supplied free of charge, and few people can resist something for nothing. Even when a purchase has to be made to obtain the free offer, the price paid is seen to be a bargain.

The presentation of the price in media advertising; direct mail; catalogues, price lists and sales literature; point–of–sale material such as crowners and price tags, window bills and display outers; and on packaging, are all promotional aspects of pricing which have to be considered at the relevant stages of the marketing mix.

Legal aspects of pricing

31. Reduced price. When goods are offered at reduced prices, whether in special 'sales' events or in the normal run of trading, the previous price must have been charged for a continuous period of twenty–eight days within the past six months (Trade Descriptions Act 1968). This is known as the 'twenty-eight–day clause'. The object of the law is to make illegal the practice of pretending goods are reduced in price when in fact they have been bought in specially for a sales event.

32. Recommended price. The government has power under the Price Commission Act 1977 to take action against the use of recommended prices (*see also* 23). However, while no action has been taken at the time of writing, the Trade Descriptions Act does lay down that a recommended price is presumed to be that of the manufacturer or other supplier and not that of the retailer. If it is merely the retailer's list price, this must be stated to avoid committing an offence. The Consumer Protection Act 1987, discussed in Chapter 15, lays down stringent rules about prices.

33. Flash packs. Special price cuts which are 'flashed' on specially printed packages must conform to the recommended price requirements stated above. Moreover, there must not be any confusion over the actual price to be paid.

34. Loss leaders. A controversial issue between manufacturers and retailers is the practice of attracting customers by the loss leader method of substantially cutting the price of a leading brand. From the manufacturer's point of view this tends to be derogatory to his product, and it can be unfair to other stockists whose sales may be impaired by their harsh competition.

The Resale Prices Act 1976 allows suppliers to stop supplying a dealer who within the previous year has used the same or similar goods as loss leaders. A loss leader is defined in the Act as a resale of goods, not for the purpose of making a profit, but to act as an advertisement for the dealer.

35. Petrol prices. Under the Petrol Prices (Display) Order 1977, the highest price for each grade or sub-grade sold must be marked on pumps, or be visible close by. This price must include all taxes and duties. If price reductions are advertised the garage must display the prices of at least two grades of petrol including four star. If a price reduction is displayed, the lowest price must be shown as well as the price from which the reduction is made. This protects the buyer against being deluded by apparently low prices, and enables him to compare the extent of a reduction.

36. Hire purchase terms. The Consumer Credit Act 1974 stipulates the information which must be carried in an advertisement for goods offered on hire purchase or credit sale. Such information must include the full cash price, the total amount on instalments, the length of the period covered by each payment, and the number of instalments which may be required before delivery of the goods. The Act also lays down a variety of other stipulations regarding deposit or no deposit, and interest rates.

Progress test 7

1. What is meant by price elasticity? **(4)**
2. What are the four basic kinds of price? **(5)**
3. How does the economic price differ from the economist's concept of supply and demand and its effect on price? **(4,6)**
4. What is meant by non-discriminatory prices? **(11)**
5. Explain what is meant by special price discrimination and give an example of its application. **(13)**
6. How can a price be distorted? **(16)**
7. Why is price stability important? Give an example. **(18)**
8. What has penetration price to do with the launch of a new product? **(19)**
9. What is a dumping price? **(22)**
10. What is meant by double pricing? **(23)**
11. Explain the difference between controlled, subsidised and guaranteed prices. **(25–27)**
12. How can prospective prices be reasearched? **(29)**
13. What is meant by the 'twenty-eight-day clause'? **(31)**
14. What is a manufacturer's recommended retail price? **(23, 32)**

8
Distribution

Aims of distribution

1. Definition. Distribution may be defined as the transfer of goods from the producer to the customer. This involves the whole process of warehousing, transportation, storage depots, advertising and sales promotion, and the organisations such as wholesalers and retailers through which goods are sold to the final customer.

2. Channels of distribution. The routes from producer to ultimate customer are called channels of distribution, shown in the form of a chart in Fig. 8.1. *A* and *B* sell through shops, *C* sells 'on the doorstep' by means of direct selling, while *D* requires neither shops nor direct salesmen and sells by post, telephone or viewdata (*see* 16).

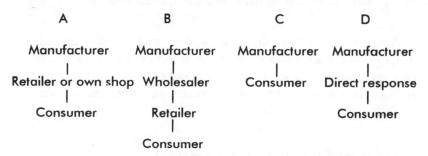

A	B	C	D
Manufacturer	Manufacturer	Manufacturer	Manufacturer
Retailer or own shop	Wholesaler	Consumer	Direct response
Consumer	Retailer		Consumer
	Consumer		

Figure 8.1. *Channels of distribution*

3. The distribution cycle. The definition in 1 describes a process of moving goods from the place of production (or source of supply) to people who will pay a price which will not only cover the cost of production and distribution but yield a profit. A great deal of money is tied up in the whole operation, it is expensive to borrow money to finance business, and it is necessary to achieve sales quickly so that money is turned round quickly. In the industrial North the biggest single cost is labour which may represent 70 per cent of the selling price.

The *distribution cycle*, i.e. the time it takes a product to reach the consumer, will depend not only on the success of selling and advertising, but on the efficiency of the method of distribution. A particular method may suit one product but not another. For one it may be best to sell through wholesalers (e.g. farm produce) but for another it may be better to sell direct to retailers (e.g. watches and clocks). To take a service as an example, insurance can be sold through brokers or direct to prospective policy holders.

It is therefore part of the marketing strategy to devise a system of distribution which allows the product to flow through distributors as quickly as possible. This does not necessarily mean that the fewer the middlemen (or the shorter the distribution channel) the shorter the distribution cycle. It does mean that in planning the marketing strategy it is essential to examine all the means of distribution and to select the channel most likely to prove efficient. There may, of course, be standard routes for certain product groups, but this may be contradicted if a more efficient method can be adopted. For instance, there are certain watches which can be bought only from direct response traders.

4. Adequate distribution. This means that stocks should be available in the shops to meet the demand created by advertising. To overcome resistance from shopkeepers who may be unwilling to invest in a new line the manufacturer may offer one or more of the following inducements.

(*a*) Special discounts or other trade terms.
(*b*) Special display material.
(*c*) Assistance with local advertising (co-operative advertising).
(*d*) A sales promotion scheme (e.g. a mail drop of premium cash vouchers).

(e) Proof of forthcoming support advertising in the press or on radio or TV.

Without such a selling-in effort the advertising would be wasted if potential customers were disappointed. It is usually poor marketing to expect distributors to stock goods because they have received enquiries. *That could be too late.* The impact of the advertising would be lost. In fact, potential customers might easily accept a rival product which *was* available.

Modern developments in distribution methods

5. Changes since Second World War. The traditional methods of distribution were either through middlemen or direct to the consumer, but since the end of the Second World War there has been a succession of innovations and revolutions. This has also brought about changes in packaging, greater varieties of goods, new methods of payment, supported by new mass advertising media such as colour TV, and changes in shopping patterns and habits. Although the customer has enjoyed many advantages there have been losses of personal service from distributors, while delivery services have either been completely curtailed or become chargeable owing to high labour and fuel costs. At one time even the local grocer or butcher would deliver orders to the home, but that is largely a thing of the past. Door-to-door sales of bread, fish, vegetables and coal have almost disappeared in the UK with only the milk roundsman remaining.

However, it is interesting that while firms like Sainsbury's and Tesco have closed town centre supermarkets and opened superstores on the perimeters of towns, there has been a re-emergence of small shops such as bakers. Also, some department stores and chain stores have reverted to free delivery services as a means of competing for business.

6. Self-service. In both large and small shops self-service has developed rapidly, partly because of staff shortages or costs and partly because the customer is more tempted to buy what is laid out for them to look at and select. Self-service has added a new dimension of freedom to shopping. The customer does not have to ask for goods, nor is he pestered by shop assistants eager to attract his or her custom.

7. Supermarket. Usually in chains of sometimes several hundred stores, but occasionally sole traders, supermarkets offer a great variety of goods (mostly fast-moving consumer goods such as foods, drinks, toiletries and household items) with self-service and a number of check-out points. Chemists and drug stores in the UK are protected from undue competition from supermarkets which are limited to selling the smaller sizes of proprietary medicines but Safeways have their own pharmacy section.

8. Hypermarket. This is a very large supermarket or superstore located out-of-town with a car-park, petrol station and often a special bus stop. It will usually occupy at least 25,000 sq.ft. (2,300 m^2) and have a minimum of fifteen check-out points. This vast shopping centre has led to what is known as *out-of-town* or *one-stop* shopping since the range of goods will extend beyond foods and household items into other domestic areas such as china and glass, kitchenware, clothing, gardening goods and so on.

The advent of supermarkets and hypermarkets (or mass merchandisers) has given such retailers a wholesaler status when buying in bulk at special prices. Big firms like Sainsbury's maintain huge warehouses which receive bulk supplies from manufacturers, and then distribute them to their large supermarkets which supply thousands of customers.

9. Malls, plazas, shopping precincts. In Singapore there are many shopping plazas with several floors of shops connected by lifts and escalators. They are indoor shopping centres. In contrast, the shopping mall in Trinidad is a ground-floor shopping area. The vertical or horizontal arrangement depends on the availability of land. Sometimes these buildings are a mixture of ground-floor and basement shops with flats and offices in a tower block above. Shopping precincts are traffic-free shopping areas with shops on one or two levels and pedestrian pavements, galleries, stairs and escalators. In a sense, these groupings of modern retail premises are a return to the market place of old, examples being found in new towns like Milton Keynes, but also in modernised shopping centres like Croydon.

10. Cash-and-carry warehouse. This is principally a wholesaler who supplies the smaller retailer. Bulk supplies may be bought at wholesale price but no credit is allowed and no transport is provided. Some issue a card so that any card-holder may be a customer. Apart from retailers, customers may include clubs, societies and individuals who wish to purchase supplies in wholesale quantities. On the other hand, if a retailer is running out of stock before supplies can be received from the manufacturer or a regular wholesaler he or she can go to a cash-and-carry warehouse for a temporary supply. Thus the cash-and-carry warehouse provides a valuable service without having to operate transport, and without having to collect accounts.

11. Symbol group. This is a term which is often wrongly applied to stores like Marks & Spencer, which is well-known for its St Michael brand. Own labels should not be confused with symbol groups.

With the growth of bulk-buying by supermarket chains — often direct from the manufacturer and, with the maintenance of warehouses, usurping the former role of the wholesaler — a special type of wholesaling has developed. In return for buying almost everything from a single wholesaler special trade terms are offered so that small retailers (mostly grocers) can compete with the supermarkets. Each shop carries the wholesaler's symbol or badge, and the wholesaler advertises the products on sale at symbol shops. A symbol group is therefore a number of identified retailers operating in collaboration with a wholesaler who supports them with advertising. Examples are Spar and Mace.

12. Discount store. By buying in bulk the discount store is able to sell expensive items like hi-fi and other electronic equipment at cut prices. The store may or may not provide servicing, and the regular dealer may defend his or her higher price by pointing to the extent of the after-sales service. However, firms like Comet not only offer a large choice of domestic appliances and home entertainment products at discounted prices but also provide servicing back-up.

13. Vending machine. Various degrees of success have been achieved with machines which sell meals, drinks, newspapers, confectionery, cigarettes, contraceptives and other items. The idea is far from new and vending machines existed on railway stations sixty or more years ago. The modern development has been into different demand locations, e.g. offices, factories and universities, and more sophisticated operations such as hot food and drinks and even ladies' tights. Vandalism is sometimes a problem, and machines for dispensing toiletries and contraceptives in public lavatories have been damaged.

14. Franchising. This has been another growth area with its appeal to the man who wishes to be independent and able to control his own fortunes. A franchise usually requires an investment and a commitment to buy the franchiser's product, while the franchiser generally gives advice or assistance in managing and promoting the business. Some franchises benefit from operating under a common name with a standard corporate identity, e.g. Wimpy bars, but others, like launderettes, merely use a certain make of machine which may or may not be significant. Franchises cover many products and services of which carpet cleaning, drain cleaning, launderettes, take-away cooked food shops, ice-cream parlours, cafés and paperback book agencies are typical examples.

Another form of franchise is the large-scale distribution of beers and soft drinks whereby brands such as Guinness, Coca-Cola, Pepsi Cola, and Schweppes are distributed by bottling companies throughout the world.

15. Home selling. This is not a completely new method, but it has been developed in original ways by firms such as Tupperware and Avon. An innovation has been *party selling* when friends are invited to a house to see a product demonstrated and make purchases.

16. Telemarketing. This is a broad term to cover a range of distribution methods using TV. At its simplest it might mean the ability to call up information on, say, flight availability so that travel may then be booked, probably by telephone. More sophisticated is the viewdata system (known in the UK as Prestel) whereby required information can be called up and goods may be ordered with an answer-back system, quoting a credit card number.

Non-store retailing or direct response marketing is a growing form of shopping, and payment is made easy by the use of credit and charge cards. Customer behaviour is therefore changing as people are prepared to exchange the ability to see the goods for the convenience of 'armchair shopping'. However, modern direct response marketing techniques are used to overcome even this disadvantage. Catalogues and many press advertisements are illustrated in full colour, so that there is realistic presentation of goods. As public transport or motoring becomes too expensive for shopping, non-store retailing has increasing attractions (*see also* 18, 9 and 10).

17. Telephone selling. This form of distribution has increased as more people have become telephone subscribers. Telephone salespeople (mostly women) are specially trained to sell, for example, advertisement space in newspapers and magazines, or to set up appointments for insurance, encyclopaedia, double-glazing and other salesmen to visit. The telephone salesperson may initiate calls, or be available to deal with enquiries and orders from callers.

Other forms of distribution

18. Wholesalers. Otherwise known as *middlemen*, wholesalers buy in bulk from manufacturers, producers or importers and sell in small quantities to retailers. They specialise in a class of goods, such as fish, meat, fruit, vegetables, food products, proprietary medicines, newspapers and magazines, stationery, books or jewellery. Some operate from central markets, e.g. the London markets of Smithfield (meat) and New Covent Garden (fruit and vegetables). Other wholesalers maintain warehouses and have travelling salesmen. In most cases the items are small unit goods (e.g. stationery supplies) which would not warrant a manufacturer's field sales force, whereas a wholesaler could supply pens, envelopes, paper clips and so on to the same shops.

19. Brokers. Rather like wholesalers, except that they do not hold stocks, brokers are to be found operating in the following areas:

(a) buying and selling on commodity markets, e.g. tea, coffee and metals;

(b) providing professional advisory services such as insurance and investments.

20. Factors. These are wholesalers who also take over the collection of accounts on a commission basis. For example, a publisher may have all orders processed by a factor, instead of despatching books direct to booksellers and handling his own account collection.

21. Multiples. Firms, other than co-operative stores, with ten or more shops are described as multiples in the British Census of Distribution. They may also be called *chain* stores, and include supermarkets as well as shops specialising in certain trades such as pharmacy, footwear, hardware, confectionery or tailoring.

22. Variety stores or bazaars. Woolworth is the best example of a variety store or bazaar, goods of all kinds being displayed on open counters. In the past these were low-price bargain stores, and in the 1930s Woolworth boasted of selling 'nothing over sixpence'. Nowadays, with higher living standards and greater spending power, variety stores have moved up-market and compete with department stores (*see* **26**). The principal ones in Britain are Woolworth, Marks & Spencer, BHS and Littlewoods. Each has its special character and kind of merchandise.

23. Co-operative stores. The original Rochdale-type co–operative society was based on customer-ownership and profit-sharing by means of dividends proportional to purchase. The Co-operative movement has seen many changes, the dividend being replaced by trading stamps, and some local societies amalgamating under national ownership. Instead of societies with many branches, Co-ops are now mostly strategically located supermarkets.

24. Department stores. These are large stores with numerous departments, usually including furnishing, soft-furnishing, clothing and household goods. Many have amalgamated into large national chains.

25. Appointed dealers. While some products may be sold through every possible outlet, others of a more specialised or high-class nature may be sold only through selected or appointed dealers. This usually means that the dealer sells no rival product, and thus provides a monopoly sales outlet for the manufacturer. The dealer may of course sell other allied products which are complementary and not competitive. For instance, a photographic dealer might sell only one make of camera, but would also sell films, tripods, cases, developing and printing materials, and offer a developing and printing service. Manufacturers may list appointed dealers in their advertising.

26. Main distributor. In the motor car trade a main distributor acts as both a wholesaler and a retailer, being a source of supply to smaller retailers who may sell a number of makes.

27. Neighbourhood shops. This expression applies to local shops, such as those in back streets or in small shopping parades in residential areas. Newsagents, grocers, chemists, greengrocers, off-licences (which sell alcoholic drinks) and hairdressing salons are typical businesses in these locations. The grocer may belong to a symbol group (*see* 11).

28. Direct selling. This is one of the oldest forms of selling, goods or services being hawked through the streets or sold from door to door, perhaps on a regular round as with bread or milk. Thus, the trader may be a casual, itinerant mobile distributor, servicing from a vehicle; a regular mobile trader who calls his or her wares and perhaps rings a bell or plays a tune to sell either coal or ice-cream; or a regular delivery salesman like the milk roundsman. For many years 'the man from the Pru' has sold 'industrial' insurance on the doorstep (i.e. life insurance with weekly or monthly payments). Canvassers also sell goods as varied as encyclopaedias, brushes, double-glazing and cosmetics.

29. Credit traders. Also known as tallymen, these are another form of direct selling, except that the method is to sell on credit, and to collect regular instalment payments.

30. Gift catalogue. Another outlet for goods is the free gift or incentives catalogue. The former includes gifts which can be obtained by collecting coupons which may be given with products such as cigarettes, confectionery, drinks or petrol. The latter is a means of rewarding successful or industrious staff, particularly salesmen.

31. Sole traders. Not all retail outlets are chains or limited companies. The one-man business with only one shop, office or workshop is called a sole trader.

32. Congeries. Collections of businesses of a similar kind are called congeries. Very often these are sole traders such as jewellers, stamp dealers or booksellers (*see also* 2, **25**).

33. Market traders, stall holders. Operating in covered or outdoor markets, again these are mostly sole traders selling fruit and vegetables, clothing and other articles. Some markets are held on certain days, others operate regularly, the stalls being dismantled and goods stored overnight. In some markets, especially in developing countries, the market stalls are small permanent lock-up premises.

34. Shopping centres. Often out-of-town, the specialist shopping centre is a means of displaying and selling goods of one type. The garden centre with its full range of plants, greenhouses, tools, fertilisers and gardening accessories is a typical example. Other centres specialise in do-it-yourself products, caravans or agricultural machinery and farm supplies.

35. Summary. The above are examples of changes and developments which have made the modern marketing scene extremely varied. The trend in industrial countries is away from the traditional shop and towards direct response and telemarketing. Direct response marketing is discussed separately in the next chapter; it is the modern form of mail order. Fast-moving consumer goods and fresh foods still require retail distribution, but even here the refrigerator and especially the deep-freezer reduce the number of shop visits that are necessary. Less frequent shopping is satisfied by late shopping nights at supermarkets and especially by one-stop out-of-town superstores or hypermarkets. The latter are no longer limited to food stores and there are such stores selling DIY and gardening products, carpets and furniture, electrical goods and children's toys and clothes.

Progress test 8

1. How would you define distribution? **(1)**
2. What is the distribution cycle? **(3)**
3. What is meant by 'adequate distribution'? **(4)**
4. How does a cash-and-carry warehouse differ from an ordinary wholesaler? **(10)**
5. How does a discount store differ from a hypermarket? **(8, 12)**
6. What problem is sometimes experienced with vending machines? **(13)**
7. Factors are wholesalers but what is their special role? **(20)**
8. Why might a manufacturer select appointed or authorised dealers? **(25)**
9. List some products which are typical of direct selling. **(28)**

9

Direct response marketing

Introduction

1. Definition. Direct response marketing is the selling of goods or services direct to customers in response to orders produced by direct mail, catalogues, press, TV or other advertising.

2. New name for mail order. Previously known as mail-order trading, this is a form of shopping without shops which has been applied to a great variety of products and services. It can be conducted on a large scale like the mail-order clubs with their warehouses or by a humble individual selling foreign stamps from his home. Almost anything can be sold by direct response marketing, and some of the reasons for its popularity will be explained later. It is a system of selling direct to the customer without the customer having to visit a shop.

3. Historical background. This method of distribution is by no means new, in spite of its recent surge in popularity. It was pioneered in the USA by Chicago traders who, more than a hundred years ago, provided the farmers of the Midwest with their every need, first by rail and then by parcel post. The names Montgomery Ward and Sears Roebuck are still famous as catalogue traders in the USA, while firms like Littlewoods, Empire Stores, Grattan Warehouses and Freemans have long been famous in the UK.

4. Modern direct response marketing. However, direct response trading has caught on in recent years in a different way from the familiar catalogues of clothes, household goods, records, books, garden plants and seeds and so on. Goods and services are now advertised in 'off-the-page' press advertisements or single offer direct mail shots. The Royal Mint markets coins and the Philatelic Bureau of the Post Office markets first day covers in this way.

Certain legislation has also encouraged use of direct response techniques. The Financial Services Act 1986 and the Building Societies Act 1987 have broadened the scope for the selling of financial services. Today, one of the biggest areas of direct response marketing, often making use of in-house databases of existing and potential customers, is that of selling financial services such as insurance, pensions, shares, unit trusts, savings schemes and mortgages. Motor insurance, for example, is sold 'off-the-page' by many companies.

Another group making great use of direct response marketing consists of large stores and fashion houses which are meeting the competition from direct response marketers suffered by their retail shops head on.

This has become a very versatile form of trading, extending far beyond the activities of the traditional mail order catalogues and clubs.

Reasons for direct response trading

5. Easily controlled. The trader can stock and offer merchandise to please a target market, and if he operates on a cash-with-order (or credit card) basis he has no cash flow problems. However, credit terms are offered by some firms, especially for costly items. It is possible to furnish a house by direct response and on long-term credit.

6. Small overheads. The trader needs no shop nor sales staff and can operate wherever and however it is most economical to do so. There are also *fulfilment houses* which will warehouse stock and receive and despatch orders.

7. Targeting. By means of neighbourhood location systems such as

ACORN (*see* 24) it is possible to aim direct mail offers at specific people. Equally, lists of regular customers can be built up for repeat offers.

8. Assessing results. The response to offers, and the pulling power of media used, is easily assessed. Expenditure can be compared with enquiries and sales.

Reasons for direct response buying

9. Original offers. The goods or services may be exclusive to the supplier, or otherwise unknown products and services may be offered. These may be unavailable or difficult to find in the shops.

10. Pleasure. People enjoy browsing through catalogues and indulging in purchases. With beautifully illustrated and printed catalogues the shop is brought into the home, and armchair shopping becomes a pleasure. The summer garden can be planned in the winter, and so can the summer holiday.

11. Convenience. Not only is it easy to buy by mail or telephone, but there is the added advantage of delivery to the home. This saves time, bus fares, car-parking charges and having to carry goods home.

12. Overcomes dislike of shopping. There is also the psychological factor that some people do not like crowds and the hassle of shopping, nor having to deal with shop assistants. Others may be elderly or infirm and find shopping a physical problem.

13. Price. In spite of the cost of postage or carriage, there may be advantageous prices, special offers, credit card or credit facilities, and prices will be stated clearly.

14. Choice. Many direct response traders offer an astonishing range of goods which the potential buyer may not otherwise know exists. This can apply to all kinds of products and services to mention only fashion goods, horticultural products, collectibles or holidays.

Methods and media

15. Catalogues. Catalogue selling remains a major form of direct response marketing. They include those of the long established mail-order catalogue firms, although some of the mammoth ones have been reduced to a number of smaller catalogues addressed to special target groups, those which specialise in particular lines such as bulbs, roses or seeds, and a number consisting of novelty items. There are also the gift catalogues circulated by charities, especially at Christmas time. Also in this category can be included holiday brochures.

It is necessary for the goods to be presented convincingly and this calls for realistic pictures (usually in full colour) and word-picture copy supported by good printing, usually by offset-photo-litho. The high quality of catalogue production is one of the characteristics of this form of direct response media.

16. One piece mailers. In contrast to the elaborate catalogue is the one-piece mailer which contains the sales message and the order form in one unit, often a folder which folds like a map. This simple type of mail shot is often preferable to the one which consists of several loose items which can confuse or annoy the recipient. Simplicity is always a sensible feature in any form of communication.

17. Direct mail. This is the advertising medium much used by mail-order or direct response traders. It depends on two things: a reliable mailing list and a good mail shot. The mailing list may consist of existing customers or enquirers, or it may be hired from a source such as a database or a list broker. Database lists often consist of other people's customers, or they could be lists of shareholders which have become available following the privatisation of state enterprises such as British Gas and British Telecom. The mail shot can consist of items such as a sales letter, catalogue and other sales literature. The one–piece mailer mentioned separately above is a simplified direct mail shot.

18. Off-the-page advertisements. These appear in newspapers and magazines, and usually explain the offer in detail with pictures as necessary, together with an order form or coupon. The coupon has to be worded very carefully so that the customer gives the right information (e.g. what they want to buy, how much they are spending and how they are paying, together with their full name and postal address) for the goods or service to be supplied. It may also be necessary to ask the customer to state a second choice in case the first is out-of-stock, and this can save needless correspondence. A telephone number may also be required.

19. Inserts. These are similar to off-the-page advertisements except that being inserted into publications they can take many forms such as leaflets, folders, brochures or catalogues. Some people object to inserts and remove them before reading the journal. On the other hand, inserts are used in increasing numbers by direct response marketers, and many publishers have installed special machines for inserting them. Their value can be judged by the value of the response they achieve.

20. Mail drops. Also known as doorstoppers, these are sales items delivered door-to-door, which is cheaper than posting them. There are firms which specialise in door-to-door distributions, a similar service is offered by those who deliver free newspapers, and the Post Office has a special service. Distribution can be targeted to cover particular places, and once again the ACORN system of selecting neighbourhoods can be used.

21. Telemarketing. A number of products and services have been sold direct to customers by using television commercials with response handling services. One method is for the customer to phone their order and credit card details to a number given in the commercial, and for the TV company's computer to process the order to the advertiser. Satellite television is likely to produce an increase in this kind of direct response marketing. For example, British Satellite Broadcasting has a direct response advertisers' package which includes a screen phone number on the commercial and respondents can obtain information by phone or mail.

22. Telephone selling. Telephone ordering and telephone selling are also part of shopping without shops, and for those who do not have the staff to attend a telephone or telephones permanently there are agencies which will generate out-going or handle in-coming calls. Telephone selling can also result from advertisements which invite enquirers and ask for telephone numbers so that enquiries can be followed up.

Targeting

23. Precision marketing. The secret of successful direct response marketing is to eliminate waste, and thereby cost, while at the same time increasing cost efficiency. One way of achieving this is to use reliable lists which have been cleaned of dead addresses, and de-duplicated to avoid wasteful duplication. With computerised mailing lists duplication is a problem because names and addresses are continually added but sometimes they can be the same address entered in a different form, e.g. 'A. Smith' and 'Adrian Smith'.

Another way to achieve accurate targeting is to select recipients according to their social grade, which is often revealed by where they live. A number of systems are available in the UK which provide *neighbourhood classifications*. These are based on census enumeration districts and postcodes and make it possible to choose certain target groups according to their residential characteristics.

24. Neighbourhood classification systems. The best known is ACORN, an acronym for *A Classification of Residential Neighbourhoods*, which identifies 30 neighbourhood types as shown in Fig. 9.1. This was created by CACI Market Analysis. Other demographic–geographic neighbourhood systems are MOSAIC (CCN Systems Ltd) which identifies 58 types; PIN (Pinpoint Identified Neighbourhoods) operated by Pinpoint Systems Ltd, which identifies 60 types; and Super Profiles from McIntyre Marketing which identifies 150 types. The ACORN system is based on the 1981 Census but with statistical adjustments to keep it up-to-date. The PIN system adopts its own classifications in preference to Post Office postcodes and Office of Population Censuses and Surveys data and locates 22 million domestic addresses.

Acorn groups		1981 population	per cent
A	Agricultural areas	1 811 485	3.4
B	Modern family housing, higher incomes	8 667 137	16.2
C	Older housing of intermediate status	9 420 477	17.6
	Poor quality older terraced housing	2 320 846	4.3
E	Better-off council estates	6 976 570	13.0
F	Less well-off council estates	5 032 657	9.4
G	Poorest council estates	4 048 658	7.6
H	Multiracial areas	2 086 026	3.9
I	High-status non-family areas	2 248 207	4.2
J	Affluent suburban housing	8 514 878	15.9
K	Better-off retirement areas	2 041 338	3.8
U	Unclassified	388 632	0.7

Acorn types			
A 1	Agricultural villages	1 376 427	2.6
A 3	Areas of farms and smallholdings	435 058	0.8
B 3	Cheap modern private housing	2 209 759	4.1
B 4	Recent private housing, young families	1 648 534	3.1
B 5	Modern private housing, older children	3 121 453	5.8
B 6	New detached houses, young families	1 404 893	2.6
B 7	Military bases	282 498	0.5
C 8	Mixed owner-occupied and council estates	1 880 142	3.5
C 9	Small town centres and flats above shops	2 157 360	4.0
C 10	Villages with non-farm employment	2 463 246	4.6
C 11	Older private housing, skilled workers	2 919 729	5.5
D 12	Unimproved terraces with old people	1 351 877	2.5
D 13	Pre-1914 terraces, low-income families	762 266	1.4
D 14	Tenement flats lacking amenities	206 703	0.4
E 15	Council estates, well-off older workers	1 916 242	3.6
E 16	Recent council estates	1 392 961	2.6
E 17	Council estates, well-off young workers	2 615 376	4.9
E 18	Small council houses, often Scottish	1 051 991	2.0
F 19	Low-rise estates in industrial towns	2 538 119	4.7
F 20	Inter-war council estates, older people	1 667 994	3.1
F 21	Council housing for the elderly	826 544	1.5
G 22	New council estates in inner cities	1 079 351	2.0
G 23	Overspill estates, high unemployment	1 729 757	3.2

Figure 9.1. *See opposite for caption*

G 24	Council estates with over-crowding	868 141	1.6
G 25	Council estates with worst poverty	371 409	0.7
H 26	Multi-occupied houses, poor Asians	204 493	0.4
H 27	Owner-occupied terraces with Asians	577 871	1.1
H 28	Multilet housing with Afro-Caribbeans	387 169	0.7
H 29	Better off multi-ethnic areas	916 493	1.7
I 30	High-status areas, few children	1 129 079	2.1
I 31	Multilet big old houses and flats	822 017	1.5
I 32	Furnished flats, mostly single people	297 111	0.6
J 33	Inter-war semis, white collar workers	3 054 032	5.7
J 34	Spacious inter-war semis, big gardens	2 676 598	5.0
J 35	Villages with wealthy older commuters	1 533 756	2.9
J 36	Detached houses, exclusive suburbs	1 250 492	2.3
K 37	Private houses. well-off elderly	1 199 703	2.2
K 38	Private flats with single pensioners	841 635	1.6
U 39	Unclassified	388 632	0.7

Area total   53,556,911 100.0

Figure 9.1. *contd. ACORN profile of Great Britain. (Crown copyright/CACI copyright.*

25. Monica. CACI also run the Monica database which predicts the likely ages of people according to their first names, and claims that 75 per cent of the British adult population have a first name which indicates age.

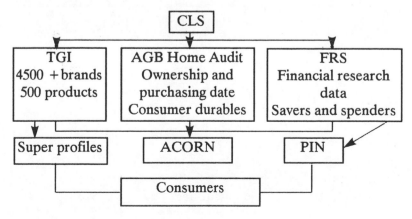

Figure 9.2 *The Royal Mail Consumer Location System*

26. Consumer location system. Developed by the Royal Mail, CLS is a computerised way of analysing people's purchasing, reading and viewing habits, and relating them to the neighbourhoods where they live. It uses data from various research sources as demonstrated in Fig. 9.2 and reveals their propensity to consume certain products. In addition to the neighbourhood classification systems already described it uses data from the Target Group Index, Audits of Great Britain and Financial Research.

Progress test 9

1. Why is direct response marketing called 'shopping without shops'?   (1, 2)

2. What are the advantages of direct response marketing to the trade?   (5–8)

3. What are the advantages of direct response marketing to the customer?   (9–14)

4. What are the principal methods and media used by direct response marketers?   (15–22)

5. How can accurate targeting be achieved?   (23, 24)

6. What does ACORN stand for?   (24)

7. What does the CACI Monica data-base reveal?   (25)

8. How does the CLS consumer profile reveal the propensity of people to consume certain products?   (26)

10
The after-market

Introduction

1. Definition. The after-market consists of all post-sale efforts to satisfy the consumer and, if possible, secure regular or repeat purchase.

2. Regular and repeat. There is a difference between regular and repeat. Regular purchase refers chiefly to small unit, mass market fast-moving consumer goods which are bought frequently. Repeat purchase could be at some time in the future as with consumer durables. In the first case habit buying and brand loyalty is involved, but in the second case long-term goodwill has to be maintained to secure an eventual purchase. The customer may buy the same brand of cigarettes every day or margarine every week, but will he or she buy the same make or motor car in a few years time?

3. Marketing strategy. It does not pay to be casual about this. Very few products or services are once-and-for-all sales. Even if they are, recommendation could be a valuable part of the after-market. The marketing strategy for the majority of things sold needs to include a definite policy on after-market tactics. Costs may be involved which have to be covered by the price. It may be poor policy to sell at a low price but have no after-sales service, and much wiser to sell at a higher price and assure the customer of back-up services. When a company offers a ten or twenty year guarantee it has usually covered the cost of this in the price.

After-marketing techniques

4. After-sales service. Few customers will spend a lot of money on a mechanical, electric or electronic item unless they can be sure that if the product breaks down, is damaged or requires a routine service, servicing facilities are available. The manufacturer or his selling agents may provide this service. This requirement applies particularly to motor cars, sewing machines, cameras, watches, radio and television sets, lawnmowers and typewriters.

In developing countries customers are apt to be careless about making sure that what they buy is covered by after-sales services. Such services may in fact be scarce because of the lack of skilled engineers. Consequently, expensive products are often discarded unrepaired.

5. Spare parts and repairs. Associated with after-sales service is the availability of spare parts and the ability for repairs to be undertaken, either by the customer or by a servicing engineer. This can be a problem with an imported product anywhere in the world, and should be a major consideration in any marketing strategy which engages in exports. Too many companies are content to export the original product and fail to ensure that adequate spares are exported with it.

This is not always the fault of the manufacturer: customers may not wish to tie up capital in stocking spares they may not want, while exchange control may restrict the volume of goods that may be imported. In some countries, a black market can exist in much wanted spares.

Another problem is that the manufacturer has to decide when to stop making and stocking spares as models age and demand lessens. It could also be prohibitively costly for the customer to obtain repairs (e.g. cost of postage or carriage), and for the manufacturer to provide them (e.g. cost of maintaining a servicing department). A necessary policy may be not to undertake repairs at all but to replace products or modules and throw away defective ones. For example, the working part of a watch or clock could be replaced completely in the original case so that, from the customer's point of view, the item had been 'repaired'. Solid-state replaceable modules are common with electronic goods, thus saving repair time and cost.

6. Manuals and instructions. Goodwill and customer satisfaction can be gained if the customer can easily understand how to use, service or repair a product, whether it be a medicine, a lighter fuel or something more complicated like a video cassette recorder or a motor car. If a product is not used correctly it may not be enjoyed fully, it may be discarded and wasted, or the customer may criticise the product among his friends, or complain to the supplier or manufacturer. This can undo the marketing strategy because either the product will become unpopular or, at the very least, the customer will buy something else next time. Much therefore depends on the instructions.

The following points are important when producing instructions.

(*a*) They should be written as simply as possible. If the product has to be assembled or used in stages, these should be explained logically so that no mistake can be made.

(*b*) Instructions should be printed as boldly as possible. Far too many instructions are printed in tiny type, and for some people they are quite difficult to read.

(*c*) Instruction manuals should be adequately indexed.

(*d*) Wherever possible, there should be accompanying pictures, cartoons or diagrams. This is essential with products sold to export markets where there are many languages, spoken languages are not written, or people are illiterate. If a product is being sold in Nigeria it is impossible to print instructions in sixty-two languages, yet one sees, for example, foodstuffs sold internationally with instructions printed in English, French, German, Chinese and Arabic on the same container! This is typical of short-sighted British attitudes to export marketing. English may be spoken world-wide, but only by a minority in any country where it is a second or third language. A businessperson may speak English (as often happens in Europe and also in Japan), but their spouse probably does not.

Cartoon pictures which are intelligible without any need for words might deter people in Third World countries from buying products like milk powder if they have no means of measurement, sterilisation and refrigeration, and so would save a lot of babies' lives.

(*e*) Where foreign language versions are used, they should be checked with nationals, as mere translations are seldom accurate.

7. Guarantees and promises. A world guarantee as given with cameras is valuable, but some of the comparatively short-term guarantees offered with motor cars are seldom compatible with the life expectancy of such a product. A ten-year guarantee on aluminium window frames may seem generous, but could suggest that such fittings cannot be expected to last any longer! Better is the simple *promise* with no small print exclusion clauses. This means of creating customer satisfaction was popularised by Corning Glass, makers of Pyrex and other heat–resistant glassware.

It is easy to give a guarantee, but what happens if the firm goes out of business? Rentokil, for instance, give a thirty-year guarantee on timber preservation work, but a trust fund exists to protect the guarantee. It may be impossible for a one-man roofing contractor to guarantee the validity of their guarantee. The old saying *caveat emptor* (buyer beware) is relevant in the grey world of guarantees.

8. Refunds and exchanges. Linked with guarantees and promises are cash refunds and willingness to make exchanges. Shoppers are right to shun tradesmen who will not give cash refunds or make exchanges if customers complain or have perhaps made a wrong or disappointing purchase.

Marks & Spencer, who do not always have fitting rooms for customers to try on clothes, overcome this disadvantage very simply by permitting cash refunds. Such refunds should be made without fuss. Some stores inflict embarrassing procedures on customers to the extent that they are deterred from seeking refunds. This can nullify the principle of refunds, and discourage purchase in the first place.

Direct response goods may be sold 'on approval' which encourages purchase, and sometimes (especially when alternative choices are invited) such sales are successful because of the simple psychological fact that 'possession' works against return of the goods. This, however, does not justify 'inertia selling' when people are sent goods they have not ordered and for which they may be held responsible. Legislation exists in Britain (the Supply of Goods (Implied Terms) Act 1973 and the Unsolicited Goods and Services Act 1975) to protect customers against such unscrupulous selling.

9. Market education. While some market education (a PR technique discussed in Chapter 4, **25**) may precede the launch or the purchase of a product, it can also be an effective after–market technique. If the customer is educated to obtain maximum benefit from a product, whether it be a cooking material like flour or margarine, a service like insurance, banking or a building society, or a quality product such as a camera, sewing machine or motor car, interest will be maintained and goodwill can be extended.

It is not enough merely to sell a product and hope that the customer will be clever enough to find ways of enjoying it. The wide-awake marketer will explore ways of encouraging the fullest possible customer usage. Road maps can encourage motorists to tour and buy petrol; recipe leaflets and cooking books interest customers in making wider use of ingredients; gardening aids help gardeners to maintain lawns, eliminate pests and grow better plants; and patterns enable knitters and needleworkers to use their talents, buy wool and materials and use machines.

10. Sales promotion schemes. Special offers and especially prize contests can encourage people to buy, say, films for cameras and so increase their use and enjoyment of photographic equipment. These are fully discussed in Chapter 11.

11. Customer clubs. Some products and services can be continuously promoted by clubs consisting of groups of customers such as owners of particular makes of motor car. Use can also be made of existing clubs with general membership such as sports, gardening, photographic and other local clubs, societies and associations. They can be supplied with speakers, videos, slide presentations, prizes and assistance with publicity such as poster blanks which can be overprinted with announcements about events. Interest can thus be perpetuated among members.

12. Pride in ownership. There is nothing like making a customer feel pleased he made a purchase. Retailers know the technique of continuing to make the sale after the sale has been made; for example, complimenting the customer on his choice as he leaves the shop. The same technique can be applied (perhaps through advertising or sponsorship) so that whenever the owner of a product sees it mentioned or promoted they congratulate themselves on already possessing it. People can be proud of the restaurant they use, the bank where they have an account, the camera, video cassette recorder or motor car they own, the deodorant or perfume they use, or the clothes they wear. This is a subtle after-market technique which leads to recommendation, and to regular or repeat purchase.

13. Brand loyalty. Many fast-moving consumer goods rely on brand loyalty to maintain capacity output, economies of scale, good distribution and profitable sales. All the time there is competition such as sales promotion schemes which seek to break down brand loyalty. Brand loyalty depends on customer satisfaction. How is this to be maintained? By consistent quality demanding quality control? By value for money pricing? By packaging which ensures easy or proper usage of the product? By good distribution? All these techniques are inherent in the basic marketing strategy.

14. Reminder advertising. Pride of ownership and brand loyalty may be induced by reminder advertising. This kind of advertising, which may mainly plug names and slogans, can do much to consolidate the after-market so that customers are not allowed to forget. If the manufacturer failed to advertise people might imagine that he had gone out of business. Moreover, a rival could easily capture his place in the market. For this reason, permanent advertisements like those seen on shop premises (e.g. metal or painted signs) can be good investments which perpetuate the name of a company, product or service.

15. Exhibitions. Not only do exhibitions provide launch-pads for new products: they enable customers to renew acquaintance with makers of goods they possess, learn new ways of enjoying these products, feel pride in possession, be reassured that the manufacturer continues to prosper, and be encouraged to repeat the purchase this year. For instance, they may visit a motor show and although they are not yet in the market for a new car their faith in their present make may be renewed when they see the current model. Exhibitions are therefore an excellent way of looking after the post-sale and the future market (*see also* 1:24).

16. Follow-ups. To help the customer obtain the fullest possible benefit from a product it can be sensible to mail reminders that the product should be serviced. This can be done by the manufacturer, if he has service depots, or by distributors if they carry out servicing. Such follow-ups are conducted by the makers of motor cars, lawnmowers, central heating systems and office machines.

17. Product recall. Occasionally a fault is detected in a product and owners are asked to return the product for modification or adjustment. The urgency and frankness with which this is done can only be to the credit of the manufacturer. In a small country like Britain the most direct way may be through advertising. In the USA, faced with a nationwide search for a product made a few years earlier, Corning used PR methods through all the mass media to recall coffee pots with faulty handles. In 1989 there was a major programme for the recall of Tricity cookers which had faulty ovens, and media such as *TV Times, Radio Times* and the *Sun* were used.

18. Public relations. The numerous techniques of public relations can be applied to the after-market. These will be dealt with in greater detail in Chapter 14, but here can be mentioned:

(*a*) the external magazine aimed at customers and users;
(*b*) feature articles in the press, and regular news about the company, product or service;
(*c*) documentary videos and slide presentations which may be seen by customers; and
(*d*) the corporate identity and the corporate image of the organisation.

19. Conclusion. The after-market is thus something of immense

importance to successful marketing. Not for nothing does the
steward or stewardess say at the end of the journey: 'We hope you
enjoyed your flight and that you will fly with us again'.

Progress test 10

1. Explain the difference between regular and repeat purchases.
(2)

2. Describe some of the problems that may occur with making,
stocking and supplying spare parts.   (5)

3. How can an instruction manual for a product sold
internationally be made to serve its purpose?   (6)

4. How can a promise be superior to a guarantee?   (7)

5. Explain how market education can be a form of after-sales
service.   (9)

6. How can an exhibition form part of the after-market?   (15)

11

Point-of-sale material, sales promotion and dealer relations

Introduction and definitions

1. Point-of-sale activities. In this chapter are discussed three activities concerning the retailer: point-of-sale material, sales promotion and dealer relations. These are, respectively, advertising, marketing and public relations activities.

2. Definitions. Point-of-sale material consists of all kinds of promotional aids displayed in retail establishments to promote sales of particular brands. As defined by the Institute of Sales Promotion, and embracing the special short-term exercises which used to be called merchandising, 'Sales promotion is the function of marketing which seeks to achieve given objectives by the adding of extrinsic, tangible value to a product or service.' Such value could be a money-off offer or a premium offer. These will be explained later.

Dealer relations consist of communication techniques and activities aimed at creating good relations between a manufacturer or supplier and distributors.

3. Value of point-of-sale material. The main value of sales promotion is that it directs attention to the product at the point-of-sale. It does so in the following ways.

(*a*) Display material identifies the retailer as a stockist of the product.

(*b*) Special packs draw attention to the product on the shelf, especially in a supermarket where the customer has to select goods.

(*c*) It consolidates advertising seen elsewhere such as in the press, on the radio or television, on public transport and on poster sites, becoming the final link in the process of advertising. This in turn is linked with the product itself and the actual sale.

(*d*) It supports the efforts of the distributor. Provided they are not overwhelmed with more material than they can usefully use, point-of-sale display material may not only help the retailer to sell the product but also encourage him or her to buy stock for resale. It can help the retailer in another way by making his or her shop attractive as in the case of some of the beautiful posters supplied by airlines, tourist centres and manufacturers of soft drinks, cameras and films. It is always sensible to think of the usefulness of this material from the point of view of the shopkeeper. This will win his or her appreciation and willingness to use it. Point-of-sale material (especially if it is seasonal) can have a short life, unless the retailer likes it so much he or she wants to go on using it. The prime example of this is an advertising clock which attracts frequent notice.

Point-of-sale material

4. Use of point-of-sale material. Material for short-term or long-term display is known as point-of-sale (POS) or point-of- purchase material, and can be a regular form of advertising.

5. Internal displays. The following forms of POS material will mostly be used for interior or window displays.

(*a*) *Showcards*. Showcards made of stout card, or metal, are usually strutted so that they can be displayed on counters, shelves or in the window display area. They are excellent for small shops such as travel agents, pharmacies, grocers, tobacconists and confectioners, or in larger shops like department stores, but are seldom suitable for supermarkets and hypermarkets where the necessary display space is scarce or absent.

(*b*) *Mobiles*. Not to be confused with mobile vehicles which travel from place to place, POS mobiles are display devices which are suspended from the ceiling. They may consist of several items which move, flutter or spin and so attract attention. Mobiles can be used in supermarkets.

(c) *Posters*. These may be of various sizes of which the double crown is the most popular (30 in. x 20 in., 762 mm x 508 mm), airline and tourist posters being good examples. One advantage of posters is that they can have additional uses, as when travel posters may be associated with a fashion or foreign food display. Another use of posters is the double-crown news or contents bill displayed by street news vendors or in wire frames outside newsagents' shops. These are sometimes called *placards*. Supermarkets make good use of silk-screen posters, printed in bright Day-glo colours, which are pasted to their street windows to announce price-cuts and special offers (*see also* billboards (7e).

(d) *Pelmets*. These are stickers fixed to the top edges of shop windows and, until they are scraped off, they may remain in position for a long time, sometimes almost permanently. Grocery, confectionery, toiletry and other fast-moving consumer goods — usually 'household names' — are promoted at the point-of-sale with pelmets. They both identify stockists and help the shopkeeper to identify his or her particular trade.

(e) *Dump bins and dumpers*. Frequently found in supermarkets and larger stores, these tubs are a means of presenting a quantity of a brand. They aim to attract impulse purchases, perhaps near the check–out or as part of a special display.

(f) *Wire stands*. Usually self-standing and portable, and ideally bearing the name plate of the supplier, wire stands can be designed in various shapes to hold magazines, paperback books, gramophone records, razor blades, drinks, confectionery and so on. There is always the risk that the shopkeeper will find such stands so convenient that he will insert rival products in them and so defeat the original suppliers' intention. However, they are long-lasting, and it is up to the supplier's visiting salesman to make sure that stands are both filled and reserved for his products.

(g) *Dummy packs*. Real products may deteriorate if placed in the window, or sufficient stock may not be held to permit use in window display. Empty dummy packs are therefore useful for window dressing, and make possible mass displays of packets, cans, jars or bottles.

(h) *Clocks*. Placed on the exterior of shop premises, or inside the shop, clocks provide good reminder advertising and identification of stockists since passers-by and customers often look at clocks to check the time. When projecting from a building a clock becomes a familiar part of the street scene.

(i) *Models and figures*. Travel agents make good use of model aircraft, trains, coaches and ships, and being portable they can be moved about the premises and used for window, counter and shelf displays. Some can be very ingenious with cut-aways to show interiors. Companies with well-known trade figures and characters use models for effective POS display, e.g. Johnnie Walker, White Horse and Black and White whisky. There are also the self-standing cut-out figures such as the swim-suited Kodak girl who adorns the doorways of shops which sell films.

(j) *Working models*. Movement attracts attention. Working models are costly, and they are therefore usually supplied for a short period to major stockists, or to those who order stocks of a certain high value. They can also be set up by businesses with otherwise static displays such as building societies, the model railway or motor racing circuit being good examples. Furniture shops sometimes use a large model animal, such as a bear or elephant, which bounces up and down to demonstrate the springing of an armchair. At Christmas, some department stores attract attention to the toy department by having working models of Father Christmas or nursery rhyme scenes. The simplest form of movement is probably a revolving table bearing a product, which is virtually guaranteed to increase sales of whatever item is placed on it.

(k) *Illuminated displays*. Whether static, moving or flashing on and off, a lighted display attracts attention, including that of passers-by and window shoppers when the shop is closed at night or at weekends.

(l) *Display stands*. These are usually specially constructed to suit the product and range from glass-windowed cabinets to padded rests for watches, jewellery and other expensive items. Another example is a panel with hooks on which can be suspended pre-packed items, e.g. gardening and do-it-yourself products. Display stands have great utility, keep goods tidy and in good condition, may assist self-service, and may be appreciated by both retailer and customer. They also tend to isolate the particular brand from its rivals.

(*m*) *Dispensers*. These may be hanging cards to which, small products are stuck and from which they can be pulled off, e.g. peanuts, raisins, dyes, foreign stamps, corn plasters, pens, pencils, erasers, aspirins and other items made up in small packages.

(*n*) *Display outers or dispenser packs*. The carton containing a bulk supply of small items such as confectionery can be folded back so that the lid becomes a display, and the product is sold from the open carton. Display outers lend themselves to small items sold from the counter, but may also be suitable for supermarket shelves for items such as packets of soup.

(*o*) *Window stickers and transfers*. Stickers can be of various sizes and may be of a temporary nature to link up with an advertising campaign, while transfers can be more permanent as when placed on a shop door. The visiting salesman may place these displays when he sees opportunities for their use.

(*p*) *Shelf edging*. These narrow adhesive strips are very effective when stuck to the edges of shelves behind the counter and facing the customer, a good example being in a bar or café.

(*q*) *Crowners*. Not to be confused with crown corks on bottles, crowners are thin card collars which are placed over necks of bottles as displayed price tags. They are very effective when bottled goods with different prices, e.g. wines or soft drinks, are set out in a window display.

(*r*) *Cash mats*. Usually made of rubber or plastic, cash mats act as useful reminders and stop coins from rolling off counters.

(*s*) *'Open' and 'closed' shop signs*. These may be either reversible cards which are hung on the inside of shop doorways, or the slotted variety which are fixed to the glass. By courtesy of the advertiser, the shopkeeper is given a means of showing when the shop is open or closed.

(*t*) *Drip mats and coasters*. These provide useful publicity wherever drinks are sold, and they also provide collectors' items.

(*u*) *Ashtrays*. Decorated with silk-screen printed advertisements, ashtrays make good give-aways or useful POS displays in bars, cafés, restaurants, hotels and other public places where the product is on sale.

(*v*) *Wrapping paper, wrapping materials, paper bags and carrier bags*. All these can be printed with advertising messages. The material is convenient for the shopkeeper and the customer, the message may be seen by others when goods are being carried home, and the message will be taken into the home. Plastic carrier bags can have a fairly long life. In some trades, special carriers may be designed to protect suits and dresses, or to carry home awkward items such as rolls of wallpaper.

(*w*) *Menu cards*. Like drip mats and ashtrays, menu cards provide useful publicity in cafés and restaurants where people are likely to buy the product. Variations range from a simple card bearing the advertiser's name to the menu card with topical magazine material which is renewed from time to time. The latter idea has been used in chain restaurants and railway dining cars.

(*x*) *Dart mats and score boards*. Used mainly to promote drink and tobacco products and found in pubs and clubs, they have both utility and publicity value.

(*y*) *Sales literature*. Leaflets, folders, booklets, price lists and catalogues really form a medium on their own, and such print can be a considerable item in the advertising budget. Most consumer durables require the back up of descriptive sales literature which can be supplied to customers, to mention only cookers and other domestic appliances; TV sets and hi-fi equipment; cameras and accessories; and motor cars and motorcycles.

6. External displays. The following forms of POS material may be displayed on premises, pavements or forecourts.

(*a*) *Shop facia boards*. Incorporating the name of the business, these are supplied and fitted by newspaper and magazine publishers, tobacco companies and others and extend across the face of the premises above the window.

(*b*) *Metal signs*. Smaller than facia boards, metal advertising signs may be attached to wall space beside shop windows and doorways. They may be fitted flat to the wall or be flanged so that they project at right angles to the premises and are visible at a distance.

(*c*) *Flags*. The advantage of plastic or fabric flags is that they will move and so attract attention, like the brightly coloured small flags on short sticks, usually fixed above window level, to advertise Walls ice cream or Kodak film. Large flags, bunting and banners may be used to publicise short-term promotions where the premises permit, e.g. a motor car showroom or petrol station forecourt.

(*d*) *Pavement and forecourt standing signs*. These are portable metal signs, flat, swinging or revolving, which can be used where space allows on the pavement outside a shop or, again, on a petrol station forecourt. The signs are often used to advertise soft drinks, ice cream, tyres, oil and petrol.

(*e*) *Billboards*. These are double-crown poster size and may be fixed to the outside wall of a shop, leaned against the shop wall, or erected in double-sided tent fashion. They are usually fitted with a wire frame to hold small placards advertising newspapers, entertainments, auctions, and various products or services, but posters may be pasted on them. (NB: In the USA and some other countries billboards refer to large posters, but in Britain they refer to small posters or placards).

7. Sales promotion overseas. The overseas student may find it hard to relate to some of the methods described in this chapter, while much of the jargon may seem strange. They may not belong to the small shop, market stall or even supermarket in his country. In industrial countries there is a greater variety of retail shops and intense competition between rival brands of fast-moving consumer goods. The use of sales promotional techniques depends very much on the spending power of customers. This also bears out what has been said about the lack of marketing in many parts of the Third World, and the emphasis instead on advertising and selling.

In some Third World countries, some of the marketing schemes mentioned below are not permitted. In others, such promotional methods could place too much pressure on poorer but gullible customers. For instance, a multinational once created a bad name for itself by offering a gift if three cans of milk powder were bought. This was an unfair inducement to poor and ignorant people to spend money they could ill-afford on a luxury product they had no means of using properly. It was therefore a psychologically bad form of promotion. Unfortunately, marketing experts planning campaigns in London, Geneva or New York can be ignorant of market conditions in continents such as Africa.

Sales promotion schemes

8. Introduction. Here we are concerned with complete and usually short-term sales promotional schemes, although gift coupons (as given by some brands of cigarettes) could be very long term and extend over many years. Another long-term form of sales promotion is the free accident insurance which has been offered at various times by newspapers, credit card operators and others. Some typical sales promotion schemes are described in **9–22** below.

9. Gift coupons. Because these have to be collected until a sufficient quantity has been accumulated to exchange for an item in a gift catalogue, regular and repeated purchase of the product is encouraged. A variation is the collection of coupons or tokens which the customer sticks on a card and sends in for a cash payment. Collecting valuable coupons or tokens both appeals to the acquisitive instinct and achieves brand loyalty.

10. Picture cards. Collecting sets of picture cards again induces regular, repeat purchase and creates brand loyalty. As cigarettes have become more expensive and the market has shrunk, this once popular way of promoting sales has disappeared, although it has been used from time to time by various food and confectionery firms. In the 1930s there were famous sets of fifty cards on different subjects, given away in packets of Players Navy Cut and Wills Goldflake cigarettes. Another card collecting scheme was a set of cards which, like a jigsaw, could be collected to complete a picture, a print being exchanged for a set of cards, while yet another required the collection of miniature playing cards which were exchanged for a pack of full-sized cards. These sets were of fifty or fifty-two cards, but post-war sets as given with teas and iced lollies have been shorter series. To encourage collection, free albums have been supplied.

Another interesting series consisted of pairs of photographic cards which could be viewed through stereoscopic lenses producing a three-dimensional effect. This device was used to promote De Reske cigarettes in the 1930s, and was revived as a television programme in 1982, viewers enjoying a 3-D effect when watched the programme through plastic lenses supplied in *TV Times*.

11. Matching halves and bingo. Petrol companies have operated a scheme of giving dissected coupons or pictures with purchases, cash or prize awards being made to those holding matching halves. Again, collecting is necessary, and the customer is encouraged to go on buying the same brand in the hope that they will eventually get a matching half. It appeals to the gambler and has a certain entertainment quality like bingo.

Actual bingo has been used to promote newspapers, readers being given cards with games printed on them, the numbers being 'called' by printing them each day in the paper. Each card may contain many weeks of games so that the reader buys the paper regularly to play the weekly games. The *Sun* in particular has used this form of promotion, with other papers copying and dropping out as they found it too expensive to buy readership this way. Each weekly prize may be as much as £50,000.

12. Cash premium coupons or vouchers. These may be printed in press advertising or on the pack, or delivered as house-to-house mail drops, either as individual vouchers or in the form of shopping magazines made up of a variety of cash voucher offers. Few people can resist taking advantage of such cash benefits. Not to use the voucher is like throwing money away!

High Street redemptions are an interesting development, the package carrying a cash voucher to be redeemed as a discount against a purchase at another store, or against the price of a railway fare, or as a discount on the cost of a holiday at a travel agency.

Charity schemes provide a variation on money-off offers, tokens on packages serving as a donation to a charity, the company promising to pay the value of the token. A similar idea is for tokens to be collected by, say, a school in order to obtain a contribution to the sports fund.

13. Free samples. Again, few people can resist something for nothing. Samples may be actual products or miniature packs such as a small sachet of tea, coffee, soup or shampoo. It is a good way of encouraging people to try something they might otherwise not buy on a first-time trial basis. Sampling can take many forms, as follows.

(*a*)   Goods such as books may be offered 'on approval'.

(*b*)   A restaurant may offer courtesy meals to prospective business clients.

(*c*)   Holiday camps sometimes have 'open days' for non-residential visitors.

(*d*)   Free trials or demonstrations may be offered by distributors of motor cars, TV sets and video cassette recorders, and consumer durables such as ironing boards, washing machines and cookers.

(*e*)   Wine merchants may hold wine–tasting sessions.

(*f*)   Many food, drink and confectionery products may include on-the-spot samples as part of in-store demonstrations.

14. Self-liquidating premium offers. This was a favourite form of sales promotion, and is not to be confused with liquidating old stock. The expression means that with the payment made by the customer, the cost of the scheme is liquidated and no profit is made. However, so many of the goods offered on this basis are now available quite cheaply in the shops that unless it is an exclusive offer it may fail to have appeal. Moreover, schemes not requiring the trouble of mailing in and sending money have become more popular. With such offers, care has to be taken about stating their 'worth' because often the items, e.g. a coffee table, towel, set of chinaware or cutlery, are manufactured solely for the offer and are not on sale in shops where comparison can be made with a retail price. Nevertheless, the offer can be a bargain and while the promoter of the scheme will gain extra sales he or she can also enhance goodwill through the offer. However, if the offer is so poorly packed that it arrives in a damaged condition, or if there is a delay in delivery, customers will react unfavourably. It is therefore an important aspect of the scheme that the customer is entirely satisfied.

15. Free gifts and mail-ins. 'Free' is the magic word in all advertising and sales promotion, even if it is only a free leaflet. Nowadays the concept has been extended to Freephone and

Freepost. Free gifts can be attached to products, for example a razor given away with an aerosol of shaving cream, or customers may have to send away for a gift offered in a press advertisement or advertised on the pack. The free razor is an instant gift requiring only purchase in the shop. Advertised gifts require the sending in of some proof of purchase, usually cut from the wrapper or carton. Sometimes a number of such tokens may be required, and a small payment may be requested for packing and postage.

The 'send away' gift is called a *mail-in* i.e. people have to mail in to obtain the gift. Care is necessary not to attract applications which exceed supply of the gift, a certain quantity of which the brand manager has to order against an estimated likely demand. A time or quantity limit should be printed on the offer. It is very frustrating for customers to receive a cash voucher because supplies of the gift have been exhausted. This has happened, and the result has been customer ill-will. Marketing managers have to recognise that sales promotion offers can create either a good or a bad reputation (*see also* 23 and 12:25).

16. Trade characters. Live versions of trade characters — people dressed in costume — may tour stores or even call at people's homes, travelling round in decorated vehicles. They have been used to promote tea, cheese, scouring powder, confectionery, cigarettes and beer.

17. Cash awards for use of product. People are stopped in the street, or are called upon at home, and asked if they possess certain products. If they do, they receive a cash award. The most famous of these was the Blue Cross matches award which resulted in many men habitually carrying a box of Blue Cross in their pockets in case they were stopped in the street by the 'Blue Cross man' asking for a light. The method has also been used by newspaper publishers during the holiday season, a character (such as the famous Lobby Lud) having to be spotted during his visit to a different resort each day. This is announced in the newspaper, and challengers have to carry a copy of the newspaper. A modern version is to advertise a range of products which housewives are encouraged to stock in case they are called upon by the representative making cash awards.

18. Banded, multiple or jumbo packs. These may or may not be seasonal, either taking advantage of, say, a holiday time to sell in bulk items which are especially popular then, or offering a number of items at a bargain price. The products may be in a special box or bag, or be taped together. For example, a number of different chocolate bars may be packed together in a plastic bag with a window which reveals the contents, or three bars of soap may be banded together and sold at three bars for the price of two. There can also be economy packs when a number of small items, like razor blades, are sold in packets of five or ten instead of being sold singly. Such packaging devices both increase the volume of sales and, by inducing repeated usage, encourage habit and repeat buying.

19. Flash packs. A flash is a special announcement printed on the package, usually declaring a price-cut, e.g. '5p off'. This is a short-term offer only for as long as stocks last. It attracts both impulse buying and switching from other brands. The method may be adopted instead of spending money on advertising, to boost falling sales or to compete with rivals. However, there is the danger that customers will simply buy the product because of its offer but next time buy another product which is making an offer (*see* **23(d)**).

20. Competitions. These can be major sales promotion schemes involving much money and administration.

(*a*) *Prizes.* There are so many big prize competitions nowadays, such as the Irish Sweep, football pools and state lotteries, that a commercial contest must offer a substantial prize. The kind of prize or prizes will depend on what potential competitors are likely to value most, and this could vary from country to country. Care is necessary to avoid offering a prize which could be embarrassing to the winner. A holiday in Tahiti might sound exotic, yet be a nuisance to a winner who has to pay for his family to accompany him or her. A motor car might be an ideal prize in some countries, but too expensive for the winner to run in others. Some prizes can have a cash alternative, and this is easy with a car but less possible with a holiday since an airline will not give the cash equivalent of an air ticket. Cash prizes are often the simplest and best.

(*b*) *Extra prizes*. There should be sufficient funds to permit at least second and third prizes, and perhaps a number of consolation prizes. This encourages entries because the chance of winning something is increased.

(*c*) *Content and rules*. Competitions should have an element of skill, and there should be sufficient permutations of answers to minimise the likely number of correct answers, and even then a tie-breaker (e.g. a written statement on why the competitor wishes to win the prize, or the invention of a slogan) may be necessary to arrive at an outright winner. Slogans make excellent tie-breakers since original and clever slogans are rare, and it is easy to discard the majority of attempts. It is usually unsatisfactory (and it may be physically impossible) to divide a prize. Rules should be clear and beyond dispute. The contest should conform to the gaming and lottery laws of the country (*see* 15, **21**).

(*d*) *Entry requirements*. It is usual to expect entrants to show proof of purchase so that the contest does promote sales. Tokens cut from packages thus form the 'entry fee'. Sufficient entry forms should be available. They may be printed in press advertisements, available in leaflet form at the point-of-sale, or inserted in or printed on the pack (e.g. reverse side of a label).

(*e*) *Judging*. It may enhance interest and credibility if well-known people are announced as judges.

(*f*) *Publicising results*. As short a time as possible should exist between the closing date for entries and announcement of the winners, and the names of winners should be published in a stated publication on a given date. A fault with some contests is that while they are promoted generously, and the promoter achieves extra sales, little regard is paid to publicising the results. Goodwill can be gained or lost at this final stage, and the announcement of the results should be planned as carefully as the launch of the contest. This is another area where the 'maximising profits' approach of some marketers shows disregard for public relations.

(*g*) *Institute of Sales Promotion*. The Institute operates a Standard Rules for Competitions system whereby promoters may apply for a licence, on payment of a fee, to print abbreviated copy supplied by the Institute rather than the full rules. ISP Standard Competition Rules, which are approved by the Advertising Standards Authority, are copyright property of the Institute and may not be reproduced in whole or in part without the prior written permission of the Institute. The system is available to ISP members only.

The recommendations contained in this section are the author's, based on practical experience of running competitions, or on observation of competitions which have been held.

21. Dealer contests. Prize contests within the trade can be another worthwhile sales promotion scheme. Dealer contests usually take one of two forms:

(*a*) a straight sales contest based on sales figures, often operated on a monthly basis;

(*b*) a special contest for the best window or in-store display, retailers submitting photographs.

In some trades the prizes can be linked to the product as when a wine producer offers a prize of a holiday for two in the wine-growing area.

22. Children's contests. These vary according to the type of promoter. Painting and colouring contests may be promoted through press advertisements or mail drops. More educational contests such as handwriting tests and essay competitions may be conducted through schools and the teacher press. There can also be contests involving the ingenious use of products which may suit older and more technically - minded students.

23. Problems with sales promotion. Because promotional schemes are usually short term, too much promotional pressure can cause problems which undermine goodwill. Loss of goodwill is bad public relations. The following are some potential problem areas.

(*a*) Retailers may resent having to collect coupons or vouchers from customers and then having to reclaim refunds from their suppliers.

(*b*) Malredemption occurs when retailers accept money-off coupons and cash vouchers for goods other than those being speeially promoted. Some supermarket chains, whether officially or unofficially, give their customers refunds on any vouchers presented provided the promoted products are stocked. Frustrated by the abuse of malredemption, some manufacturers state on the pack that the money–off offer is limited to that product. The following are examples of manufacturers' attempts to prevent malredemptions:

20p coupon towards your next purchase of Persil Automatic liquid any size.

TO THE CONSUMER: This 20p coupon entitles you to a saving of 20p on your next purchase of Persil Automatic Liquid. Redemption of this coupon against any other item would constitute fraud.

TO THE RETAILER: Lever Brothers Limited, Department 874 (NCH) Corby, Northants, NN17 1NN, will refund the face value of this coupon provided that you have accepted it in part payment for Persil Automatic Liquid and not otherwise. Lever Brothers Limited reserve the right to refuse redemption of coupons if they have cause to believe they have been accepted other than in accordance with their terms.

PLEASE DO NOT CAUSE EMBARRASSMENT BY ASKING YOUR SHOPKEEPER TO ACCEPT THIS COUPON AGAINST THE PURCHASE OF ANY OTHER PRODUCT.

Coupon worth 8p off your next purchase of Fairy Snow.

TO THE CUSTOMER: This coupon entitles you to a saving of 8p when you buy Fairy Snow. Most stores will accept it. Only one coupon may be used per pack purchased.

PLEASE DON'T EMBARRASS YOUR RETAILER BY ASKING HIM/HER TO ACCEPT THIS COUPON AGAINST ANY ITEM OTHER THAN FAIRY SNOW.

TO THE RETAILER: Procter & Gamble Limited will redeem this coupon at its face value, provided you have accepted it from your customer in part payment for a purchase of Fairy Snow and not otherwise. Only one coupon may be accepted per pack purchased. Coupons for redemption should be sent to Procter & Gamble Limited, Coupon Redemption Centre, P.O. Box 160, Corby, Northants.

PROCTER & GAMBLE LIMITED RESERVE THE RIGHT TO WITHHOLD PAYMENT IF THEY HAVE CAUSE TO BELIEVE THAT THIS COUPON WAS REDEEMED AGAINST ANY ITEM OTHER THAN FAIRY SNOW.

(*c*) Banded offers (e.g. three bars of soap at the price of two) may be nullified by shopkeepers removing the bands and selling all the items at the full price. This is more likely to occur in the smaller shops, whereas malredemptions are more common in larger shops where they can be swallowed up in bulk purchases and fast sales.

(*d*) Brand loyalty can be lost if customers adopt what is known as 'cherry picking', and buy only the brands with special offers. They could, for instance, buy a different brand of toothpaste every time they made a purchase.

(*e*) In some cases where the premium offer is very attractive, customers may tend to buy the offer and be oblivious to the brand, especially where a number of brands may be similar in performance or quality.

(*f*) When new packs have to be printed to accommodate 'flashes' announcing offers, or other special wording, this can be costly. It is less costly to ask customers to submit as tokens standard parts of the pack such as the address, trade mark, logotype or barcode.

(*g*) Because the extent of demand has not been fully forecast, or because the supplier cannot deliver quickly, some premium offers are delayed and this annoys applicants. If the premium offer is a seasonal one such as a beach ball, a Christmas carol record or spring bulbs, delay in delivery can be disastrous. To overcome this it is wise to state something like 'please allow twenty-eight days for delivery'. When such offers are despatched by a specialist firm, and the sponsor of the original offer is not identified, a delayed delivery may mean that the customer will forget who made the offer! This has happened too often! Brand managers responsible for premium offers need to make sure that their product enjoys the fullest publicity and goodwill benefit from the scheme. The initial extra sales are not everything.

(h) Too many offers (and a visit to a supermarket or hypermarket will reveal their multiplicity) may have the counter effect of:

(i)   destroying the credibility of regular prices; or
(ii) boring and confusing customers who may become blasé about so many offers.

(i) Retailers may be annoyed if they are still carrying old stock, and customers are looking for special offers which have been advertised.

(j) Advertising must be carefully co-ordinated with adequate distribution (see 8,4). This may require that special offer goods are in the shops before and after the advertising campaign.

This links with the problem noted in (i) above. There have been fiascos when advertising has appeared on TV and in the press, but the selling-in and delivery process has not preceded the advertising.

24. Role of the merchandiser. The merchandiser visits retailers who have agreed to support a sales promotion scheme, and arranges the special POS displays. This may include window dressing, or the setting up of displays and stands for demonstration purposes and the supply of stocks for sale by the demonstrator. In the case of a self-liquidating premium offer or a prize contest, displays of sample offers or prizes will be arranged. In other words, the merchandiser is the organiser of the sales promotion scheme at the point-of-sale, and he supports the company's sales representative who has received orders and obtained the willingness of retailers to co-operate in the promotion.

Encouraging dealers to stock up and sell

25. Introduction. The sales promotion techniques described so far all help to move the dealer's stock. They push through sales in the pull-push process. However, other techniques may be necessary in order to sell-in stocks to the retailer. He may be impressed by POS support and schemes to encourage customers to purchase, but he may be even more impressed by special selling-in efforts addressed to himself. These are mostly forms of dealer relations, or public relations aimed at the trade. Some of the possible schemes are described in **26–36** below.

26. Special trade terms. Quantity discounts, a 'free case' with so many cases, thirteen for the price of twelve (known as a baker's dozen) and a free quire of copies of a newspaper are among the inducements that may be used to attract orders. 'Introductory offers' may be made to open up new accounts, or to achieve distribution of a new product. With a new product, or prior to any advertising campaign, it is essential to have adequate distribution to satisfy the demand produced by advertising.

27. Special displays. (*See also* 6(*j*).) Working models and other special displays can be offered against volume orders, or these more expensive or elaborate displays can be toured from one main stockist to another. They can be offered on loan for a short period. A modern device is the video cassette and recorder which can provide a miniature film show on retail premises which have sufficient space such as a motor car showroom or a department store. British Telecom, for instance, have demonstrated Prestel in this way.

28. Publishing of stockists' names. This can be done in press advertisements, sales literature and catalogues, or lists of stockists may be supplied on application perhaps by sending in a request coupon from an advertisement. This can be a service to potential customers, and encouraging support which will be appreciated by stockists.

29. Training of sales staff. Uninformed sales assistants at the point-of-sale can frustrate sales, especially when the product provokes enquiries, explanations or demonstrations. It is no use the shop assistant saying that everything is explained in the instructions supplied with the product. The shop assistant should know those instructions backwards. It is not like selling a fast-moving consumer good which can virtually sell itself off the supermarket shelf without any aid from the shop staff.

Typical products for which training is necessary are mechanical, electric and electronic goods from typewriters to sewing machines, i.e. the more expensive consumer durables, although manufacturers of other very different goods such as cosmetics also often run training schools. Those trained usually receive certificates such as those seen in the service department of a motor car trader, and these display convincing proof of the efficiency of the staff, especially when a product requires servicing.

30. Works visits. Visits to the production plant (or to a tourist centre in the case of travel agents, or a wine-growing area in the case of wine merchants) provide sales staff with authentic background knowledge which can help them to talk convincingly to customers.

31. After-sales service. Retailers will find it easier to sell a product if they can promise a good servicing, repair or spare parts service, whether this is provided by themselves or the manufacturer. This may be bound up with the training of staff already mentioned in **29** above. Chapter 10 deals with this aspect in detail.

32. Buffer stocks. The manufacturer's travelling sales representative may carry a small stock of products in his car or van so that if, on calling, he finds a dealer is temporarily out-of-stock he can replenish stocks until an order is delivered.

33. Dealer loaders. Mainly associated with sales promotion schemes, dealer loaders are gifts of, say, the self-liquidating premium offer which the dealer has been displaying. This can be an inducement to the dealer to display a sample of what is being offered to customers, e.g. a coffee table, tea-set, glassware and so on. It is probably more convenient to leave it with the retailer than collect it, but it is a benefit which repays the stockist's co-operation.

34. Co-operative advertising schemes. The form of co-operative advertising relevant here consists of the manufacturer co-operating with his stockists to promote the product in or on local media such as the press, radio, cinema, direct mail or even TV if the retailer has branches throughout a TV region. The manufacturer may pay a proportion of advertising media costs; supply artwork for local newspaper ads; insert the dealer's name in radio tape commercials or in advertising videos or slides; or organise direct-mail advertising bearing the local stockist's name and address.

35. Commando salesmen. When a new line is being launched, or when there is a special promotion for an existing product, it may not be wise to interfere with the journey cycles (*see* 3:**19**(*b*)) of regular travelling sales representatives, or the journey cycles may be too long for regular salespeople to cover the territories quickly. To overcome such problems, the sales force can be augmented by a temporary and supplementary sales force hired from a firm which specialises in providing 'commando salespeople'. These salespeople also act as merchandisers and set up displays. They will usually concentrate on shops of a certain size, such as those with double-windows and a minimum of, say, six sales staff, which, of course, coincides with the likelihood of getting large orders and having space for displays.

36. Aids to travelling sales representatives. Dealers can be encouraged to buy if the visiting salespeople have convincing back-up material. This may include:

(*a*) *samples,* especially ones which can be left behind for the dealer to examine or enjoy using himself;

(*b*) *portfolios, promoters or presenters* in ring-binder or album form;

(*c*) *audio visuals* i.e. portable desk-top projectors (*see also* 3:**19**(*d*)).

Progress test 11

1. Define sales promotion. (1)

2. Define point-of-sale material.   (2)

3. Why are mobiles particularly useful in supermarkets? (5(b))

4. What are display outers?   (5(n))

5. How can crowners assist with displays?   (5(q))

6. What is the difference between a self-liquidating premium offer and a mail-in?   (14,15)

7. What are jumbo packs?   (18)

8. Describe a flash pack.   (19)

9. What important considerations are necessary when deciding on the prize or prizes for a competition?   (20(a))

10. Describe some of the problems with sales promotion.   (23)

11. What is the role of the merchandiser?   (24)

12. Describe some of the methods which may be used to encourage dealers to stock up and sell a manufacturer's products. (26–36)

13. What is co-operative advertising?   (34)

14. What is the role of the commando salesperson?   (35)

12
Advertising and the marketing mix

The role of advertising

1. Need for advertising. Fast-moving consumer goods (e.g. foods, drinks and toiletries) will tend to rely more on advertising than will consumer durables (e.g. motor cars and domestic appliances) and luxuries (e.g. jewellery). This is because it is necessary to obtain regular repeat sales of FMCGs, create brand loyalty and maintain factory output at an optimum level which will permit a competitive mass production price. In other words, volume production and rapid turnover depends on advertising.

Advertising becomes necessary when there are many potential customers existing at a distance from a manufacturer who is capable of supplying a large market. This is very different from the small producer who can sell directly to customers simply by displaying his goods and perhaps shouting his wares like the market stallholder. He does not need advertising beyond his price tickets, and he may not even use those.

Advertising is, therefore, the product of mass production, transportation, urbanisation, shopping centres and communication media. In fact, goods can be produced in one country and advertised and sold all over the world. This applies to many things ranging from oranges to television sets. Without advertising, mass marketing would be impossible. Advertising is an essential part of any kind of economy − not merely capitalist − in which goods and their availability have to be made known if they are to be sold. People cannot buy what they do not know exists.

2. Is advertising wasteful? Advertising is an agent of competition. Competition provides choice, and choice is the essence of a free economy. There are critics of advertising who believe it to be parasitical and wasteful. Advertising is wasteful only if it is badly planned and executed, and fails to sell. Advertising cannot gain repeat sales for a bad product or service, and by branding a product and advertising it the manufacturer stakes his reputation on it. The public are quick to reject a bad product and to ignore advertising for it. There are also laws and codes to protect the public from unscrupulous advertisers (*see* **22–26**). There is nothing wrong with advertising itself. It is a useful marketing tool, but one which can be misused by disreputable advertisers.

3. Who pays for advertising? This is a question which puzzles some people. The advertisers obviously budget their advertising expenditure and pay the bills. They may even talk about spending what they can 'afford', when they probably mean what they 'need to spend'. The advertising agent pays the media and various suppliers on behalf of the advertiser. In fact, he or she is responsible at law and acts as 'principal'. If an advertiser goes bankrupt the agent is still responsible for payment of any bills incurred on the advertiser's behalf.

Advertising is a *distributive cost*, just like packaging, commission to company sales representatives, transportation and discounts to wholesalers and retailers. The manufacturer has to recover all these costs and make a profit if he is to run a successful business. Consequently, all these costs plus profit must be met in the price. From this it becomes clear that if the product is successful the customer pays for advertising. If the product fails the manufacturer has to pay for advertising along with all the other costs he has incurred.

Let us look at this more closely. If it is a new product, or an expensive slow-moving one, the cost of advertising may be high simply because selling costs are high. On the other hand, with fast-moving consumer goods which do not have high unit prices, the price may be as low as it is because advertising can produce mass sales and justify economic volume production.

It used to be said that advertising produced price reductions through economies of scale, and to some extent this is still true as has been seen in the fall in prices of fairly new products such as calculators. However, real prices are nowadays sometimes obscured by the inflationary costs of labour, raw materials, packaging and energy or by the imposition of taxes including VAT and import duties. When looking at prices inflated in these ways it will be seen that advertising is only a minimal fraction of the selling price.

4. Advertising and the standard of living. It will be noticed that the volume of advertising reflects the standard of living of a country. As the economies grow in developing countries so does the volume of advertising. One of the reasons for the scarcity of newspapers in some countries is not the low level of literacy or the inability of people to buy them but *the low buying power* of people and the resultant *small amount of advertising* to provide newspapers with income.

5. Definitions. Two definitions are worth remembering for two different reasons. The first emphasises the selling purpose of advertising while the second brings out the expertise of the advertising agency.

(*a*) 'Advertising is the means of making known in order to sell goods or services.' (Advertising Association.)

(*b*) 'Advertising presents the most persuasive possible selling message to the right prospects for the product or service at the lowest possible cost.' (Institute of Practitioners in Advertising.)

The first definition distinguishes advertising from anything that merely makes known such as a shop facia board bearing only the tradesman's name, a brass plate outside a doctor's surgery, the name of a house or street, or a directional sign. They all make known but they sell nothing. The second definition not only emphasises the selling intent of advertising but shows that effective and economical advertising depends on creative skills, market research to define prospects, and efficient media planning and buying.

6. Effective advertising. As stated in **1**, fast-moving consumer goods depend on advertising more than technical ones, and so advertising plays a greater or lesser part in the marketing strategy depending on the product involved. It plays a big part in the successful marketing of a product which depends on repeat purchases in a highly competitive market. Other products and services, such as goods bought as gifts or holidays and travel, are likely to require seasonal advertising. Technical and industrial goods may use little media advertising, relying more on exhibitions, technical salespeople and PR techniques such as market education (*see* 16, 12).

From the above remarks it will be seen that advertising is not a cure–all that can be used indiscriminately. Its cost has to be justified by results. A lot will depend on the media used and their ability to reach and influence prospective customers. Television may sell foodstuffs to housewives, press advertising may be better for savings and investments, posters for entertainments, and direct mail for business courses. Even then, it depends on how the media are selected and exploited, the creative techniques employed, and the timing and the volume used. Planning, budgeting and executing an advertising campaign is a very skilled business, as the IPA definition implies (*see* 5(*b*)).

7. Advertising and distribution. It is important to consider the question of *adequate distribution*. The mistake is sometimes made of using advertising to create demand so that when dealers receive enquiries from interested customers they will be encouraged to order stocks. But this can be too late and false marketing policy. There is no point in spending money on advertising to create demand which cannot be satisfied. Nowadays, retailers may stock up only if there is promise, of advertising which will produce customers who will buy their stock (*see also* 8, 4 and 11, 23(*j*)).

8. Advertising and the DMU. The 'DMU' is the decision-making unit which is made up of all those people who, at different times, effectively influence the final buying decision. The people in this unit play various roles. They may advise, cajole, specify or actually buy. A data processor may demand certain hardware but the chief executive signs the cheque. A child may desire a toy, parents may approve and an aunt may buy it as a present. A client may prefer certain fittings in a building, an architect may specify them, and a builder may buy them. Whose finger is really on the buying trigger — or how many fingers are there and again whose?

A combination of advertising, sales promotion and public relations may be necessary to reach all those people at the appropriate moments when their influence is greatest. Advertising aimed at the final buyer may not be sufficient. In some trades, 'back selling' is important to create or maintain demand for, say, a particular make of component which a secondary supplier provides to the assembler of a finished product. In planning an advertising campaign, and its media schedule and copy platforms, it may be necessary to consider a number of either stage-by-stage or simultaneous advertising approaches. The simplest example may be a combination of trade and consumer advertising to ensure adequate distribution to meet consumer demand.

9. Public relations and market education. An advertising campaign could be wasteful if there has been no preliminary PR or market education to educate potential buyers prior to the launch of the product. For example, in the early days of car ferries neither holidaymakers nor travel agents appreciated the merits of the Thoresen route from Southampton to Le Havre. Advertising proved a waste of money. A PR programme took a Viking car ferry round Britain and travel agents were brought to various ports for a first-hand inspection. Next year, Thoresen had no problem in promoting their service.

Today, drive-on drive-off car ferries sail from many British ports to Irish and continental destinations. Thoresen's pioneer PR campaign, conducted by Infoplan, virtually created the modern car ferry service.

In more recent times manufacturers of products as varied as non-drip paints, computers and dairy spreads have found it necessary to educate the market before plunging into advertising. It is very necessary to understand who is involved in the decision-making unit, and not rely entirely on advertising aimed at a limited target audience. It is no use propelling the customer into the shop if the retailer has no faith in the product, or insufficient knowledge of it, which has happened with some new products.

Other examples have been the government's privatisation

schemes, involving the selling of shares in small lots on an instalment system to millions of new investors. Preliminary PR was necessary, first to convince the big institutional share buyers (e.g. pension funds, unit trusts) of the value of the shares, and second to explain share buying to those who had never bought shares before. Typical examples were British Telecom, British Gas, British Airways and Rolls-Royce.

10. An advertising disaster. A disaster of recent times was the attempted launch of NSM (an unattractive abbreviation of New Smoking Mixture). It was assumed that since 50 per cent of adults were anti-smokers a safe cigarette – not made from tobacco – would be a great success. It was overlooked that these people would not smoke any cigarette, and that smokers would prefer a 'real' cigarette, might not like the taste of NSM, and would object to paying the same rate of tax as that imposed on normal cigarettes. The product had to be withdrawn from sale and millions of pounds were lost on its promotion. Nevertheless, a build-up PR programme over two or three years might have prepared the market for a product which could well be a popular big seller today. Advertising alone will not work miracles.

Another failure was the ill-fated launch of the Sinclair C3 which people had expected to be an electric motor car, but which turned out to be a sort of tricycle which was lampooned on the TV puppet show *Spitting Image*. Had there been frank prior knowledge the machine might have been modified and might have survived.

11. The three sides of advertising. There are three closely interrelated but quite separate and distinct sides to advertising, namely:

(a) the advertiser;
(b) the advertising agent;
(c) the media owner.

These are examined in detail in the following sections.

The advertiser

12. The company advertising organisation. The advertiser will usually have an executive in charge of advertising called the advertising manager, product manager or brand manager, but sometimes the marketing manager may deal with advertising himself. There may be a nominal advertising department which does no creative work, or there may be a large functional advertising department. The in-house advertising department will depend on the kind and size of business. Here are a few examples.

(*a*) A large consumer product company may have a number of executives (brand or product managers) responsible for the overall promotion of a single brand or groups of products. For example, Reckitt Colman have food, wine, household and toiletries divisions with group product managers attached to each. Such large companies also have media managers even though they make use of advertising agents.

(*b*) A direct response company may be self-sufficient with its own creative staff for the production of catalogues and print, and for the conducting of direct mail, but it may also use an advertising agency for press or TV advertising.

(*c*) A large travel agency or a department store may be fully self-sufficient, either because it is advertising continuously, or has to produce advertisements quickly.

(*d*) A large advertiser may use an agency for above-the-line advertising, but produce its own print, sales promotion material, exhibitions, direct mail and other below-the-line advertising (*see* Chapter 13, 22).

(*e*) Technical and industrial firms, which may engage in little media advertising, may have a general communication department with perhaps more emphasis on PR than advertising.

13. Different advertising needs. The examples in **12** are generalisations, and each company will develop whatever advertising organisation is best suited to its needs. For instance, if advertising is conducted regularly and in volume it will pay to employ the necessary specialists such as copywriters and artists on a full-time basis; otherwise it will be more economical to share the services of agency specialists. If the work is very urgent and concerned with rapid price movements, as with a department store or supermarket chain, it may be impractical to use an agency.

Again, if there is a large volume of creative work such as producing mail-order catalogues or travel brochures, it will be more practical to do this inside the company. Alternatively, a direct response company may well use the assigning, printing, addressing and despatch services of a specialised direct response agency.

14. Use of an agency. Generally speaking, an agency will be used for the following reasons:

(*a*) Because expenditure on advertising has reached a level when it pays to use an outside agency service, and also when the account is worth accepting by an agency. This works both ways. Accounts can be too small for an agency to handle profitably.

(*b*) When expert media planning and buying services are required.

(*c*) When independent and expert creative services are required.

(*d*) Because the advertiser is remotely situated and needs a service close to the media, or where ancillary services such as art studios, photographers, research units, printers, typesetters, TV production units and so on are conveniently available.

(*e*) Because a new product is being introduced which needs specialist advice and ideas.

(*f*) Because expertise in the production of TV commercials is required.

(*g*) Because specialist services are required, as already mentioned in respect of direct response companies.

The advertising agent

15. Historical development. The historical development of the advertising agent is worth recalling because it helps to explain why he has this anomalous title of 'agent' (and also why it is wrong to speak of a PR consultant as a PR agent). Strictly speaking, the advertising agent is the agent of the media owners who pay him a commission on space and airtime, although he is appointed by the advertiser. This does not mean that he sells the advertiser as much space and airtime as he can in order to earn commission, for he is a most critical and selective buyer on behalf of his client (*see* IPA definition in **5**).

Originally — some 200 years ago — the agent came into being as a space-broker, hawking advertisement space on which he earned commission. As trade and commerce and the press developed in the nineteenth century, as more space-brokers set up business and competed with each other, and as printing techniques improved to permit different sizes and kinds of typeface and also illustrations, the space-broker began to offer advertisers creative services in return for booking space through them. Gradually, the service agency evolved with large agencies offering marketing, marketing research, print design and eventually radio and TV services.

16. Benefits of agency system. The advertiser and the media owner have both benefited from the development of agencies. The advertiser receives many services free-of-charge (paid for out of the agent's commission), his only extras being physical supplies such as artwork, photography, typesetting or camera–ready copy, and additional services such as print or marketing research. The media owner has to deal with only a comparatively small number of agencies who are obliged to pay promptly (in order to get commission) instead of having to wait months for payment from thousands of advertisers. Cash flow is vital to the media which are producing a daily, weekly or monthly product with huge production costs. A one-day strike can cost big circulation daily newspapers at least £1 million.

The media owners also deal with people who are capable of producing advertisements at the right time and in the right form. The latter can apply to the kind of copy or artwork required for letterpress, photogravure, lithographic or flexographic printing processes as the case may be. Most national newspapers are printed by web-offset litho, although the *Daily Mail* has adopted flexography. Some, like *The Independent*, use contract printers. Most women's magazines are printed by photogravure, but the newer women's magazines and many other classes of magazine are printed by web–offset. Free newspapers are printed by web-offset, as are most regional newspapers. Letterpress has been largely superseded by offset-litho.

'Agency recognition' agreements (*see* **19**) require that the agency should obey the British Code of Advertising Practice which applies a self–regulating control over advertisements, and helps the media to publish advertising which is ethical and unlikely to produce complaints from readers (*see* **22**).

In the UK there are some 600 advertising agencies; about half belong to the IPA, but these members represent the bulk of agency business.

The situation today is a changing one brought about by economic circumstances including the high cost of employing large staffs in expensive city centre offices, the different needs of advertisers, new marketing techniques, and to some extent moves away from traditional media.

17. Kinds of agencies. There are today a variety of agencies, such as the following.

(*a*) *Full service agency.* This is the traditional post-Second World War agency which offers clients ('accounts') a large range of services. Many of them, like J. Walter Thompson and Foote, Cone and Belding, are of old-established American origin, while newer ones, like Saatchi & Saatchi Advertising and especially Allen, Brady and Marsh, have grown rapidly in recent years. Agencies tend to split up or amalgamate and over the years there have been numerous name changes.

(*b*) *Creative agencies or 'hot shops'.* These 'à la carte' agencies specialise in creativity, i.e. launching new products, inventing new names or handling the purely creative side (e.g. design and copywriting) for an advertising campaign, and do not buy media direct. Because they do not need recognition by media owners they have not been inhibited by the finance needed to set up full service agencies. Some of these à la carte agencies have been so successful that they are no longer small units, and a new generation of 'third wave' creative agencies has emerged.

(*c*) *Media independents.* These agencies specialise in buying media and claim to do so more efficiently than full service agencies. There are about thirty of them. Some of their clients are the 'à la carte' creative agencies mentioned in (*b*). Some clients prefer to use an à la carte agency and a media independent rather than put all their advertising with a full service agency, thus getting the best of both worlds. Or, a client may produce creative work in-house, and place the advertising through a media independent. (They are usually recognised and may either accept commission as their remuneration, or rebate the commission and charge a fee.)

A variation on this was introduced by Saatchi and Saatchi in 1988 when they set up Zenith as a media buying (but not media planning) company servicing the various agencies in the Saatchi and Saatchi conglomerate.

(*d*) *Poster agency*. Because clients do not always use outdoor advertising all the time it can be uneconomical for full service agencies to have an outdoor advertising section. Poster agencies are usually owned by a consortium of service agencies, commission being shared.

(*e*) *Industrial agency*. This is similar to a full service agency except that it handles technical or industrial accounts rather than consumer ones. Because advertising is placed in smaller circulation specialist journals which usually pay a lower rate of commission, arrangements can be different regarding payment from clients. There may be service fees instead of or in addition to commission, and clients may be expected to pay more promptly and even pay into an advance fund.

(*f*) *Studio agencies*. Mainly used by industrial clients, the emphasis is on creative work such as catalogues and sales literature with some trade and technical press advertising. They seldom require or qualify for the national and regional newspaper agency recognition awarded by the Newspaper Publishers Association (NPA–nationals) or the Newspaper Society (regionals), but usually have recognition awarded by the Periodical Publishers Association (PPA).

(*g*) *Product development agencies*. A number of these have emerged in recent years, and they have often been successful in their handling of the whole process of creating, packaging, pre-testing, researching and promoting new products.

(*h*) *Direct response agencies*. With new concepts of mail-order trading (including the use of TV advertising) there has been a development of the direct-mail house as a direct response marketing agency, with services ranging from use of the ACORN and other locational systems (*see* 9) to database mailing lists.

(*i*) *Sales promotion agencies*. These range from agencies which produce entire sales promotion schemes, such as contests, in-store promotions and premium offers, to agencies providing incentive schemes for employees.

(*j*) *Sponsorship agencies*. These agencies bring together organisers who are seeking sponsors and companies which wish or are willing to sponsor sports, arts, events, celebrities, educational interests and so on. They will then organise the sponsorship on behalf of the client. Major sponsorships organised in this way are the Football League, test cricket, the London Marathon and support for symphony orchestras, yacht races and mountain climbs. This is not to be confused with sponsoring a programme on television. Well-known sponsorship consultants are Alan Pascoe Associates.

(*k*) *Overseas press agencies*. These are agencies which specialise in placing advertising in the foreign press, e.g. Joshua B. Powers, who are the London representatives of many overseas newspapers and magazines.

(*l*) *Recruitment agencies*. Recruitment agencies (and recruitment divisions of service agencies) specialise in the placing of displayed situations vacant advertisements. Austin Knight is a well-known recruitment agency.

(*m*) *Financial agencies*. As the name implies, these specialise in financial advertising such as annual report announcements, takeover campaigns and the publishing of prospectuses for new share issues. Dewe Rogerson Ltd. is such an agency.

(*n*) *Radio, television and telephone selling agencies*. These agencies are concerned with three media which have grown considerably in recent years. Britain has seen the advent of commercial radio and new independent local radio stations continue to be opened. As a result agencies have emerged which specialise in writing scripts for radio commercials. There has also been a rapid development in telephone selling and telemarketing (see 8, 16 and 17) which can be organised on a campaign basis, and agencies have been set up to provide services in this area.

(*o*) *Through-the-line agencies*. There has also been a revival of the comprehensive agencies which handle both above-and-below-the-line media. Known variously as through-the-line or one-stop agencies, they offer to undertake total promotional campaigns.

From the above breakdown it will be seen that there has been a distinct move away from the service agency except for major campaigns using the national press and/or networked TV. In addition, it is common in the service agency world to have fewer specialists (e.g. copywriters, visualisers) in-house and to employ freelance services. This both saves office space and allows the agency to use varied talent.

18. Agency personnel. Advertising agencies employ teams of specialists, and the full service agency is likely to have those listed below. Other agencies may have some of them, depending on the nature of their business.

(*a*) *Account executive.* Sometimes also called the account controller or agency representative, he or she is not an accountant but acts as the liaison between the agency and the client, who is called an 'account'. He or she is more than a seller of the agency's services and should be an all-round well-qualified practitioner. He or she is responsible for representing the agency to the client, giving him advice and bringing the client's needs back to the agency. Here the account executive may chair the Plans Board, made up of departmental heads, direct the planning of the advertising campaign, or head a group of specialists. Then a presentation of the agency proposals will be made to the client, and, having got the client's approval or amendments and authority to execute the campaign, he or she will supervise the creation and placing of the advertising. Throughout the preparations the account executive will be the contact between the agency and the client, presenting media schedules, copy, artwork and proofs for approval, and ensuring that work is done and approved on time so that the advertising campaign runs smoothly.

(*b*) *Marketing director.* Clients often like to work with an agency which has a marketing executive who can advise on special marketing aspects such as branding, new product development, pricing, packaging and marketing research. This may be because the client has no marketing manager, or because it does have one who welcomes working with their counterpart in the agency.

(*c*) *Creative staff.* Different agencies are organised differently. Some have creative directors who control both copywriting and artwork, others have separate copy and art departments, while some rely on freelance creative people. There may also be creative groups which concentrate on major accounts. The main creative people are as follows.

(*i*)   The *copywriter* produces the copy platform or theme and the words.

(*ii*)   The *visualiser* creates the artistic presentation.

(*iii*)   The *typographer* specifies type.

(*iv*)   The *layout artist* draws carefully measured plans or layouts of advertisements (including adaptations for different sizes of span) for the printer to follow. For litho printing camera-ready copy will be prepared based on the layout.

(*v*)   There may also be a *script-writer* for radio or TV commercials. For television a storyboard will be drawn showing the sequence of actions to be filmed. This looks like a cartoon with a series of sequences drawn in shapes like TV screens.

(*vi*)   Agencies which handle television will also employ a *producer* who is responsible for conceiving ideas for commercials, and for working with the director of the outside production company responsible for the actual filming or video-taping.

(*d*) *Media planning and buying.* Covering space in the press and airtime on radio and television, there will be media planners who prepare prospective schedules for approval, and media buyers who negotiate the purchase of space or airtime to fit the approved media schedule.

(*e*) *Production and progress chasing.* It is necessary to control the work flow so that the campaign takes place at the specified time, and systems of control vary according to the size of the agency. The production manager (sometimes called the mechanical production manager) usually produces a timetable of operations and checks progress daily. She is also responsible for buying production materials and, if there is no separate print buyer, she also buys print. Large agencies usually have a 'traffic' department which controls the work flow, while small agencies may put creative and production responsibilities together.

(*f*) *Other staff.* According to the size of the agency and the nature of its business, other agency personnel may include:

(*i*)   *the voucher clerk* who sends the client proof of the insertion of press advertisements in the form of voucher copies;

(*ii*)   *the librarian* who operates an internal information service and stocks relevant books, directories, research and government reports, newspapers and so on;

(*iii*)   *the accountant* who bills the client and pays agency accounts.

19. Agency recognition and the commission system. In Britain until 1979, agency recognition by the media owners gave the advertising agency the right to stated commission on media purchases. For example, if £1,000 of space or airtime was bought the agency was billed for £850 (if the commission was 15 per cent). The agency then billed the client for £1,000 and so earned the 15 per cent. There were some variations as when agencies added a further $2\frac{1}{2}$ per cent because 15 per cent was considered inadequate remuneration.

However, under the Restrictive Practices Act 1976, and a ruling of the Office of Fair Trading in 1978, the old commission system was held to be a monopolistic practice. As a result, recognising bodies such as the NPA, Newspaper Society and PPA (*see* **17**(*f*) and the Independent Television Contractors Association (now Independent Television Association) (commercial TV) and the Association of Independent Radio Contractors (commercial radio) offer more limited recognition. This new form of recognition, introduced in 1979, approves the credit-worthiness of an advertising agency, and requires adherence to the British Code of Advertising Practice (*see* **22**).

Advertising agencies make their own commission agreements with individual publishers and broadcasting companies. Some agencies charge their clients fees, as in the case of the à la carte agencies described in **17**(*b*).

In most overseas countries the commission system persists, with various forms of recognition or accreditation. It must be emphasised that recognition does not imply excellence, and is concerned with ability to pay accounts promptly. Recognition is not awarded by professional or trade bodies such as the Advertising Association, Institute of Practitioners in Advertising or Advertising Standards Authority, as is sometimes misunderstood by students. Recognition is mainly a system whereby media owners can ensure prompt payment.

The media owner

20. Types of media owner. Inevitably we have already strayed into the third side of advertising, which only demonstrates the interrelationship of all three. The above-the-line or traditional media owners consist of the following (*see also* 13, **12– 21**).

(*a*) Newspaper and magazine publishers.

(*b*) The fifteen regional TV programme contractors who are awarded contracts by the Independent Broadcasting Authority (IBA). They both present programmes and sell airtime. In London, two companies operate, Thames Television from Monday to Friday at 7.00 p.m., followed by London Weekend Television from late Friday to closedown on Sunday, plus TVam and Channel 4.

However, new television legislation will change this in the 90s with prospective programme companies bidding for franchises. The IBA will be replaced by the Independent Television Authority (ITA). In addition, as from 1989, satellite television programmes have been broadcast from continental transmitters by SKY and BSB, these being received either by privately-owned dish or via cable television.

(*c*) The twenty-six independent local radio programme contractors (plus others in the future) which are at present awarded contracts by the IBA, together with Radio Luxembourg and Manx Radio. In London there are two companies, LBC News Radio and Capital Radio. Like television, radio is experiencing changes with the replacement of the IBA for radio purposes by the Radio Authority, the introduction of community radio (with certain stations for ethnic audiences) and, in recent years, a totally different approach to sponsorship. The latter is discussed more fully in Chapter 13, **14**.

(*d*) Poster or outdoor advertising contractors, and transportation advertising contractors dealing with advertising on public service vehicles and properties.

(*e*) Cinema advertising contractors, who also cover advertising on ships and Forces cinemas.

21. Sale of space and airtime. The space salesman of old has been redesignated a marketing executive, but the media owner's role in advertising is essentially to sell media, whether it be space in the press, time on the air, or sites for posters. The distinction is best seen if we describe the company *advertising manager* as a buyer and the media *advertisement manager* as a seller. The media do not just wait for orders to come in. They are actively organised as selling organisations, and they have to compete for sales. To this end they use statistical information gained from the JICNARS (press readership), JICRAR (radio audience) and BARB (television audience) surveys. They sell by making claims and comparisons of cost–per–thousand circulation (ABC), cost–per–thousand readers (JICNARS), cost–per–thousand listeners (JICRAR) or cost–per–thousand viewers (BARB) and Opportunities To See (posters) (*see also* 13, **33–36**).

The rate card states various rates for sizes, positions or times and gives mechanical data, and then details are reproduced in the monthly bible of the media buyer, *British Rate and Data*.

To increase their sales ability, special features are run to attract press advertising while the broadcasting contractors offer packages which are a mixture of prime and less popular times. It is a highly organised competitive business.

Self-regulatory control of advertising

22. The Advertising Standards Authority. Advertising professionals have long been jealous of the good name of their business. Credibility and trust are vital to successful advertising. As long ago as 1926 The National Vigilance Committee established the voluntary control of advertising. This Committee became the Advertising Association (AA), which first held professional examinations in 1931 and ultimately became one of the founders of the CAM Education Foundation. In the 1930s the director of the AA, Russell Chapman, campaigned against some of the abuses of advertising at that time, especially the large ads for dubious proprietary medicines which used to appear in the popular Sunday newspapers. For years, until the creation of the Advertising Standards Authority (ASA) in 1962, the AA ran its own Advertisement Investigation Department. Now, the self-regulatory control of advertising is performed by the independent ASA, and since 1974 this has been financed by the Advertising Standards Board of Finance (ASBOF) which collects a 0.1 per cent levy on advertising expenditure, this being paid to ASBOF by the media. Since 1975, the ASA has been financially independent of the Advertising Association, its original financer.

The basis of voluntary control is the British Code of Advertising Practice (BCAP), which in recent years has been continually expanded to deal with particularly troublesome drink, cigarette, slimming and other advertising. The 8th edition was published in December 1988. The ASA is serviced by the Committee of Advertising Practice (CAP), and it has subcommittees which specialise in health and nutrition, financial, mail order and sales promotion. There are also five copy advisory panels which meet every week to consider complaints.

The ASA runs a regular advertising campaign inviting the public to submit written complaints about any advertising which they consider to be unethical (*see* Fig. 12.1). It also issues a sheet of advertisements for free space insertions, which are used as fillers in the trade press, especially papers such as *Campaign, Marketing* and *UK Press Gazette*, where they not only invite complaints but remind the industry! Every month the ASA publishes its *Case Report* on complaints rejected or upheld. This contains some very well-known names, for leading advertisers and their agencies do, mostly unintentionally, offend against the Code simply through carelessness or over-enthusiastic promotion. Such malpractices are quickly controlled by either withdrawing or amending the offending advertisements. The ASA has no power to exact penalties.

23. Disadvantages of the voluntary system. While it is proper that the good name of advertising should be protected, and this is good PR for advertising, the inviting of complaints itself leads to abuses. One gentleman who was a teetotaller objected to every advertisement for alcoholic drinks and submitted 150 complaints in one year. *ASA Case Report* lists everyone, innocent and guilty

M ost advertisements are legal, decent, honest and truthful. A few are not, and, like you, we want them stopped.

If you would like to know more about how to make complaints, please send for our booklet: 'The Do's and Don'ts of Complaining'. It's free.

The Advertising Standards Authority.

We're here to put it right. ✓

ASA Ltd , Dept 7, Brook House, Torrington Place, London WC1E 7HN

This space is donated in the interests of high standards of advertising.

Figure 12.1. *Typical ASA advertisement*

alike, so it can be embarrassing and poor PR if one is subject to a frivolous or unjustified complaint.

24. Benefits. However, the Code does have a preventive effect in that it helps to stop unethical advertising being produced or published, even though certain advertisers may wish otherwise. An agency can refuse to offend against the Code on the grounds that it could lose its right to commission. In some delicate areas, an agency may seek the advice of the media or the ASA on whether an advertisement is acceptable (*see also* 15, 1–3).

25. Problem media and advertisers. Unethical advertisements often appear in publications which are hard up for revenue, e.g. small circulation regional newspapers, religious publications, and minority interest or 'alternative' journals. A big worry to the ASA are the give-away job and entertainment magazines, and especially the hundreds of free newspapers which are delivered house to house. The publishers are usually outside the bodies which are signatories to the BCAP. Another worry has been the arrival of new, inexperienced advertisers in the computer world who may not be able to meet demand for software.

26. Broadcast advertising. The ASA controls only press advertising; indoor and outdoor posters; aerial advertisements; cinema and video-cassette advertisements; advertisements on viewdata services; brochures and leaflets direct mailed or distributed door-to-door; inserts in publications, and sales promotion. Television and radio advertising has a similar but more wide-ranging and stringent code which has the power of law because it is part of the Independent Broadcasting Act 1973. All TV commercials are vetted by the Independent Television Association (ITVA), and this copy control deals with more than 8,000 scripts and 5,500 commercials annually. The television code extends into other areas because of the intrusion of television into the home and family circle. Advertisements for cigarettes, betting, money-lending, contraceptives and anything to do with religion or politics are banned. Advertisements must avoid portraying anything which would encourage a child to behave dangerously.

Copy control of radio advertisements is conducted by the Association of Independent Radio Contractors (AIRC). Commercials need not necessarily be misleading to provoke objections. One wine merchant had to restrain his commercials because listeners were irritated by the raucous voice of a character who attempted to sing the sales message.

Progress test 12

1. How would you define advertising?   (5)
2. What is meant by adequate distribution, and how is advertising related to this?   (7)

3. What sort of people make up the DMU? **(8)**

4. What are the three sides of advertising? **(11)**

5. For what reasons might a company use an advertising agency? **(14)**

6. What is a full service agency? **(17)**

7. How does a media independent differ from other advertising agencies? **(17)**

8. What is a product development agency? **(17)**

9. Who are the main personnel of an advertising agency? **(18)**

10. How does a television commercial producer differ from a director? **(18)**

11. Explain what is meant by agency recognition. **(19)**

12. What are the roles of the ASA and ASBOF? **(22)**

13. Why does the television and radio advertising code have legal power whereas that for the press and sales promotion is voluntary? **(26)**

14. Name some of the classes of advertising which are banned on British television. **(26)**

13
Creativity and media

Introduction

1. Interaction of ideas and media. Two things go together in advertising:

(*a*) the ideas which give the advertising its originality and sales appeal; and
(*b*) how that sales message is conveyed to the right people at the right time.

Clever advertising will not work if it is misplaced, while good media will be wasted if the sales message is poorly created. It is not a question of deciding which is most important, the donkey or the cart — both are necessary.

2. Cycle of advertising development. In an article in the Advertising Association journal *Advertising*, Autumn 1980 issue, David Stewart Hunter, of Saatchi & Saatchi, set out the following useful four-stage cycle of advertising development.

(*a*) Moving strategy definitions. (What to say and to whom?)
(*b*) Creative development. (How to say it?)
(*c*) Communication assessment. (Have we said it?)
(*d*) Campaign evaluation. (What was the effect of what we said?)

3. Different media, different needs. As will be seen as each medium is discussed, the creative needs will be different. One may need colour, another sound, another vision; one may permit a lot of words, another may require few, while yet another will require words and construction that read or sound well. Thus creativity has to be married to media characteristics.

4. Essentials of creativity. These can be summarised in the following five-point 'AIDCA' formula.

(a) An advertisement must first of all attract *Attention* to itself, generally in competition with other attractions which may be very powerful, especially if they were the subject of the person's original attention.

(b) It must command *Interest* if the message is to be absorbed.

(c) It must create *Desire* for the product or service.

(d) It must inspire *Confidence* so that people believe the product or service is worth buying.

(e) It must urge *Action* so that people respond to the advertisement.

5. Agents of creativity. Creativity can adopt many devices according to the medium. Some media may be static like a newspaper or lack colour like a black and white newspaper or radio; or again lack movement like a poster or radio; or, as in the case of television, be blessed with everything, movement, sound and colour.

Creative skills

6. Words. The words in a press advertisement are called the *copy*, while in a radio or television commercial they are called the *script*. Good copywriting is at the heart of most creative advertising. The *copy platform* is the theme for an advertising campaign, and the *visualiser* will produce his visual ideas for layout and illustration from the basic copy theme.

Words are therefore very important in advertising, whether in a press advertisement, on a poster, in a mailing shot, or in a radio or TV script including the jingle. Critics of advertising sometimes attack it for its banality and abuse of the English language. This is often deliberate for words, sentence construction and punctuation

can all be used to special effect. Advertising messages would not
be read, and they would be ineffective, if they were verbose.

Buzz words are short and powerful – the clichés of advertising –
such as the most successful word in all advertising, 'free', and its
runners-up, 'now', 'new', 'here', 'at last', 'today', 'look' and so on.
Buzz words are also very often *action words* of which the following
are typical:

See	Ring	Pick
Get	Write	Start
Do	Call	Give
Use	Go	Send
Tell	Take	Taste

7. Headlines and straplines. Headlines are nowadays often
displayed copy – whole sentences or paragraphs – while slogans
are used as pay-off lines, straplines or signature slogans.
Associated with the name and logo, they help to create a corporate
image. Well-known examples are 'You'll always come back for
Knorr' (Knorr soups), 'Good food costs less at Sainsbury's' (J.S.
Sainsbury), 'The Ultimate Driving Machine' (BMW) or 'Top
Breeders Recommend It' (Pedigree Chum).

8. Copy techniques. The following are some of the special
techniques employed in writing advertisements.

(*a*) *Repetition*. This is one of the secrets of successful
advertising. Brand or company names are repeated throughout
advertisements, while advertisements themselves appear regularly.
The public memory is short, as any entertainer knows who steps
out of the limelight for a while. Sometimes the brash and vulgar
may be necessary for survival.

(*b*) *Alliteration*. Pleasant sound, easy reading and a sense of
motion all stem from another form of repetition, alliteration.
Examples are 'Mars are marvellous' and 'Let the train take the
strain'.

(*c*) *Colloquialisms*. Even in technical and prestigious
advertisements, the use of colloquialisms such as 'you'll', 'we're',

'I'd', 'wouldn't' and 'don't' are common. They help to give the copy pace and warmth.

(*d*) *Invented words*. 'Drinka pinta' and 'Beanz Meanz Heinz' are typical examples of distorted or invented words which may offend the purists but which are effective copy devices.

The above examples all emphasise the tight, catchy style of copywriting which does not waste words or space in getting the sales message across as quickly, pungently and convincingly as possible. Unlike the preceding sentence it sticks to short words and short sentences, even paragraphs containing but one word! This may irritate the pundits of grammar, but it sells goods — fast.

9. Artwork. Advertisements are enhanced by artwork which may, of course, be the chief means of gaining attention. Photographs, line drawings and wash drawings may be used. To overcome the poor quality of newsprint, photographs can be converted into lines and dots by the scraperboard, quarter-tone and the newer Asline system of screen effects.

10. Typography. The use of typographical effects can add to both the attractiveness and the legibility of an advertisement. The selection, blending and specification of typefaces calls for a skilled typographer. Copywriter, visualiser and typographer should work together as a creative team, for good copywriting will be wasted if it is not set in an attention-getting advertisement which is easy to read. These are the sort of creative skills which the advertising agency can provide.

Above-the-line media

11. Introduction. Advertising media which normally pay commission on purchases made by advertising agents, traditionally the press, radio, television, cinema and outdoor, are termed *above-the-line*. They are the media on which agents depend for most of their income (*see* Chapter 12, **19**). Use of above-the-line media is known as *media* advertising.

All other media such as direct mail, exhibitions, sales literature, point-of-sale, sales promotion and sponsorship are known as *below-the-line.* They do not usually pay commission, and those agencies which do provide below-the-line services do so on a fee and costs basis. Most below-the-line advertising is therefore handled by the company in-house advertising department but there are, as explained in the previous chapter, some agencies which specialise in providing these services.

Below-the-line media are not necessarily, if at all, inferior to above-the-line media, although service advertising agencies may naturally regard them as being of lesser importance because they do not contribute to their commission income. For some advertisers, however, they can be vital media, and for direct response traders direct mail and sales literature will be primary media. The mistake should not therefore be made of regarding above-the-line as *primary* advertising media and below-the-line as *secondary.* Their values could, with some trades, products and services, be reversed.

Let us consider the characteristics of each of the five traditional media whose existence, abundance, scarcity and advertising value vary in different parts of the world.

12. The press: in Britain. Newspapers, magazines and other regularly published publications abound in the literate, industrialised and urbanised countries and, in spite of television, the press remains the dominant medium. This may change as television becomes fractionalised, or de-massified as Alvin Toffler has put it in his book *The Third Wave,* and the viewer can receive specialised advertising from a multiplicity of channels via cable or satellite, or as satellite television provides advertisers with more airtime.

The press can be broken down into the following categories.

(*a*) *Newspapers*, national, regional or local, published morning, evening, weekly or on Sunday. They may be sold, or (as free newspapers) delivered door-to-door free of charge.

(*b*) *Consumer magazines* such as women's and those on a variety of topics and sold through newsagents.

(*c*) *Trade, technical and professional magazines* aimed at distributors, technicians and manufacturers, and professionals respectively. Some may be retailed, others sold on postal subscription, while many others are mailed free-of-charge under the controlled circulation (CC) method. The advantage of CC journals is that they have greater penetration of their markets than those with cover prices, and advertisers are willing to pay for this bigger circulation and wider coverage. However, there has been a tendency for journals to start as CC journals and then to revert to subscription sales as has occurred with *Marketing, Marketing Week* and *PR Week*.

(*d*) *Directories, annuals, year books and membership lists.* These cover every subject, trade and profession and if constantly referred to (like *Advertisers Annual*) can be valuable media. Included here are telephone directories and *Yellow Pages*.

(*e*) *House journals.* These are privately published internal or external journals. A few have very big circulations which make them useful advertising media.

In the UK there are, according to *Benn's Media Directory*, some 12,000 newspapers, magazines and directories published in the UK. This means that through the press it is possible for advertisers to reach almost any kind of reader.

13. The press: in developing countries. As countries in the South develop, both educationally and economically, so does the press. Indeed, the number of publications and the size of their circulations is a barometer of development. Nevertheless, in a large and populous country like Nigeria the circulation of a national newspaper will be no more than 400,000 (*Daily Times*) which is similar to the small circulation London *Times*, whereas a popular British daily such as the *Sun* sells 4 million copies daily. Newspapers in developing countries may have small circulations for the following reasons (but *see also* 12, 4).

(*a*) Widespread illiteracy so that perhaps no more than 20 per cent of the population can read.

(*b*) Widespread poverty so that even literate people cannot afford to buy a newspaper. This happens in India.

(*c*) Foreign exchange problems which limit import of expensive newsprint, as in Zambia.

(*d*) Great distances and poor transport facilities which limit distribution.

(*e*) Numerous ethnic groups and languages which either limit the number of people who can read newspapers printed in English or some other national language, or mean that vernacular newspapers are expensive because of small circulations. In contrast, Hong Kong boasts some one hundred Chinese language dailies!

From the above remarks it will be seen that some countries of the South suffer difficulties not to be found in industrialised countries where there is often only one language, most people are literate and able to afford newspapers and magazines, and road, rail, sea and air communications are excellent. The continual growth of the press in developing countries is therefore a commendable achievement, and there are some splendid publications in these countries.

In contrast to the above remarks, there has been a growth in international circulations of newspapers and magazines such as the *International Herald Tribune, Wall Street Journal, USA Today*, and the *Economist* which have world-wide circulations thanks to satellite transmission to overseas printers.

14. Radio: in Britain. Since the passing of the Sound Broadcasting Act 1972, and the renaming of the Independent Television Authority as the Independent Broadcasting Authority, independent local radio (ILR) commercial stations have come into being. By 1982, sixty-nine stations had been designated and twenty-six were operating. To these may be added Manx Radio and the English language programme of Radio Luxembourg. Unlike most other countries of the world, commercial radio is a comparatively recent innovation in Britain.

In the 1990s, commercial radio and television will be separated, and for radio the IBA will be replaced by the Radio Authority. There will also be community radio stations, aimed at smaller local and in some cases ethnic audiences.

A major change in IBA policy in the 80s was its relaxation of the rules about sponsorship. A number of commercial radio items are credited to sponsors, e.g. stock market reports and air travel information, while the aircraft which flies over London giving traffic reports is sponsored. Some concert services are networked with a sponsor such as NatWest, and there is the Nescafé sponsored weekly Network Chart Show. A company which specialises in 'funding programmes' (the official term for radio sponsorships) is PPM Radio Waves. Sponsorships are usually 12-week deals.

15. Radio: overseas. Commercial radio has operated in the majority of overseas countries for a long time, sometimes since the origins of radio. In developing countries radio is often the principal advertising medium, having the advantages that it can penetrate distances and reach rural populations, it can be listened to by people who may not be able to read, and programmes (and advertising) can be broadcast, often regionally, in different languages. However, even in these encouraging circumstances, radio can have the following weaknesses.

(*a*) There may be too many ethnic groups and local or tribal languages for programmes to be broadcast in them all. If programmes are transmitted nationally, airtime has to be divided between a number of languages so that there is limited listening time for each language group.

(*b*) People in remote places may not be interested in programmes about happenings in distant cities.

(*c*) There is a tendency for people to use radio as a pleasant, companionable background noise. They may prefer 'pop' music, and switch on to foreign stations in neighbouring countries if they meet this need.

(*d*) Most sets are operated by batteries which are expensive to replace, while sets which are out of order are expensive to repair or replace. Many sets are therefore not operating. Diffusion services or 'box' radio can overcome this, including radio in public places. Some people cannot afford to buy sets anyway.

(*e*) Reception may be poor in some areas.

16. Television: in Britain. In 1982, Britain extended its television with ITV'S Channel 4, and 1983 saw the arrival of commercial breakfast TV presented by TV-am. Britain is served by fifteen commercial stations, with two in London (one operating during the week and the other at the weekend). Advertisers can use single stations, groups of stations or the national network. The British television audience is vast, and the national audience for a very popular programme could be 20 million viewers. This is a very powerful medium which is ideal for advertising consumer goods, but it has become noticeable in the 1980s that advertisers of more expensive goods and services such as video cassette recorders (VCRs), cruises and motor cars are also using the medium.

However, in Britain and America, there is great awareness of a revolution that is occurring in television, not unlike that which destroyed the big Odeon and Gaumont cinemas of the past. The mass television audience is being fragmented by *alternative TV*, which consists of the following.

(*a*) *Viewdata* (British Telecom–Prestel) and *teletext* (ITV–Oracle) plus the non-advertising BBC Ceefax systems of providing shopping and general information on the television screen as called up by the viewer. Viewdata is an interactive system so that the viewer can buy off the screen (*see also* 18, **10**).

(*b*) *VCRs* which enable the viewer to record programmes and view them instead of regular programmes; show his own video tapes shot on his own camcorder like home movies; or show films on video tape which he has bought or hired in video cassette form. Advertisements can be placed on commercial videotapes.

(*c*) *Video discs*. This is another method of showing private programmes on the home TV receiver, provided one has a special video disc recorder. However, this method has been slow to develop.

(*d*) *Video games*. Video cassettes consisting of games to be played on the TV screen can be bought or hired.

(*e*) *Cable TV*. Well established in the USA and spreading in Britain is the ability to receive special programmes from cable TV operators. Again, advertisers may use this medium.

(*f*) *Satellite TV*. A small earth station can be attached to the domestic TV set, and this means that numerous channels become available from other countries or from private broadcasters aiming at special audiences. Satellite programmes can be received by cable. In 1989, Sky and BSB satellite programmes were launched so that Britain had a surfeit of available channels.

We are rapidly approaching a demand information situation whereby the viewer can decide what they want to see, and for what purpose they wish to use their TV set. Another development is electronic mail, correspondence being conducted on the office computer screen without the need for a postal service. Some of these topics are reviewed again in Chapter 18.

17. Television: overseas. There are interesting developments in countries of the South where television has its problems and yet its innovations. The following are some special aspects.

(a) *Small audiences*. In some developing countries, the cost of a TV set is prohibitive, and it remains an élitist medium. This has a detrimental effect on television production standards since stations cannot afford the best equipment, and may have limited outside broadcast facilities. However, they do benefit from the availability of video cassettes, and some can receive satellite broadcasts. The Gulf states and Indonesia have satellite facilities.

(b) *Lack of electricity*. This is a major deterrent to widespread viewing, especially in Africa.

(c) *Use of 12-volt car batteries*. In Asia, e.g. Indonesia, which has its own satellite and some ninety earth stations, lack of electricity is overcome by the use of 12-volt batteries. Since batteries are costly to recharge, viewers are very selective. On Indonesian television, commercials were grouped together as one programme slot, interspersed with pop records to attract an audience. Now they are banned because they incite the expectations of the poor.

(d) *Community viewing*. In many parts of the South, community viewing in halls has brought TV to people who could never afford to buy sets. However, in some societies women do not go out at night, so there are all–male audiences.

(e) *Urbanisation*. Countries like Nigeria have growing town and city populations which increase the overall audiences.

18. Outdoor and transportation: in Britain. Outdoor advertising, and that on public transport vehicles and property, is a universal medium provided there are sites. A large city like London has every kind of site, i.e. hoardings, supersites, pedestrian shopping precinct posters, illuminated signs, buses, bus shelters, taxi-cabs, railways and of course the London Underground railway system with its miles of walls, quite apart from the train carriages. A large population, travelling about its business or for pleasure, provides a huge audience for this type of advertising. Not for nothing was poster advertising in the 1930s dubbed the 'poor man's art gallery' for posters are usually beautifully designed. Modern advertising also goes aloft with ads painted on hot air balloons and small airships.

Arena advertising at sports stadiums, race tracks and other sporting venues has become a very popular form of outdoor (and indoor) advertising. Such advertisements are seen not only by the spectators but also by television viewers at home since the camera inevitably picks them up from time to time.

19. Outdoor and transportation: overseas. Outdoor advertising sometimes takes different forms outside Britain, although Britain has borrowed from the East the idea of the flutter sign made up of spangles. On the Continent one sees circular poster sites on the pavement, while lines of fluttering advertising flags are popular, and banners trailed by aircraft are common.

However, in the developing world, in spite of a scarcity of sites, posters are noticeable as a first-class means of advertising to people who may be illiterate or who speak different languages. The characteristics of posters are their dominant size, coloured pictures and brief wording. Cartoon pictures, or the very explicit pictures seen on Malaysian posters, can convey sales messages very effectively to the people who crowd the cities and highways. It is significant that in China, where one might expect little advertising, large solus posters are common, many advertising Japanese products but some advertising even Mackintosh's Quality Street!

In the East, advertising signs, lit up at night, are projected overhead from buildings, and are a familiar sight in places like Hong Kong and Tokyo. Even in Moscow and Leningrad the night sign proclaims that advertising is indispensable.

The painted bus or train, less often seen in Britain nowadays, is a popular medium in places like Hong Kong.

20. Cinema: in Britain. Advertisers may make a cinema version of their TV commercial, and it can look far more powerful on the wide screen. British cinema audiences have changed: this has become mainly a very young people's medium but while cinema audiences dwindled with the arrival of television, the late 80s saw a revival of cinema-going.

21. Cinema: overseas. In developing countries there are two forms of cinema, static and mobile, and the former can include both theatre and open-air drive-in. The medium tends to suffer from the perhaps inevitable use of non-local actors since the commercials are mostly made by multinational companies which are advertising in a number of countries. It can be offensive if a black actor or actress is wearing the wrong national dress, which can happen when a commercial is shown simultaneously in a number of, say, African countries. This problem is less prevalent in the Caribbean where populations are of varied descent such as African, Indian, Chinese or European.

The mobile cinema is frequently used in developing countries to take commercial film shows, perhaps supported by product demonstrations and entertainers, from village to village as with the monthly tours in Kenya. To people with no sophisticated entertainments the mobile cinema van brings a welcome novelty. Again, the problem of literacy and language is overcome by the visual demonstrations on the screen. Pack recognition is helped by the ability of illiterate people in the literary sense having the remarkable capacity to enjoy visual literacy and a pictorial memory.

Below-the-line media

22. Introduction. As already stated (*see* 11), below-the-line media consist of all those other than the five just described: the list is endless. Their values vary. Some are used as primary media. Someone will attempt to sell advertising on anything that will accept it. The question is, is it worth buying? Advertising on the backs of deck-chairs at the seaside, even on toilet rolls and clouds in the sky could be valuable to someone! On a building site the builder does not hesitate to hang a lighted name sign from a tower crane, while the shopkeeper sends the customer down the street carrying a plastic bag advertising where he or she has been shopping. Advertising is very much the art of exploiting opportunities. It must be placed right before their very eyes!

Some typical below-the-line media are described below.

23. Direct mail. Given a reliable mailing list or database of prospective buyers, this can be one of the most effective media when it is necessary or possible to appeal to individuals direct, and especially when a lot of information has to be given. Press advertisements contain limited copy, and the size of the space is restricted by its cost, whereas a direct mail shot can include an entire single- or full-colour folder, brochure or catalogue. Mailing lists can, of course, be built from the response to press advertisements.

The following are some important considerations when using direct mail.

(a) *Minimum mailings.* Mailing lists should be pruned of repeated addresses, wrong addresses, non-buyers and doubtful buyers. Broadcast mailings can be wasteful, costly and annoying. It pays to update regularly, and if the list is held on a computer a system of de-duplication should be used (*see* 18, 7).

(b) *Timing.* Precise timing is important so that the mailing shot will obtain the best response. For instance, holiday brochures may be mailed to arrive just before Christmas because family holidays are often discussed over the holiday and people may have Christmas bonuses with which to pay deposits. Again, some mailings may be made to avoid clashing with holidays such as Bank Holidays, festivals and early closing days. Or it may be necessary to give people time to make arrangements and final decisions, and arrival of the offer or information must be so many days, weeks or months in advance. A charity marketing Christmas cards has to mail a catalogue early enough for people to receive personally printed cards in time to meet last posting dates.

(c) *Enclosures and one-piece mailers.* It can be irritating to the recipient if the envelope contains so many loose items that he or she does not know which to look at first, and he or she may discard the lot out of sheer frustration. More effective can be the simple one-piece mailer. A typical one-piece mailer is a broadsheet which folds down like a map, and contains all the required information including an order form which may be detached.

(d) *Weight, size and postage.* The cost of the mailing should be budgeted carefully. Contributions to production costs and postage include the size of the mailing material (and the necessary envelope size); the number of items (if a one-piece mailer is impractical); the weight of paper used (60 gram paper may be ample instead of 80, 90 or 100 g. and could halve the postage); and ultimately the postal cost. The latter may depend on whether Post Office discounts are feasible, and whether time will permit surface mail instead of airmail on international mailings.

(e) *Is a sales letter necessary?* For some mailings a well-printed (and well-produced!) sales letter is the primary element in the shot, but a covering letter may be needless, especially with a self-explanatory one-piece mailer. If a letter is to be used it should be composed seriously by a professional copywriter. Too many sales letters are poorly-written business letters composed by incompetent authors who do not really appreciate that sales letter writing is a highly skilled craft. With modern word-processing and laser-printing techniques, letters can be produced immaculately, personalised and given special colour and typographical effects (*see* 18, **5**).

(f) *Are printed envelopes necessary?* It depends on whether the recipient is likely to see the envelope so that the selling can start even before the envelope is opened. If the recipient has their mail opened in the post room or by their secretary, they will never see the printed envelope, but it may be important that the secretary sees it. Mail received at home may have an added impact if it arrives in a printed envelope, for example a holiday brochure, but it could be a disadvantage for some unsolicited mailings, resulting in the envelope not being opened at all.

24. Exhibitions. Indoor or outdoor, public, trade or private, exhibitions enable participants to display or demonstrate products or services, and to meet existing or prospective customers face to face. There is a pleasant atmosphere of semi-entertainment since the event is an outing for visitors, while goodwill is fostered by face-to-face contact. Trade exhibitions are often opportunities for company leaders to meet their distributors in hospitable circumstances. The many different types of exhibitions include the following.

(a) *Public*. Perhaps the most famous is the Ideal Home Exhibition run by the *Daily Mail* for more than fifty years and held, usually in London, for a whole month during the Spring. The Motor Show, run by the Society of Motor Manufacturers and Traders, comes a close second; it serves the motor trade in addition to the public. The Boat Show is also very popular.

(b) *Trade or business*. These may lack the hundreds of stands of a major public show, and the million or so visitors to the Ideal Home Exhibition, but they will have specialist exhibits for a quality attendance by people limited to invitation ticket or to turnstile ticket on presentation of a business card (*see also* Chapter 1, 16). Free tickets may be distributed in trade magazines, or by exhibitors.

(c) *Conferences*. A number of annual conferences have associated exhibitions at which suppliers to the industry, trade or profession show exhibits. Trade union and professional institute conferences often have these exhibitions.

(d) *Private*. Usually held in a hotel or other public rooms, private exhibitions are usually small, specialised ones attended by invited guests. They may be either sales or PR orientated.

(e) *Outdoor*. The nature of the subject may require an exhibition to be out-of-doors as with agricultural shows, while in hot countries it may be both possible and desirable to hold outdoor shows.

(f) *International*. Overseas trade fairs and Expos, Joint Ventures and British Exhibitions sponsored by the Department of Trade and Industry, plus famous international motor car, aviation and book exhibitions, are all part of the world marketing scene. In some countries there are permanent exhibition sites (e.g. at Frankfurt in West Germany and Cairo in Egypt) for both national and foreign exhibitors. Exhibitions have become increasingly popular in the Middle East, Bahrain for example.

(g) *Portable*. Some organisations have portable exhibitions which are travelled from place to place and set up in hotel rooms, foyers, concourses, lobbies or shop windows. Building societies welcome small window exhibits which help to overcome the dull, static nature of their own displays. Portable exhibits can also be incorporated in events such as works visits, open days, school careers evenings, press receptions and sales conferences.

(*h*) *Travelling.* On a larger scale are travelling exhibitions associated with transportation such as caravans, trailers, buses, custom - built mobile exhibition vehicles, exhibition trains, aircraft and ships. These have the advantage of taking the show to the people. In developing countries, as already mentioned in **21**, the mobile cinema van (usually a Land Rover) can be combined with travelling exhibitions and demonstrations. In this category can also be included the demonstration tours, based on international airports, by aircraft manufacturers.

(*i*) *On-site demonstrations.* This is a good method of demonstrating to an invited audience a piece of equipment, e.g. farm machinery or building equipment such as systems for concrete formwork. It involves finding a satisfied customer who, acting as an innovator (*see* 2, **20**), is willing to have potential buyers (adopters) attend a demonstration on his property or premises. The farm demonstration was probably originated by the American McCormick who demonstrated his ploughs and the first combined harvesters on Midwestern farms in the mid-nineteenth century.

25. POS material and sales promotion schemes. These have been fully described in Chapter 11. The sheer power of sales promotion, and the dangers if this power is not fully appreciated, are demonstrated by the experience of John Player and Sons with their lighter offer in February 1980. (A full account of this appeared in *Marketing* April 15, 1982).

(*a*) *Player's free lighter offer.* A free cigarette lighter worth £3.75 was offered for only fifteen pack fronts from John Player King Size, Player's No.6 King Size and John Player King Size Extra Mild. It was expected that a few thousand applications would be received. In fact Player's had to satisfy a demand for 2,225,000 lighters costing £1 each! The first ad on a Sunday produced more than 3,000 applications by the Wednesday and 50,000 by the end of the first week, while at one point 38,000 applications a day were coming in. The promotion had to be extended from two to six months to cope with this avalanche of responses, and the advertising had to be cancelled. Moreover, it displeased the retail trade whose sales of lighters were frustrated by the offer.

(b) *Illegal gifts*. In some countries, such as Germany, it is illegal to offer a free gift which is so valuable that it represents a threat to retail sales. There has also been hostility in some developing countries to sales promotion gifts which mislead poor people into buying more of a product than they can really afford; this has applied, for instance, to the over-zealous promotion of powdered baby milk. The Single European Market in 1992 will require observation of conflicting laws.

(c) *Avoiding these difficulties*. Without doubt, free gifts and mail-ins for free gifts are a very effective way of boosting sales although the modern trend is to run schemes where offers can be supplied or redeemed at the point-of-sale.

To avoid provoking a demand which exceeds the budget for a promotion it is wise to declare a limited number of gifts. Better still is the self-liquidating offer that involves a payment which at least recovers costs. Player's might well have achieved their target of a few thousand applications had they charged £1 instead of offering the lighter free.

26. Print. All forms of sales literature come under the heading of below-the-line, including leaflets, folders, brochures and catalogues, many of which are indispensable at the point-of-sale. Most consumer durables require sales literature. Give-away print is also required to meet the response of couponed press advertisements, or to be handed out at exhibitions. The catalogue or brochure is an essential advertising medium for direct response firms, horticultural suppliers and package tour operators.

27. Calendars. Whether individually produced, or stock calendars from one of the calendar producing firms such as Bemrose, Eversheds or Lockwoods which can be overprinted with the sponsor's name and address, calendars have the distinct merit that they are likely to occupy a permanent viewing position for a year. They are a blend of advertising and PR combining reminder value with usefulness and decorativeness. Lockwoods have produced calendars illustrating historical advertisements for the History of Advertising Trust.

28. Diaries. Whether pocket or desk, these have merits similar to those of calendars, and the gift can be perpetuated by means of a refillable cover.

29. Sponsorship. There are several reasons for engaging in a sponsorship and it is important to be clear about the purpose, and then to select the kind of sponsorship most likely to achieve that purpose, *see* 12, 17(*j*), regarding sponsorship agencies. Since sponsorship can involve considerable expenditure, maximum benefit should be sought. The following are some of the purposes of sponsorship.

(*a*) *Advertising.* The aim may be purely promotional, linked with ability to be seen as the sponsor by spectators at the event or watching it on television. For instance, when Coral sponsor a horse race – which may occupy only a few minutes of screen time – advertisements will be sited strategically so that cameras will not miss them, and the commentator will name the sponsor in naming the race. There will be additional mentions on the sports pages of national and regional newspapers, and in the programme magazines (*Radio Times* and *TV Times*).

The coverage will be repetitive. When motor sport is sponsored – and support for a motor racing team is the costliest of all sponsorships – the coverage will be continued through a series of international events. The actual races occupy a lot of screen time with repeated viewing of cars bearing sponsors' names, while posters and banners will be evident round the track. Big sponsors such as Canon, John Player, Marlboro and Goodyear achieve immense coverage. Since Grand Prix racing takes place at race tracks all over the world this form of sponsorship, although costly, suits companies whose products are sold world-wide.

This type of sponsorship will be of great advertising value to firms like cigarette manufacturers who are banned from commercial television advertising, although this is a controversial point, especially when such firms associate themselves with healthy pursuits. On the other hand, it is 'natural' for Coca-Cola to sponsor young people's sports like swimming.

(*b*) *Marketing.* It may be marketing policy to associate the product or service with certain demographic groups by sponsoring activities which interest them or by positioning a product by sponsoring an interest associated with a certain market segment, e.g. a ladies' product and a ladies' golf tournament.

One of the most direct marketing-plus-PR sponsorships has been that of test cricket by Cornhill Insurance which has successfully used this medium to widen the market segment for its domestic insurance service (*see* 3, 11).

(*c*) *Public relations.* Even the sponsorships already described have their PR content, but some are directed entirely at creating goodwill, establishing reputation, creating awareness and understanding, showing social responsibility or providing a service for customers. Arts sponsorships such as giving financial support to symphony orchestras, local theatres, art exhibitions and book awards are not unlike the patronages given by the royal or the wealthy to the arts in the past. Without such sponsorship, the arts would probably not survive and such behaviour enhances corporate images. The Booker and Whitbread book prizes produce a lot of publicity.

30. Miscellaneous media. There are countless minor media which may have special value to particular advertisers. Money should not be spent frivolously, and it is easy to squander a valuable appropriation on fringe media, but there are times when some of the following may have distinct merits.

(*a*) *Book matches.* These can provide an appreciated customer service, as in hotels.

(*b*) *Balloons.* Children love balloons, and they may be useful to a retailer anxious to please parental customers.

(*c*) *Trolley-ads* placed on supermarket trolleys can provide prominent in-store reminders.

(*d*) *Advertising gifts.* Key-rings, pens, badges, playing cards, calculators, cuff-links, letter-openers, pennants, dart flights, lighters and ashtrays are useful in different trades and for promotional events.

(*e*) *Drip mats or glass coasters.* Obviously, these have their special users such as brewers and other drinks manufacturers and make good POS material. They are also collectors' items.

(*f*) *Plastic records and compact cassettes. Readers' Digest* have made excellent use of plastic records to sell records, while Linguaphone have used both plastic records and audio cassettes to promote language courses. Both audio and video cassettes have been used to promote financial services such as unit trusts.

(g) *Plastic carrier bags*. Such bags, including the more elaborate ones supplied by Marks & Spencer for the packing of suits and other large garments, not only provide a long-lasting advertising medium but save the cost and trouble of wrapping up goods with paper and string or tape.

Media research

31. Introduction. Reference has been made to the media planner (*see* 12, **18**(*d*)), and he is assisted in his work by statistical information available from the following seven sources.

32. Media owners. The larger media owners may conduct their own surveys in order to inform advertising agencies and advertisers about the circulation, readership or audience profile of their medium or media. They will also interpret and present extracts from the independent surveys (e.g. JICNARS, BARB) described below, demonstrating cost-per-thousand (CPT) figures for net sales or readership, or, in the case of broadcast media, listeners and viewers. They will also indicate the ability of their media to reach particular demographic groups, or the buyers of certain products or services (*see also* 12, **21**).

33. Audit Bureau of Circulations (ABC). This body supplies its member publishers with forms of audit which are completed by these publishers in order to arrive at average net sales for periods such as six months. If satisfied, the Bureau issues an ABC certificate. Net sales means that all returns, free copies and copies sold at special prices are deducted from the number printed. ABC figures are then announced monthly.

34. Joint Industry Committee for National Readership Surveys (JICNARS). This is representative of advertisers, advertising agents and publishers. A continuous national random sample of 30,000 households is surveyed to produce readership figures for newspapers and magazines, including a demographic breakdown of these readers. Whereas the ABC figure will record individual purchases, the JICNARS figure will be considerably larger and show how many people read each publication. The circulation of a popular national newspaper might be 4 million but the readership figure could be as high as 16 million.

35. Broadcasters' Audience Research Board (BARB). Television audiences, both BBC and ITV, are researched continuously by means of a sample of households keeping diaries and using set meters. The system has been modified and extended to record use of second receivers, VCRs, and reception of satellite television. Each week a Top Ten list of programmes is published. Advertisers can aim to achieve a certain volume of television ratings (TVRs), and then withdraw commercials or rest them for subsequent showings.

36. Joint Industry Committee for Radio Audience Research (JICRAR). Similarly, radio audiences are surveyed to provide advertising agencies and advertisers with breakdowns of audience figures throughout the day, including a demographic profile of listeners. There are usually annual surveys.

37. Media schedules. With such statistics the media planner can calculate economic media schedules aimed at reaching the target audiences required by the advertising campaign. When the campaign is presented to the client the agency can justify its recommendations, not on the basis of value judgments, but as a result of carefully assessing the figures supplied by mainly independent research sources.

The client's managing director may wish to advertise in a newspaper which he reads or likes, but the agency can challenge this by quoting published research figures. It is this facility to understand and use reliable data which makes the agency service valuable to the advertiser. This, coupled with buying skill, has led in recent years to the setting up of many media independents which are non-creative agencies specialising in media planning and buying (see 12,17(c)).

38. Target Group Index. Owned by the British Market Research Bureau, the TGI has a panel of 25,000 adults who are interviewed annually between April and March concerning 400 brands, including the media exposure and demographic breakdown of respondents. This is useful for planning TV advertising since TGI examines TV viewing in half–hour segments from before 9 a.m. to after midnight so that viewing profiles of any target audience can be defined. Larger segmentations of the audience, e.g. 24,000 adults compared with BARB's 2,900 homes with set–meters and viewing diaries, is possible. However, BARB varies its methods when awarding new contracts to research companies.

Progress test 13

1. What is David Stewart Hunter's four-stage cycle of advertising development? **(2)**
2. What are the five essentials of creativity as expressed in the AIDCA formula? **(4)**
3. What are buzz words? **(6)**
4. What is a strapline? Can you quote one? **(7)**
5. Why is repetition so important in advertisement copy? **(8)**
6. What are the five above-the-line media? **(11)**
7. Are below-the-line media inferior to above-the-line? **(11)**
8. What are primary and secondary media? **(11)**
9. What is a free newspaper? **(12)**
10. What are controlled circulation journals? **(12)**
11. Why may newspapers in developing countries have small circulations? **(13)**
12. What are the weaknesses of radio in developing countries? **(15)**
13. What is alternative television? **(16)**
14. What are the three characteristics of posters? **(19)**
15. Describe the important considerations when using direct mail. **(23)**
16. What is the value of a portable exhibition? **(24)**
17. What kind of travelling exhibitions are there? **(24)**
18. What danger should be avoided when making a free gift offer? **(25)**

19. Describe the three main purposes of sponsorship.   (29)
20. How does circulation differ from readership?   (33, 34)

14
Public relations

Scope and importance

1. Importance. Public relations is a bigger and more important subject than is sometimes admitted or accepted in marketing circles. It is in fact the subject of the author's companion Handbook *Public Relations* (Pitman, 3rd Edition, 1988).

Public relations embraces the total communications of any organisation, commercial or non-commercial, in both public and private sectors. In fact, the greater part of the PR profession probably operates outside organisations involved in marketing, e.g. local and central government, the health services, voluntary bodies, educational establishments, the police and the Armed Forces. Its span of activities consequently exceeds those of marketing, advertising and salesmanship. This may be obscured by the fact that expenditure on PR is far less than it is on these other mainly commercial activities.

2. Areas of communication. Even in an industrial or commercial undertaking, public relations concerns the following areas of communication.

(*a*) *Community relations:* maintaining a 'good neighbour policy' can be sensible and beneficial.

(*b*) *Management-employee relations:* a major growth area in public relations as it was realised that the old 'them and us', management versus trade union situation was destroying industry.

(*c*) *Distributor relations:* educating the dealer and bringing the dealer closer to the supplier.

(*d*) *Financial relations:* informing the investment world about the performance of a company, which can help to maintain share prices and prevent take-over bids, or justify take up of new share issues. Shareholder and investment relations have become increasingly important since the Big Bang deregulation of the London Stock Exchange in 1986.

(*e*) *Issue or advocacy PR:* usually in the form of institutional or corporate advertising to declare a company's stance in relation to a political, economic, social and ecological issue of the day.

(*f*) *Customer relations:* to maintain goodwill and also to counter the criticisms of articulate consumerist bodies.

(*g*) *Market education:* to prepare the market for new products and services, either before advertising breaks or as support for an existing product. This includes preparing people for the new life-styles which products of the microchip and space-travel age are creating, coupled with new ideas about unemployment and leisure (*see* 12, 10).

This broad span of PR activity is rather different from that sometimes attributed to PR by marketers who see PR as no more than creating favourable images, favourable climates of opinion and free advertising. Sensible PR recognises that things cannot always be favourable for there are bound to be accidents, fires, strikes, financial losses, product recalls and other disasters. In fact some organisations, like those in the energy industries, have evolved contingency PR plans to deal with disasters and crisis PR has become a very important PR function. Nor is PR free advertising or any kind of advertising. The two are totally different. Public relations educates and informs but advertising persuades and sells.

3. PR transfer process. This is demonstrated by the author's much quoted PR transfer process which shows that the object of PR is to effect change by converting four classic negative states into four preferable positive ones, this resulting in the essential objective of PR which is *understanding*, (*see* Fig. 14.1).

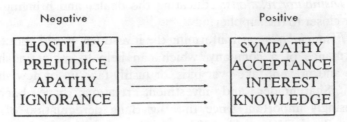

Figure 14.1　*The PR transfer process; knowledge leads to understanding*

How can this be expressed in marketing terms? If there is *hostility* towards flying because it is considered dangerous, people will not buy tickets. This is still a problem in developing countries, particularly with domestic airlines. If people are *prejudiced* about indigenous products they will continue to prefer imports which may embarrass a foreign exchange situation. If there is *apathy* about hygiene, there will be health problems which could lead to the misuse of food products. And if, as is often inevitable, there is *ignorance* about products or services, they will not be bought. In developing countries there is often ignorance about banking and insurance. In fact, the marketing of products and services in developing countries suffer from all four negative states. However, ignorance is inevitable when people in any society are confronted by new and puzzling concepts. They can be as diverse as satellites, AIDS or the Channel Tunnel.

Numerous problems have been encountered in industrialised societies over the years. Sophisticated products and services such as cameras, central heating, double glazing, life insurance, holidays abroad, pest control, computers and even television have been subject to hostility, prejudice, apathy and ignorance. Marketing, advertising and salesmanship alone have not succeeded in making all these things acceptable, desirable, adopted or popular.

Definitions

4. IPR definition. The first definition is the well-known one used by the Institute of Public Relations:

'Public relations practice is the planned and sustained effort to establish and maintain goodwill and mutual understanding between an organisation and its publics.'

It is significant that PR is not seen as something haphazard but as an organised programme, which means that like the marketing mix, a factory production programme, an advertising campaign or a sales campaign, *it must be planned in advance.* Something planned obviously seeks to achieve an objective, and that gives the lie to the false idea that PR is intangible. The objective, as we showed in discussing the PR transfer process (see 3), is to create *understanding*, but more than this is required by the IPR definition. It must be *mutual* understanding. The aim is not only to create understanding of our subject but to gain understanding of our various *publics* since in PR the audience is broken down into many categories. These PR publics are more numerous than the target audiences of advertising. They could be as diverse as children and politicians. Some of these publics are indicated in the areas of communication set out in 2 above (*see also* 11).

5. The author's own definition. This develops the IPR definition a stage further by the introduction of 'objectives':

'Public relations consists of all forms of planned communication, outwards and inwards, between an organisation and its publics for the purpose of achieving specific objectives concerning mutual understanding.'

Here we extend the IPR's 'planned and sustained effort' more purposefully, and in justification of the claim made above that PR is tangible. If, at the planning stage, objectives are set — whether qualitative or quantitative — the results are capable of being assessed. Either those objectives are achieved or they are not, and the degree of success or failure can be assessed.

If the objective is to increase awareness of a company, a product or a service, opinion surveys carried out before and after the PR campaign can measure the extent to which awareness has or has not increased. Some results can be observed: are there fewer complaints? Or if a company has diversified into new product areas, to what extent is this now known? And in press relations, if there were misunderstandings or hostile attitudes in press reports, have these now been corrected after a campaign to gain proper understanding? All these issues are far removed from 'free advertising' and they are very measurable cost-effective tangible achievements.

6. The Mexican Statement. Resulting from an international conference in Mexico City in 1978, with representatives of national PR institutes, this definition extends the explanation of PR in both directions:

> 'Public relations practice is the art and social science of analysing trends, predicting their consequences, counselling organisation leaders, and implementing planned programmes of action which will serve both the organisation's and the public interest.'

Now we are really into researched, planned, advisory, objective, accountable and socially responsible public relations. For all the slightly flowing language (it did have to be translated into several languages) it is a businesslike description of professional PR.

First, it requires the analysis of trends, that is, research such as opinion or awareness surveys or image studies (*see* 4, 14 and 15). *Second*, the results of these preliminary studies have to be analysed and interpreted. *Third*, management is advised. *Fourth*, planned programmes are carried out. *Fifth*, the action must serve the organisation's interests, that is, achieve results. *Sixth*, this PR action must be responsible and must not abuse the public interest.

That sixth point is important because PR is sometimes maligned as a dubious business which hoodwinks the public. If it attempts to do so it will be a waste of money because credibility is fundamental to the success of PR. There are, of course, management and marketing people who want to misuse PR, but that is rather like the misuse of advertising. Both are tools of communication. Sometimes PR is confused with propaganda. The simple distinction between PR and advertising/propaganda is that PR will work only if it is impartial, but advertising/propaganda must be partial.

7. **PR and sales success.** The object of PR is not to sell anything. It is to create knowledge and understanding after which marketing, advertising and salesmanship can get on with the job of selling. It may not be possible to sell if people do not understand what is being sold. When this simple truth is recognised the value of PR becomes clear.

Six-point PR planning model

8. **Introduction.** The six-point PR planning model, described in 9–14 below, is the framework for a practical PR programme. The reader should note how it ties in with the Mexican Statement (*see* 6).

9. **Appreciation of the situation.** This is the same as analysis of trends, or what the Americans call 'PR audit'. Using whatever forms of investigation are necessary – desk research, interviews, observation, monitoring of media, marketing research – a study is carried out to establish the *current image*. This perceived image is a consensus of outside knowledge and attitudes, and it could be contrary to the mistaken *mirror image* held by organisation leaders from the chief executive to the marketing manager. The extent of the four negative and positive states (*see* 3) will be revealed.

10. **Definition of objectives.** In a full PR programme, with the in-house PRO or outside PR consultancy reporting direct to management, PR will deal with all three functions of a business, production, marketing and finance. It may concern staff recruitment (or contentment!) at one end and a new share issue at the other, but also deal with marketing (*see* 15–21). The PR function should not be locked in the marketing department. Thus, there could be a long list of possible PR objectives concerned with every function of business, and by no means limited to marketing. They may have to be whittled down because of budget, resources or feasibility. Resources, incidentally, are mostly manpower for PR is labour intensive, and the biggest cost is time reckoned in salaries or fees. There is no commission system in PR to provide free human services.

11. Definition of publics. In a general sense, the 'publics' are the adjacent community, employees, suppliers, the financial world, distributors, consumers or users, and all those people called 'opinion leaders' who in fact probably know less than they should about the organisation. We are not talking about a mere market segment or target audience, the comparative simplicities of marketing and advertising. Consequently, every organisation will have a very long list of publics or types of people with whom it should or could communicate.

12. Selection of media and techniques. In PR we are not dealing with the media people who sell space and airtime but with editorial and programme people. A PR programme can use far more media than would be economic for an advertising media schedule. It is quite likely that different media will be used, e.g. PR in the women's press but advertising in *TV Times*. In addition to commercial or public media (e.g. commercial TV and the BBC), PR makes use of much private created media such as house journals, videos, slide presentations, conferences, seminars and private exhibitions. Mass communications give way to group and personal communications.

13. Budget. Essential to the PR programme is a carefully calculated budget of man-hours, materials and expenses, of which the first is the largest unless there is a large expenditure on print or audio-visuals. Expenses for travelling, hotels and hospitality are, contrary to myth, the least of PR costs. The salesman who submits a big expenses account for entertaining and calls this PR is not in the PR business. PR is mostly hard work. The chief item in a PR budget is the workload and its cost.

14. Assessment of results. This should be related to the original research and the set objectives. While marketing may be a blend of many contributory factors, PR objectives are usually clear-cut and capable of being evaluated on their own, or at least reasonable credit can be taken for the PR effort. Even a straightforward product publicity story in the press will produce a measurable volume of space in journals of merit that can be given ratings, or will produce a measurable volume of enquiries. It is even possible to spend less on advertising, if the market has been familiarised with the product. Dealer interest and response could be heightened if PR has educated the trade.

Confusion about a new product could be lessened or demolished, as happened with St Ivel Gold, which the press had been insisting was another kind of margarine. Rentokil was able to sell its service to eradicate pharaoh's ants in hospitals because, by PR means, the service was made known to hospital management throughout the country. It was a question of convincing hospitals that palliative treatments were not cost-effective. The market was convinced not by advertising or salesmen, but by authoritative case-study feature articles in the hospital press, and the results were tangible and accountable. Other hospital managements with the same problem discovered that there was a permanent solution.

PR and marketing communications

15. An integral part. Public relations is not an ingredient of the marketing mix which can be used as an optional extra, like deciding whether to spend more on salespeople or more on advertising. An astute marketing manager accepts PR as an integral part of their job specification (so that he is at all times PR-minded and a conscious communicator), and also as an integral part of every ingredient in the marketing mix. This may be termed marketing communications, which are not limited to the promotional forms of communication, namely advertising, sales promotion and selling. Public relations is a form of marketing communications which relates to every element of the marketing mix. A few examples are described in the following paragraphs:

16. Company name, product brand names. Choice of a name may result from researching lists of names, or even using a computer, but it must still be a name which communicates readily and effectively. What image does it conjure up, is it characteristic, can it be read and pronounced easily, does it display well, is it memorable? These questions represent the very essence of PR-creating understanding. Yet some names fail to meet any of these requirements, while others are ideal. A bad, ill-conceived, obscure, misleading, hard to pronounce and remember name is bad PR.

17. Packaging. A pack which instantly identifies a product, and is convenient, protective or ensures good usage or enjoyment of the product, creates goodwill and is good PR. Some of the clever modern packages such as blister and bubble packs, aerosols, roll-on sticks, sachets and dispensers all help the customer in some way and this is good PR-thinking.

18. Pricing. The psychology of pricing has its PR aspects for people judge a lot by price. A high price may imply quality, a fair price can suggest a responsible supplier, a low price may be a pleasant bargain.

19. Advertising policy. The quality of advertising can do much for the image of a company or product whereas exaggerated (even if not unethical) or 'knocking' advertising can cause offence. The old 'whiter than white' detergent ads provoked public distrust of advertising in general. People do not like to feel that you can fool most of them most of the time. Responsible advertising is important to both the corporate and the product image. It does one's reputation no good if an over–zealous advertisement provokes complaints to the Advertising Standards Authority, and publication in their monthly *ASA Case Report*.

20. Dealer relations. Too often the dealer is treated materialistically on the grounds that he is interested only in profits. However, he does have to invest in supporting products, new or old. He can sell them better if he understands them. It is no use him answering customers' queries with a vague 'Well, that's what they say in the advertisements'. Dealer education gets goods on shelves, even in supermarkets. Trade exhibitions, dealer magazines, works visits, staff training schemes, trade press news coverage – all kinds of PR applicable to the particular trade – can overcome sales resistance by store buyers.

A number of products and services have failed initially, simply because the man behind the counter was not sufficiently convinced to sell the product. Or the salesperson sold it wrongly, like the gas showroom sales lady who told the customer she did not need a timer on her cooker if she did not go out to work. The hostility, prejudice, apathy and ignorance of people at the point of sale can be devastating, and no weight of advertising can undo it.

21. Sales force relations. There is a difference between PR education and sales training. Is this always recognised? Do the people in the field know and understand the company, or are they told only about the product, how to sell it and what they will earn? Do they actually *like* the company they work for? Replacing discontented, disillusioned, disinterested salespeople is costly and wasteful.

There is also the question of the *multiple image*. The dealer's only concept of the company may be that given him by the visiting representative. Personalities and behaviour can differ so much that dealers in various territories may have different, inaccurate and conflicting images of the company. It can therefore be an important PR exercise to see that all members of the sales force give a consistent image without actually producing uniform personalities. As an example, one has only to walk through a Marks & Spencer store to know one is not in any other store of that kind.

PR department or PR consultancy?

22. PR department. Unlike advertising where most people work in advertising agencies, the majority of people employed in PR do not work in PR consultancies. It is natural that most PR practitioners should work in-house because it is essential for them to be intimately associated with all the internal workings of the organisation. This is not necessary in advertising. A spokesman needs to know what he is talking about, and this requires close contact with people in every department and at every level who know him and are prepared to give him information.

However, this can have its own drawbacks. There is a tendency for the in-house PRO to become too biased in favour of his company and its products and services, and for management to take him for granted and not permit him the status he should enjoy. However, even these two drawbacks really depend on the calibre and professional experience of the PRO, and on where he is positioned in the organisation. Ideally, he should be independent and answerable to the chief executive while servicing all departments. It could be unfortunate if he was isolated in the marketing department, and perhaps worse still if he had to double as advertising and PR manager, unless advertising was a minor part of his duties. A number of industrial firms which conduct comparatively little advertising have general communications departments which also handle advertising, but are predominantly concerned with PR.

The success of in-house PR depends on its positioning and the status of the person responsible for PR. In most large and successful companies PR is conducted by a board director, i.e. a PR Director, not by a PRO in a marketing department.

23. PR consultancy. PR consultants should not be called PR agents, because they are not the agents of the media and do not depend on commission from the media for the bulk of their income.

The advantages of the PR consultancy are that the consultant — as an outsider — is not biased and that he can often express views and criticisms quite frankly, which might be less easy for the in-house PRO to do. In fact, he may be paid for his candid opinions and advice. The consultant also has wide experience because he handles or has handled a variety of accounts, and has used most if not all PR techniques. However, he does suffer from being remote and not having the close relationships with company personnel which are enjoyed by the company PRO.

There is also the question of fees, i.e. what the client gets for his money, and what the consultant can do with the money he receives. Whether the consultant does enough, and whether he is paid enough, are sometimes irreconcilable questions. In order to make a profit and stay in business the consultant can give to the account only the time for which he is paid. The greedy client may not be satisfied with these elementary economics. Careful planning, budgeting, time-sheeting and accountability are therefore vital to good client–consultancy relations.

In Chapter 12 many different kinds of advertising agency were described. There are also specialist PR consultancies which may deal with certain trades like fashion, foods or the motor car industry, while others specialise in particular aspects of PR such as house journals, exhibitions, corporate and financial PR, sponsorships or parliamentary liaison.

24. The choice. It is impossible to say whether in general a PR department is better than a PR consultancy or vice versa. Much depends on the nature of the company and its communication needs. It is quite practical for a company to have an in-house PRO with his own department, and also use a PR consultancy to augment the PRO for specialised tasks such as financial PR or sponsorships, or to provide overall advice on PR policy in general.

25. Market education. Preparing, informing and extending the market. References have already been made to market education or the lack of it (12, **9, 10**), but this is a subject which belongs to this chapter. Regrettably, it is something ignored by those marketeers who place all their bets on the hammer effects of advertising or the competitiveness of sales promotion schemes. This is because of the antipathy of marketeers towards public relations, a subject rarely or only sketchily discussed in most marketing textbooks.

Marketing education has, in spite of the academic sceptics, proved valuable in the real world of marketing and there are countless case studies to prove its practical role in successful cost-effective marketing. It works best, of course, when education is necessary, as with a new product or service, and probably not at all with a competitive new FMCG such as a chocolate bar. Nevertheless, even detergents were originally launched in the UK with posters announcing acceptance of this then unknown product by millions of American housewives. Other examples such as the origin of drive-on-drive-off car ferries, and privatisation schemes were described in Chapter 11, **9, 10**.

Marketing education can take two forms:

(*i*) *Pre-selling* or preparing the market to accept a new product or service when it is launched.

(*ii*) *Post-selling* to further interest in or use of a product or service which is already on the market.

In neither case are advertising methods necessary. The techniques can be those of public relations and may include:

(*a*) *Press relations* in the form of news stories, pictures, feature articles, press receptions, works visits and so on to inform the media of the forthcoming project, product or service. In recent years we have seen the examples of the use of advance media relations on behalf of the Sony camcorder, the Eurotunnel, the conversion of the Abbey National Building Society into a public limited company, and the attractions of new holiday venues for the British such as Florida, Japan and Turkey. Some, like changing over to lead–free petrol, insuring household contents adequately or adopting a healthier diet may take longer.

(*b*) *Videos*. The documentary video has largely replaced the documentary film and its range of uses can include loans to societies, home showings on domestic VCRs, and showings in shops and showrooms, at exhibitions, at press receptions and to any audience representing suitable publics.

(*c*) *Discussion on TV* in a variety of programmes dealing with new ideas such as *Tomorrow's World*.

(*d*) *Adoption by innovators* is an excellent way of introducing a product so that case studies can be built up of its successful application. This has occurred with hospital equipment which has been tried and proved in workaday circumstances, e.g. a new kitchen dishwasher. One of the first exercises in damp-proofing buildings by means of electro-osmosis was undertaken on the stonework of Gloucester Cathedral.

(*e*) *External house journals* issued to appropriate publics can prepare the way for a new product, or introduce new ways of enjoying an existing one.

(*f*) *Dealer education* can be included because the trade must be sufficiently familiar with the product to be able to convince customers at the point-of-sale when advertising breaks.

The effect of these and other PR techniques will pave the way for the arrival of the new product or service which will be greeted as something known, expected and, ideally, looked forward to and welcomed. And yet so many products just come out of the blue, and it is no wonder that 50 per cent of new products fail to sell. There is a lot of hostility, prejudice, apathy and ignorance facing a new product or service which a market education programme can minimise or dismiss altogether.

Similar techniques can be used to educate the market about how to benefit from a product once purchased, or how to enjoy new benefits. Products such as motor cars, gardening aids, DIY materials, sewing machines, knitting wools and cooking ingredients such as flour and fats can all gain from educational PR efforts which help to continue and prolong their use.

Progress test 14

1. What is the PR transfer process?   (3)
2. How would you define public relations?   (4, 5, 6)
3. Is PR tangible or intangible?   (4, 14)
4. How can the results of a PR programme be assessed?   (14)
5. How can PR be an integral part of the marketing mix? (15, 21)
6. What are the advantages and disadvantages of the PR department and the PR consultancy?   (22, 23)
7. What kinds of specialist PR consultancies are there?   (23)
8. How can market education improve the effectiveness of advertising?   (25)

15
Introduction to codes of practice and law

Codes of practice

1. Legal versus voluntary controls. There are two forms of control of advertising, sales promotion and public relations activities: legal and voluntary. Legal controls are necessary for the protection of the consumer, whereas voluntary controls not only protect the consumer but serve to establish professional standards and to protect the reputation of the industry, business or profession. There is, therefore, an important public relations element in voluntary controls.

It may be thought that voluntary or self-regulatory controls are weaker or less efficient than legal restraints. This is not necessarily true. They operate differently and to some extent for different purposes. In some cases it is better to avoid legislation, and discussions between industry and government have had useful results, as with the Clutter Code of 1962 which succeeded in reducing the excessive number of advertisements on and about shop premises.

The weakness of legal control is that it may not be effective until after the offence has been committed, and court cases can drag on for years. Voluntary controls can be more preventive, and can often be applied very quickly, as when, for instance, the Advertising Standards Authority upholds a complaint.

2. Some examples of codes. The Institute of Public Relations Code of Professional Conduct is very much a set of behavioural standards with which members are expected to comply. A significant point here is that membership of the IPR requires acceptance of the Institute's code: the non-member is not so constrained and membership (which also implies considerable practical experience) therefore confers professional status. Similarly, members of the Public Relations Consultants Association have to undertake to comply with the PRCA Code of Consultancy Practice.

Members of the Institute of Practitioners in Advertising (advertising agencies) are required to maintain high professional standards in advertisement content, financial matters and business conduct, and to observe strictly the advertising and sales promotion codes of practice. The British Direct Marketing Association requires its members to do likewise. The Association of Mail Order Publishers operates a Mail Order Publishers' Authority which has its own code of practice for the mail order industry, and members of the public may submit complaints to this Authority for investigation.

3. Relationship between official and voluntary control. Despite the existence of these codes, the Office of Fair Trading acts as an official watchdog in the interests of the public. It was effective in urging the Advertising Standards Authority to make itself more effective and better known to the public, this leading to the regular appearance of ASA advertisements inviting written complaints from the public (MIsee 12, **22**). It was an OFT ruling which led to changes in the system of recognised advertising agencies and commission (*see* 12, **19**). The mail order code was approved by the Office. In many areas there is considerable co-operation between official and voluntary forms of control.

Law

4. Introduction. There is a labyrinth of legislation concerning marketing which cannot be fully discussed in this short chapter. Here, the subject will be confined to certain essential legal considerations. Table 15A lists some of the most important statutes which apply to marketing. Some topics are discussed in other chapters (*see* 8, **31–36** and 12, **26**).

Statute	*Date*
Advertisements (Hire Purchase) Act	1967
Betting, Gaming and Lotteries Act	1963
Business Advertisements (Disclosure) Order	1977
Consumer Credit Act	1974
Consumer Protection Act	1987
Control of Misleading Advertisements Regulations	1985
Copyright, Designs and Patents Act	1988
Defamation Act	1952
Data Protection Act	1984
Fair Trading Act	1973
Food and Drugs Act	1955 (as amended)
Independent Broadcasting Act *	1973 (incorporating the IBA Code of Advertising Standards and Practice)
Labelling of Food Regulations	1970 and 1976 amendments
Lotteries and Amusements Act	1976
Medicines Act	1968
Medicines (Labelling and Advertising to the Public) Regulations	1978
Misrepresentation Act	1967
Prices Act	1974
Race Relations Acts	1968, 1976
Restrictive Trade Practices Act	1976
Sex Discrimination Act	1975
Supply of Goods (Implied Terms) Act	1973
Trade Descriptions Act	1968
Unsolicited Goods and Services Act	1975

*N.B. To be replaced by new legislation setting up the Independent Television Authority and the Radio Authority

Table 15A

5. Types of law. There are two kinds of law.

(*a*) *Common law* includes contracts and torts or civil wrongs, for which an aggrieved party or plaintiff can seek damages by suing in the civil courts.

(*b*) *Statute law* consists of Acts of Parliament and Regulations, and offenders are liable to prosecution, fine and/or imprisonment as a result of criminal proceedings between the Crown and the accused. Under the Trade Description Act 1968 prosecutions may be instituted by local weights and measures (or consumer protection or trading standards) authorities to whom complaints may be made.

Law of contract

6. What is a contract? So that proof may be shown if necessary, a contract *should* be in writing, but a verbal contract, even on the telephone and not necessarily confirmed in writing, may be held to be a legal contract on the grounds that there was implicit intent to enter into a contract. Hands may be shaken and a contract may be entered into in this way too.

Three things are necessary to make a contract valid. An *offer* must be made, there must be an *acceptance*, and both sides must sacrifice a *consideration* (e.g. a cash payment and a product supplied). If the acceptor makes amendments to the offer, this now becomes the offer which has to be accepted by the maker of the original offer. A gift is not a contract since nothing is surrendered by the recipient. There must be no *mistake* or *misrepresentation* which could invalidate the contract.

7. Practical implications. When buying or selling services such as those of an advertising agency or PR consultancy there should be a letter of contract setting out the services to be provided, their cost, the method of payment, the period of contract and the period of notice agreed for cancellation. In addition, if copyright material is involved it should be clearly stated whether the servicing company retains the copyright wholly or assigns it, say, when all accounts have been paid (*see also* 15).

When a printer submits an estimate (an 'offer') and this is accepted, the customer should make it clear that he accepts the offer as described in the estimate of a specified number or date.

Better still, he should repeat the details of size, colours, quality of paper, quantity, cost and delivery. However, if he changes any details, even the quantity, this constitutes a fresh offer which the printer now has the responsibility of accepting.

Defamation

8. Definitions. If a person, organisation or product is intentionally or unintentionally brought into disrepute, an action may be brought for damages, or an injunction may be sought to prevent re-occurrence. There are two legal forms of defamation, the spoken or transitory known as *slander* and the published, broadcast or permanent which is called *libel*. The former includes *slander of goods*.

A libellous or scandalous statement must be:

(a) defamatory;
(b) false, unless the contrary is proved;
(c) understood to refer to the plaintiff;
(d) made known to at least one person other than the plaintiff.

9. Slander of goods. Slander of goods is an interesting example where there can be either legal or voluntary control. The British Code of Advertising Practice prohibits knocking copy (or ash-canning), which occurs when a statement in an advertisement denigrates another product (which is different from making a fair comparison). There has been a lot of this in motor car advertising, and one manufacturer was obliged to buy space to make a public apology. In addition to voluntary control, legal action could be taken for slander of goods.

10. Attributed statements. Care must be taken to see that statements are not attributed to people who would not make, or would not permit, such statements. It has happened that a successful action has been taken by a person of the same name and similar address who was not the actual person quoted!

On the other hand, if a person is photographed in a crowd, and he should not have been there, it is embarrassing, and he suffers some penalty as a result of being recognised, he has no claim.

People in hospital or prison scenes usually have their faces obscured to avoid embarrassment.

These situations can occur in advertising unless everyone concerned is vigilant.

11. PR articles. When writing PR articles in which products other than the company's are mentioned care is necessary to avoid slanderous implication. For instance, it *could* be held to be slanderous to say that a company has replaced one fleet of vehicles with another because the first had proved unsatisfactory, if the unsatisfactory make was named.

12. Employee references. When preparing references it may be safer to write a purely factual statement about employment rather than make any critical comments which could disadvantage the person when applying for another job. Damages can be based on loss suffered by the plaintiff as a result of the defamation.

Again, we have a voluntary control parallel in the IPR Code which says that 'a ·member· shall not maliciously injure the professional reputation of another' so that an IPR member may have redress without going to law.

Copyright

13. Legal basis. Under the Copyright Acts copyright subsists in any original work, but not in an idea. This broadly covers 'literary, dramatic, musical or artistic work'. Copyright exists for fifty years from the end of the year in which the author died (with certain special provisions), but can be assigned to someone else who then owns the copyright. The new Copyright, Designs and Patents Act extends the rights of copyright owners, and includes other creative forms which did not exist at the time of the original 1956 Act.

14. Fair dealing. This means that an insubstantial part of the whole may be used for educational purposes, or in such an uncommercial way that the copier enjoys no financial gain. However, this is a very tricky area and various owners of copyright such as authors, publishers, gramophone record companies and broadcasting organisations are very busily demanding their rights.

Educational establishments are permitted to record broadcast or cable programmes, e.g. by making a video recording, but there is actionable ingfringement of copyright if the video is made available for sale or hire.

A new element in the 1988 Copyright, Designs and Patents Act is that the copyright of a photograph now belongs to the photographer.

The Act also introduces *moral rights*. The author of a copyright literary, dramatic, musical or artistic work, and the director of a copyright film, has the right to be identified as the author or director of the work.

15. Advertising. It is necessary for the advertiser to understand his rights. If he employs an advertising agent to produce advertising which includes pictures, the copyright belongs to the agency as the employer of the artist (unless the work was done outside the employer's time, in which case the copyright belongs to the creator). Even though the work is done for the advertiser, the copyright does not belong to him unless it is ultimately assigned to him, and this should be stated in the letter of appointment or contract.

16. Public relations. When PR pictures are submitted to the press it is important that the copyright is owned by the sender, and that pictures are not submitted which were taken by someone else, such as when a local newspaper photographer happens to take a nice picture of the PRO's managing director. Editors print PR pictures on the understanding that no reproduction fee is required. If a PRO submits a picture which is someone else's copyright the editor is unlikely to be willing to pay a fee, and so will not print the picture.

There is no copyright in a news release which is distributed in a broadcast fashion. In fact, an editor may cut, rewrite or discard it as he wishes. On the other hand, there is copyright in a single PR article written exclusively for one journal, or even syndicated to any number of journals.

17. Advertisements. There is no copyright in an advertisement published in a newspaper since it is placed there for all to see. The copyright exists only in the original artwork used to produce the advertisement. Advertisements are frequently reproduced without permission in textbooks, in newspapers or on television (e.g. Esther Rantzen's *That's Life*). It is the advertiser's bad luck if he is crucified for making a boob.

18. Protecting copyright. Some people are very fussy about either infringing or protecting copyright. Some copying shops will not copy pages from books. The *Harvard Business Review* charges fees for the reproduction of various parts of its issues. If a PR documentary is to be used in a television programme there is a copyright expert who will want to know which sequences are original, and which (like 'library' shots) were hired or borrowed and have copyright belonging to someone else who is entitled to a fee. Yet another example occurs when music is played in a public place and a fee has to be paid to the Performing Rights Society, something to remember when running events although this will usually be taken care of by the owner of the premises.

19. Passing off. If a product is packed in such a way that it resembles another, and is bought in mistake for another, the owner of the original may sue for damages representing loss of business provided he can produce evidence that:

(*a*) the trade name or get-up is associated with his goods in the public mind;

(*b*) the acts objected to have interfered or are calculated to interfere with the conduct of business or sale of goods in the sense that there is confusion in the public mind.

20. Examples. The following are some examples of passing off.

(*a*) Misuse of a trading name. Sometimes there may be a very slightly different spelling.

(*b*) Misuse of the trade name of the goods.

(*c*) Imitation of the get-up of the goods. This may be the shape of the container, or the colour scheme of the label or package, so that buyers are easily misled.

There are also a number of dodges and rackets which are frustrating to exporters who find they have to compete with apparently identical goods, which are either inferior or cheaper. In some parts of the world makers of engineering goods have found fraudulent spare parts on sale in their export markets. In the East, publishers have to contend with competition from identical copies of their books, these pirated editions being sold at low prices which discourage imports of the genuine books at normal prices. Some foreign governments have taken the view that if the public can benefit from these cheaper books their sale should not be discouraged!

Competitions

21. Lottery or competition? Competitions are popular forms of sales promotion (*see* 11, 20), but care is necessary to avoid committing an offence under the Betting, Gaming and Lotteries Act 1963 or the Lotteries and Amusements Act 1976. A lottery has been defined by Lord Hailsham and others as 'a distribution of prizes by lot or chance'. It is a lottery if competitors are asked to determine, say, the most popular pet foods because they will have no idea what other competitors' guesses will be.

Competitions, to be legal, must have an element of skill, correct answers must not be prejudged, and in a two-stage contest intended to provide a tie-breaker skill is necessary in both parts.

22. Rules. Before acceptance of a competition, editors usually insist on seeing the rules. In drawing up rules the promoter should make the conditions as fair as possible, allowing sufficient time for the screening and judging of entries, and stating when and where the results will be published. The Institute of Sales Promotion has its Standard Rules for competitions (*see* 11, 20(*g*)).

Such stringent rules do not seem to apply in some parts of the world. In some parts of Africa, for instance, it is common to see competitions with hardly any element of skill, being used as devices for giving away large numbers of so-called prizes. A contest should really have so many possible permutations that only a small number of ties will result. There are professional contestants who submit so many entries that they win a considerable number of prizes. One television programme was based on a visit to a man's home which was crammed with sales promotion contest prizes.

Trade descriptions

23. Trade descriptions. In the marketing of goods, great care is necessary to identify them correctly as stipulated by the Trade Descriptions Act 1968, while the Trade Descriptions Act 1972 has been replaced by the important Consumer Protection Act which concentrates on product liability, consumer safety and misleading price indications. The ramifications of trade descriptions legislation need not be gone into here beyond the copious definition of a trade description in the 1968 Act.

A trade description is an indication, direct or indirect, given *by any means whatever*, of any of the following matters with respect to goods or parts of goods:

(*a*) quantity, size, gauge;

(*b*) method of manufacture, production, processing or reconditioning;

(*c*) composition;

(*d*) fitness for purpose, strength, performance, behaviour or accuracy;

(*e*) any physical characteristics not included in the preceding paragraphs;

(*f*) testing by any person and results thereof;

(*g*) approval by any person or conformity with a type approved by any person;

(*h*) place or date of manufacture, production, processing or reconditioning;

(*i*) person by whom manufactured, produced, processed or reconditioned;

(*j*) other history, including previous ownership or use.

24. The wine industry. A particularly sensitive area is the wine industry where certain products such as champagne, port and sherry traditionally originate from particular countries or regions. When similar products are produced elsewhere, such as in Australia, Cyprus, South Africa or the USA, it is necessary to make such a place of origin very clear. In 1982 one of Britain's largest wine importers had to withdraw a press advertising campaign which committed such an offence. The advertising had likened a French wine to champagne, and action was brought by Moet et Chandon on behalf of the champagne industry. It is very easy for the copy in such advertisements to be written in good faith, and the obligations placed on the advertiser can be onerous.

25. Role of legislation. Such legislation calls into question traditional descriptions which may be imaginative to say the least such as milk stout, or that artful one of old, 'art. silk' for artificial silk meaning rayon. To what extent is a product such as a watch or raincoat waterproof or only water resistant? There was a time when 'standard' jam really meant that its contents included vegetables as well as fruit. Most of these anomalies went out with the original Merchandise Marks Acts 1887–1953. Such descriptions which may be understood as the jargon of the trade, but which can be given literal meanings by the public, have provoked consumer protection legislation, and are therefore outside the scope of voluntary controls.

26. Responsibility of marketers. In the motor car industry we have seen great changes in marketing attitudes since the time when an American automobile tycoon declared that 'safety is a negative selling factor'. It is a sad commentary that marketing misbehaviour has had to be contested by Ralph Nader and other champions of consumer rights. Over-zealous marketing based on maximising profits at the expense of the customer has proved to be not only bad public relations but suicidal business. It has opened the door to the torrent of Japanese products based on the simple marketing dictum of value for money. Fitness for purpose is the hallmark of so many Japanese products, which could evoke crushing criticisms if they failed to please.

It is not good enough to say that the British marketing manager is · the victim of poor production technology and poor workmanship. The fault lies in top management not being sufficiently marketing- and PR-orientated to make the Trade Descriptions Act and the Consumer Protection Act unthinkable and redundant. Such legislation should never have been necessary. However, as pointed out in Chapter 14, public relations does not rate very highly in British marketing thinking, and hardly at all in American if we judge by the Philip Kotler best-sellers. Articulate consumerism and consumer protection legislation is the price of public relations being ignored by marketers.

Progress test 15

1. What are the strengths and weaknesses of legal versus voluntary controls?   (1)

2. What is the difference between common law and statute law? (5)

3. Can a verbal contract be legal?   (6)

4. Give the three requirements of a legal contract.   (6)

5. What four conditions make a statement libellous or slanderous?   (8)

6. Explain the term slander of goods.   (9)

7. How long does copyright last?   (13)

8. What is meant by fair dealing?   (14)

9. How can passing off be effected and what is meant by the 'get–up'?   (19, 20)

10. What is the essential requirement which a competition should meet if it is to be legal?   (21)

11. Name some of the most important aspects of trade descriptions covered by the Trade Descriptions Act 1968.   (23, 24)

16

Industrial marketing

Products and customers

1. Introduction. The marketing of industrial products and services has its own special characteristics, and is often quite different from the marketing of consumer products and services, including consumer durables, even though these may also be very technical.

2. Types of products. Industrial products and services are those bought by industry, commerce and business, and not just by heavy industry. The expression 'industrial' differentiates them from products bought by the general public. They can be divided into the following five groups.

(*a*) *Capital goods*. These include machinery, transport and what accountants call 'fixtures and fittings', e.g. furniture and office equipment. Some of this equipment may be bought, but nowadays items ranging from aircraft to computers are leased.

(*b*) *Raw materials*. Here we have the basic materials such as metal, timber, chemicals or ingredients, which may be primary products in their natural state or, as with metals and alloys, processed as steel, tinplate, wire or rod.

(*c*) *Components*. Sometimes called secondary supplies, these are sold to firms which assemble them in finished products such as motor cars, ships, television sets and electronic equipment. A clock-maker may buy in cases from a case-maker, a furniture-maker will buy in covering fabrics from a textile mill.

(*d*) *Supplies*. Industries and businesses cannot run without supplies of energy, water, lubricants, detergents, disinfectants, paints and other materials which are usually sold in bulk quantities at special prices.

(e) *Services*. Banking, insurance, accountancy, legal, architectural, printing, packaging, exhibition, photography, research, recruitment, advertising and public relations are among the services which various organisations may need. Today there are numerous specialist consultancy services.

3. Customers. In many cases industrial customers may differ from those for consumer goods for the following reasons.

(a) Customers may be few in number. For example, there are only a certain number of manufacturers in an industry. They are not like grocers or chemists.

(b) Customers may be scattered all over the country, like paint manufacturers.

(c) However, they could be concentrated in a certain area or areas like the jewellery trade (*see* 8, 32).

(d) Buyers are likely to be technical or well-qualified people, such as specifiers, formulators, designers, architects and scientists. Or they may be professional purchasing officers.

(e) They could be people with considerable buying power and of top management status.

(f) Purchases may be made irregularly or infrequently so that a system of regular calls by salespeople will not be practical.

(g) Sales interviews could be once-and-for-all events as when an enquiry is being dealt with for capital equipment.

Sales staff

4. Size of sales force. The sales force for industrial products is likely to be much smaller, mainly because the goods or services are usually more costly and sales are concentrated on fewer buyers than occurs with consumer products. This is not absolutely true because retailers will also be sold goods for their own use such as shop fittings and cash registers. Nevertheless, a lot of industrial sales are to manufacturers, consisting of raw materials, machinery or components.

5. Technician or salesperson? Although there are unresolved arguments as to whether the industrial salesperson should be a technician first and a salesperson second, or vice versa, it is generally the case that he or she should be able to talk intelligently about essential technicalities. This may require special sales training rather than reliance on the salesperson being, say, a qualified engineer.

Problems do arise over the issue. An image study of a chemical company showed that it was considered to be old-fashioned because its representatives were boffins rather than salespeople. In contrast, another survey showed that architects thought building materials salespeople were unable to discuss their products properly.

6. Advice and service. The customer may be better pleased with the printer who offers ideas and makes constructive suggestions than with one who merely accepts a job and prints what they are given. *Advice* and *service* can be important attributes of the industrial salesperson. Regular business is more likely to develop when the salesperson is able to help the customer. This entails patience, and the willingness to try to understand the customer's business.

To take a further example, this time from advertising – and selling an agency service is also a kind of industrial marketing – one advertising agent lost an account because he attended client meetings, listened to what various executives wanted, and produced advertising that pleased everyone but which failed to produce results. His successor said quite bluntly: 'Do as I advise or fire me.' In the event he produced a completely unorthodox campaign which was a great success. The lesson here was that one does not buy a dog and bark oneself.

The industrial salesperson must guide his or her customer. His or her skill will reflect on the image of the company. They will be called in to give advice. The eventual business may have to be earned over a period of time, and will not depend on sales gimmicks.

Marketing and product research

7. Samples. Techniques different from those used in consumer research are used for industrial products. Such research can be less expensive because the sample size for surveys is smaller. Paradoxically it may be cheaper if respondents are scattered and cannot be visited easily. When the customer list is comparatively small, and locations are scattered, a sample can be interviewed by telephone, appointments being made in the first place by letter explaining the purpose of the enquiry. Some studies can be carried out in go/no-go stages so that if a project is found at an early stage not to be feasible further investigation can be abandoned.

8. Prototypes. Another form of research involves prototypes which can be loaned for test purposes to customers. This was done, for instance, with a large dishwashing machine which was tried out for a year in a hospital. It has also been done with marine and fire retardant paints, the product being tested under actual use. Flooring material has been tested in a holiday camp throughout a summer season. Products can also be sent to a private, trade association, university or government test laboratory for independent trials.

Advertising

9. Trade press. Budgets for industrial marketing are usually slim, and sometimes traditional media advertising may be uneconomic simply because insufficient weight of advertising can be afforded to have the required impact. Money is sometimes wasted on ineffectual trade press advertising. It is therefore advisable to evaluate such advertising very critically.

However, this is not to deprecate trade press advertising if used skilfully. Many such journals, for example, provide reply cards so that readers can apply for literature offered in advertisements. Controlled circulation journals (*see* 13, **12**(*c*)) may offer the advertiser excellent penetration of specialised markets.

However, he may do better with some of the other media discussed in **10–12** below.

10. Direct mail. This will provide the opportunity to send detailed information such as technical data sheets, price lists and catalogues to selected prospects. Ring binders can be supplied to customers so that they can collect data sheets which are mailed periodically. It can be helpful to someone like an architect to have information readily on file. Samples of some products can be sent by post. Print for direct mail, response to press advertising, exhibiting and other purposes will be an important medium.

11. Directories. These can be an indispensable medium, and most trades have at least one reputable directory in which a company may place its name, address, telephone and telex or fax number and so make itself readily accessible. If felt necessary, black letter entries or display advertisements can be used to draw attention to one's products or services. In the advertising business, *Advertisers Annual* is a valuable directory often used daily by its subscribers. There are also more general directories such as telephone directories, Yellow Pages and Kelly's trade directories, while for detailed information about the people in an organisation there are seven volumes of the *UK Kompass Management Register*. Not only do such directories provide business leads but they are mailing lists for direct mail purposes.

To be absent from a directory can be suicidal. Here are two examples from the author's experience. He was asked to do a communications audit for a foreign bank. Enquiries produced attitudes that the bank was disreputable. Finally, it was discovered that the reason for this was that the bank was not listed in the international banking directory, *Polk's*. In the second instance, a company could not get contracts from local authorities. It was eventually discovered that the reason was that its materials were not among those in a very out-of-date directory to which reference was made by buyers. If you are not listed it may be thought that the publishers did not consider you worth listing, but sometimes it may be that when invited you did not complete and return an information form sent to you. It is surprising how many important names are missing from *Advertisers Annual* and the *UK Kompass Management Register*, simply because the information was not supplied.

12. Trade exhibitions. These enable the industrial marketer to demonstrate products and talk to customers, and most trades have regular shows which are focal points for the industry to show new products and for buyers to seek what is new. Exhibitions are sometimes criticised for being costly, but it all depends on how well the participant exploits the event, e.g. by sending tickets to customers and inviting them to visit him or her on the stand.

There are also PR opportunities which are often overlooked, such as co-operating with the exhibition press officer and issuing stories to the associated trade press so that news of exhibits is extended to people who may not attend the show. Important stories can also be sent to the Central Office of Information for overseas distribution. There are many such ancillary benefits when exhibiting. A fork-lift truck manufacturer used a helicopter to fly people from a London exhibition to his factory in the Home Counties.

Smaller, more private exhibitions can be set up in building centres, hotels, libraries or railway station concourses, or toured by caravan, bus, trailer or train (*see also* 13, 24).

Public relations

13. Relative importance of public relations and advertising. In industrial marketing, public relations could be more cost-effective than advertising. The need to inform and educate fairly small groups of customers, or individuals, invites the use of PR techniques, and private rather than commercial media will be more appropriate. There are three reasons for this:

(*a*) Industrial buyers need facts, not promotion.

(*b*) Industrial buyers are fewer and can therefore be approached more directly and personally.

(*c*) Technical products and services need detailed explanation.

14. Media and techniques. In the light of the above, public relations methods may consist of the following.

(*a*) *Press receptions*, works visits and outside visits to, say, installations.

(*b*) *Feature articles* in the trade, technical, professional and business press as the case may be. The authoritative case study can help readers to learn how the product or service can also solve their problems. A typical article could demonstrate how a customer had a problem, installed or used a product, and after a certain time was satisfied that the problem had been solved. The article can be given dramatic impact by comparing the earlier inferior situation with the present one. This technique can be applied very successfully to industrial marketing, and if the article is written professionally and commercial references are kept to a minimum the article will be published on its merits. It should, of course, be discussed with the editor in advance, not written speculatively. This has nothing to do with advertising, and does not have to be supported by purchase of space.

(c) Good technical *photographs* are also appreciated by the press, provided there are no blatant name displays.

(d) Documentary *videos* of about twenty minutes maximum length and, like the feature article and photograph, kept free of blatant 'plugs', can be shown to invited audiences. *Slide presentations* with synchronised audio tapes, or better still slide presentations using two projectors with cross fade effect, are also useful. The cost of production can be a good investment if the video or set of slides is used repeatedly at receptions, client meetings or press receptions, in showrooms or on exhibition stands.

(e) *External house journals* containing authoritative material, and aimed at specific readers, can be an excellent way of educating the market. Such a journal should be produced in a practical way so that it resembles the kind of publication produced by commercial publications. If it is too glossy and prestigious it will lack credibility. When ITT Europe issued their magazine *Profile* they deliberately designed one which looked like a typical business magazine.

(f) *Sponsored books:* a good, well-written and well-illustrated technical book, published with the imprint of a well-known publisher, can help to establish the reputation and image of a company. An example is the Rentokil library of textbooks on pest control published by Hutchinson, first launched over twenty-five years ago, and developed with new volumes being added year by year from the pens of company scientists.

(g) *Seminars, conferences, teach-ins.* Face-to-face activities with potential clients can be convincing if undertaken educationally and with an absence of salesmanship. Presentations can be made by technical experts, supported by audio-visuals and displays.

All this is similar to the market education proposals set out in Chapter 14, 25 except that this is not only a pre-selling exercise, but can be a continuous programme, year after year, and is likely to be more effective than the advertising which would be essential with FMCGs.

Channels of distribution

15. **Introduction.** Again, distribution will tend to differ from that in the consumer sphere, unless there is a large number of customers. The most likely channels are discussed in the following paragraphs:

16. **Direct to user.** This is very natural when there are few buyers, or when technical services and advice, and perhaps a custom–built design service, is necessary. The producer is able to exercise control over every aspect of customer relationships including tenders, prices and discounts. It is also easier to forecast demand when one is directly communicating with buyers.

17. **Agents.** Manufacturers' agents are a feature of industrial marketing where it is more economical to sell things through a specialist who handles a number of allied products which can be sold to the same market. Such agents are usually given exclusive selling rights. The benefit here is that the selling role is relinquished by the manufacturer who can concentrate on what he knows best and leave marketing to outside experts. This does, however, have the weakness of distancing the manufacturer from the market, its trends and wants.

18. **Brokers.** These are used in certain businesses; insurance being a good example. The broker will have clients whom he or she will advise on all kinds of insurance such as fire, accident, indemnity, pension funds and so on.

19. **Distributors.** Unlike agents, distributors will usually stock a

variety of makes and will not have exclusive rights. They are useful in providing regional depots as in the case of machinery which can be displayed at vantage points in the market. A typical example is farm equipment, distributors having showrooms or yards in market towns.

Progress test 16

1. What sort of products or services may be termed industrial? (2)

2. What are the characteristics of those who buy industrial goods or services? (3)

3. Should industrial salespeople be technicians first and salespeople second or vice versa? (5)

4. What special forms of marketing research can be applied to industrial marketing? (7,8)

5. Why are controlled circulation journals useful? (9)

6. Why should a company be represented in trade directories? (11)

7. Why is public relations especially valuable in industrial marketing? (13)

8. Which media and techniques are most useful for public relations in industrial marketing? (14)

17
Overseas marketing

Introduction

1. Definition. The expression 'overseas marketing' has been chosen for this chapter because it will deal with a number of different ways of marketing outside the domestic (which is not necessarily the 'home') market. There are three main kinds of overseas marketing, as follows.

(*a*) *The home market.* This is more than the domestic market within political frontiers. It is rather the regional market, e.g. the countries within the EEC as will become more apparent with the advent of the Single European Market and the opening of Eurotunnel. Satellite television will place emphasis on Eurobrands.

(*b*) *Exporting.* This means selling home-produced goods abroad.

(*c*) *International marketing.* Here we have something far more complicated. Motor cars may be exported for assembly in factories in other countries where there are joint venture plants with shares held by local nationals. Or a local company may have a franchise or licence to produce a branded product, importing the essential ingredients, as with Coca-Cola. Ready-made products are not exported, but final production or assembly takes place in the overseas market.

2. Antipathy to overseas marketing. Not every company takes eagerly to overseas marketing; some lazily prefer to concentrate on home sales. They are frightened of the complications which they see in documentation, foreign languages and currency, overseas selling and promotion, special packing and freighting, extended credit and foreign exchange problems. They regard exporting as a nuisance so why should they bother?

3. Reasons for overseas marketing. The reasons for wishing to market abroad are more complex than just wishing to expand sales, although that may be one factor. They may include the following.

(a) *Saturated home market*. The company can sell no more in the home market so it seeks new markets abroad.

(b) *Desire to expand sales*. A company wants to expand its sales and sees or seeks opportunities overseas.

(c) *Opportunities in developing countries*. The company may produce goods which are needed in developing countries, and may be approached by buyers or their agents.

(d) *Use of resources overseas*. Available and economic labour forces may exist in other countries so that it is worth while producing there, e.g. Hong Kong and Taiwan or countries with free trade zones like China and Mauritius.

(e) *Investment of profits*. Opportunities may be sought to invest profits, and developing overseas markets, especially by setting up manufacturing units abroad, may be a good way of doing this. This is sometimes regarded as economic imperialism. American companies such as Ford and IBM do this, but so do British companies such as ICI and Unilever. The Japanese have done this all over the world, Nissan in Britain being an example.

(f) *Multinational policy*. Multinationals such as IBM are very astute at straddling continents like Europe with factories in various countries. They have been dubbed 'supranationals' since they superimpose themselves across normal frontiers. In the case of ITT, each factory is responsible for a complete piece of equipment, receiving components from its factories in other countries while also supplying them with components.

(g) *Home market unable to absorb volume production*. Countries like those in Scandinavia have small populations so cannot absorb industrial production. Consequently, they produce for overseas markets as is seen with such companies as Volvo and Saab. This is also true of Italian companies such as Necchi sewing machines, while Indesit was able to mass produce washing machines by taking Europe as its market. It is interesting to note, however, that where there is a large home market the national product may predominate, e.g. German, French and Italian cars predominating in their own countries while still selling abroad, or being built abroad.

(h) *Export-import need.* Some countries require a high level of exports for one of two reasons:

(i)   to maintain a high standard of living; or
(ii) to obtain a balance of trade which will make imports possible.

There is a difference between the two. Japan has a sophisticated economy but scarcely any raw materials so it has to manufacture and export high trade technical products in order to import raw materials to provide Japan with the same goods. On the other hand, oil-producing countries have been exporting oil in order to create infrastructures and new societies, as in Nigeria, India, Mexico, Indonesia and the Gulf States.

4. Is there a global market? It is rare that a product will have universal appeal, and perhaps one of the fortunate few is Coca-Cola. Many products will suit only certain countries. Other products may have the wrong name, colour or shape for some countries. A company which is considering overseas trading for the first time will probably need to select the most promising countries, and gradually build up overseas markets rather than attempt to sell to the world at large. It depends on the product. A new printing machine might be sold at the rate of one machine to each of seventy different countries simply because very large printers are not commonplace.

So, generally speaking there is seldom such a thing as a global market. There may be a number of *different* foreign markets. This handbook could be taken as an example. It is quite likely that outside the UK it could be found in bookshops in Cyprus, Hong Kong, Kenya, Malaysia, Nigeria, Singapore and Trinidad but perhaps not in some neighbouring countries. The reasons for this are related to the education system, language, income, foreign exchange and other factors.

The existence of a market in a particular country may depend on the religious, ethnic or political situation. It is difficult to sell alcoholic drinks to Muslim countries, the Russians are unlikely to import Bibles, the Chinese would not favour white motor cars, the Arabs would probably object to the opening of branches of Marks & Spencer, and the Israelis would probably object to the import of dates from Libya. These are perhaps rather obvious limitations but it is surprising how naïve would-be exporters can be.

One of the biggest unforeseen drawbacks is that while a company may be a household name in its own country it could be totally unknown beyond that country's frontiers. It is sometimes hard for new exporters to accept this nasty truth, and unless properly organised a marketing exercise in a foreign country could be like the proverbial drop in the ocean. Before the early 1970s, who outside Japan had heard of Datsun? Overseas markets have to be researched and chosen carefully, and then cultivated with patience and sustained effort. The rest of this chapter will be devoted to the stages and techniques involved in developing an overseas market.

Developing an overseas market

5. Right product or service. While it is a somewhat 'chicken and egg' situation when selecting both the right product and the right market, we start here with what we plan to sell abroad. The following questions have to be asked:

(*a*) Is there a market for it? If so, where?

(*b*) Will it need to be adapted for foreign markets?

(*c*) Will it need to be packed differently for special protection?

(*d*) Can the present name be used, or could it have unfortunate connotations?

6. Selecting foreign markets. Research of two kinds may be necessary. A good deal of desk research is possible because much expertly gathered information already exists. Most international banks can supply economic reports on individual countries, and a series of booklets is also published by the British Overseas Trade Board. Really detailed reports are produced by *The Economist*

Intelligence Unit, Metra Consultancy and other specialists in overseas market research.

Such *secondary research* may, however, be too general when what is needed is *primary* or original research to establish the feasibility of marketing the product in a particular market (*see also* Chapter 4). There may be no similar product, so will anyone buy it? How will they buy it – are there retail outlets? How will it reach these outlets – are there wholesalers, is there transport? Are there any legal restrictions on this kind of product, and if so what are they? Are there any ethnic problems or taboos, or special requirements of certain sections of the population? How will potential customers know the product is available; what media are available for advertising? The situation in the foreign market is likely to be different in every respect from that in the home market. Basic to this will also be the fact that a company or product well-known in its own country may be unknown abroad.

To conduct primary research it will be necessary to commission a survey. However, conditions may be very different from those in the UK. If it is not an industrial country it is unlikely that there will be a local research organisation. Statistical information such as a population census or an electoral roll may not exist. Sampling by the quota or random methods may be impossible. The typical solution is to commission a British research unit with overseas experience, and if normal sampling is impractical qualitative group or individual discussion surveys may be necessary. Such studies have been carried out in Nigeria.

7. Selecting distributors. As already said, a product can be assembled by a joint venture company or manufactured under licence by an indigenous company, but many products will be handled by export/import agents. Part of the research (which is likely to require visiting the territory) will be to find reliable agents who will distribute to retailers in the chosen country. In some trades it may be possible to sell to a chain of stores (e.g. Kingsway Stores in Nigeria) who have a buying agency in the UK. It is most important to find distributors who will physically distribute and not leave goods in a warehouse waiting for orders.

8. Advertising. The following are some important considerations when preparing overseas advertising:

(*a*) *Cost*. The volume of advertising which can be afforded will depend on the volume of potential sales. A big problem in many overseas markets is that media are scarce and costly, and the cost of an advertising campaign can be disproportionate to the value of sales. Local agents will press for budgets to promote sales, and it is very easy to dissipate non-cost-effective sums to please overseas agents.

This does depend on the country or continent. Media comparable to the British will be found in other industrialised countries. The above remarks depend on whether one is selling to Europe, North America or Australia, or to countries where the marketing situation is very different.

(*b*) *Use of home or overseas agency?* Advertising campaigns can be organised through an agency in the home country, or by an agency in the overseas market. The one may be remote from the market, the other may be small and relatively unskilled. The exporter has to balance the pros and cons very carefully. Does he keep control of the advertising, or does he trust his overseas agent? A compromise may be to use an international advertising agency which has branch offices in the chosen foreign markets, e.g. Lintas.

(*c*) *Choice of media*. The advertising may be quite different from that used in the UK. There may be few newspapers, they could be in a variety of languages, and much of the market could be illiterate. Television could be an élitist medium, quite unlike that in industrial countries. Radio may be the principal medium, and although poster sites may be scarce, pictorial posters could be an excellent way of reaching people of different ethnic groups, speaking different languages, with the majority being illiterate. But even in industrial countries the media may not be the same as in Britain. For example, national newspapers, like those of Britain, are not likely to be found elsewhere, although by means of satellite *US Today* and the *Wall Street Journal* have brought the first national newspapers to the USA. Television can also be a very different advertising medium outside Britain (*see also* 13, **12–13**).

If one were selling to Europe, North America or Australia there could be very different regional advertising situations. The market would not be as compact as it is in Britain and therefore not so easily reached by mass circulation popular newspapers, magazines or by networked TV.

9. Public relations. It may be necessary to pave the way with PR before embarking on advertising. When a company or a brand is popular in the home country it is easy to forget how long it took to arrive at that happy situation. An unknown product in a foreign market is something the exporter may find difficult to imagine. There are billions of people, e.g. most of the Chinese, who have never heard of most of the brands we take for granted in the UK.

(a) *Media and methods.* Depending on the type of product it is planned to introduce to this overseas market, a PR programme must be prepared. Again, however, the situation is likely to be different, whether it be in nearby Europe where the market is more uncommon than common, or in an African republic where communications can be frustratingly difficult. It is unlikely, for instance, that one will find anything corresponding to the British press, radio and television with their multiplicity of opportunities of nationwide coverage. The media tend to be more regionalised (*see* **8**(*c*) above and 13, **12–21**).

It is more likely that we shall have to create media. House journals may be welcome, mobile exhibitions and video shows will be popular, talks and seminars may go down well, and the innovator system (*see* 2, **20**) may operate extremely well. People may expect more hospitality, not because they crave free drinks but because when people gather together it is natural to have a party. A lot of PR may be on a one-to-one basis, talking to opinion leaders who will act as innovators whose advice will be listened to.

(b) *Role of salesperson.* One of the criticisms of the British export salesperson is that he or she does not stay long enough in the country. In other words, he does not allow sufficient time for people to get to know, understand, like and trust him or her. He or she resembles the person who moves into a village where he is regarded as a foreigner, an outsider; it may take years before they are accepted. The salesperson who rushes from airport to hotel, sets up a meeting and hopes to catch the next plane home with a briefcase full of orders is going to be disappointed.

(c) *Grass roots campaign.* The PR programme may begin with a video show organised in advance through the British High Commission, Embassy or Consulate, or through a chamber of commerce. There may be local PR consultants who can advise on how to set up a communications and market education programme.

10. Customer satisfaction. The easiest way to sell a product is to have people recommend it. People will recommend a product that gives satisfaction. The more complicated the product the more likely it is to break down, while misuse, climatic conditions, poor maintenance and so on will cause it to break down more quickly than in normal circumstances. The manufacturer must recognise the existence of these different circumstances, and realise that the after-market (*see* 9) is all important. Overseas marketing can fail if there are no spare parts, no trained service staff, no back-up service which will give people the confidence to buy in the first place. This requirement applies everywhere in the world. It is an aspect of overseas marketing the Japanese have excelled in, whereas some British firms have been negligent.

Government and other aid to exporters

11. Role of the British Overseas Trade Board. World trade is vital to the balance of payments and the health of the national economy, and so there is considerable official encouragement to British firms to sell abroad. Much of this is by encouraging participation in exhibitions, joint ventures and trade missions. The British Overseas Trade Board (BOTB) helps exporters in the following ways.

(*a*) *Joint ventures*. A minimum of ten firms must be sponsored by an approved trade association, chamber of commerce or similar body. The BOTB supplies them with space and a shell stand at special rates at an overseas exhibition, and also assists with travel costs if the event is outside Western Europe.

(*b*) *British pavilions*. At international trade fairs, mostly outside Western Europe, the BOTB sets up British pavilions provided enough British companies are taking part. In Eastern Europe, in co-operation with the British Embassies in these countries, the

BOTB has run pavilions at the Leipzig, Budapest, Poznan, Brno, Plovdiv and Bucharest trade fairs. Further afield, the BOTB has in recent years had pavilions in international shows in places like Nairobi, Baghdad and Kaduna. In a single year the BOTB helps some 7,500 British firms at more than 300 events in some 50 countries.

(c) *Supporting publicity.* The BOTB organises press coverage for participants in overseas exhibitions and sometimes arranges supplements in newspapers and magazines in the countries where events are taking place.

(d) *UK events.* Support is also given to some sixty British shows at which British firms can show the world their products, e.g. the International Plastics and Rubber Exhibition and the International Spring Fair. *Trade Fairs and Exhibitions in Britain* is an annual BOTB booklet printed in English and six other languages (including Arabic). Its 100,000 copies are mostly distributed through the commercial attachés at British embassies.

12. The Export Credits Guarantee Department. The ECGD offers attractive insurance rates, from date of contract acceptance or from date of shipment, with a special introductory scheme for new small exporters. Cover provides collateral for usual bank financing, and the risks covered include:

(a) insolvency of the buyer;

(b) failure of the buyer to pay within six months of acceptance of goods;

(c) war, civil wars and revolutions;

(d) cancellation of UK export licences or new export restrictions; and

(e) delay in the transfer of sterling to the UK.

Further details of these services can be found in handbooks published by the Department.

13. Central Office of Information. In addition to its work for government departments in the UK, the COI operates an international information distribution service of great value to British exporters. If they have news which is good news about

Britain the COI will use it in the form of news stories, photographs and videos.

14. International and overseas advertising agencies and PR consultancies. Details of these will be found in *Advertisers Annual*, and other information can be obtained from organisations such as the Institute of Practitioners in Advertising and the Institute of Public Relations in London.

15. BBC External Services. The Export Liaison Unit at Bush House in the Aldwych (*not* Broadcasting House) broadcasts a number of programmes featuring British products, events and achievements. These go out in many languages on the overseas service, and are well monitored round the world. Information supplied must be fully detailed (especially about the despatch of export orders), and the company must be capable of handling a volume of enquiries from abroad.

16. EIBIS International Ltd. (*See* Appendix II.) One way to educate overseas markets is to publish feature articles, pictures and news stories in the foreign press. These need to be translated by experts if foreign language journals are being supplied with editorial material. Although editors of foreign journals may speak English they are publishing in their own language, and therefore need PR material which is translated ready for editing and printing. EIBIS International is probably the only international PR organisation of its kind, and over many years it has built up contacts and established its reputation with overseas editors. Great care is taken by EIBIS to write, have translated (and have the translation checked) and distribute stories about British companies, products and services. Its record of success is commendable.

17. Universal News Services. Long established and well known in the UK for its wire service for company news (clients pay for the service whereas the Press Association and Reuters are financed by the press which receives their news), UNS also offers an overseas news distribution service. UNS is now owned by the Press

Association and has access to its computerised news distribution services.

Progress test 17

1. Name the three main forms of overseas marketing.   **(1)**
2. What are the eight reasons for wishing to market abroad? **(3)**
3. Is there such a thing as a world market?   **(4)**
4. What questions must be asked when considering whether a product is suitable for an overseas market?   **(5)**
5. Describe the forms of secondary and primary research which can be undertaken.   **(6)**
6. What sort of advertising agency would be chosen?   **(8)**
7. How can PR techniques help the exporter?   **(9, 13, 15, 16, 17)**
8. Describe some of the government services available to exporters.   **(11, 12, 13)**

18
The computer in marketing

Introduction

1. Increasing use of computers. Computers have been with us for decades but, in their various forms, they are fast becoming essential facets of modern marketing. Computer costs have fallen so dramatically in recent years that even the smallest of offices can now afford personal computers and word processors. Each organisation will have its own application whether or not it has its own hardware. This chapter can therefore be no more than an introduction to a large and ever growing aspect of marketing.

2. Main advantages of computers. The two main advantages of computers are:

(*a*) their speed of operation;
(*b*) their ability to store, sort and perform tasks with large volumes of information which can be displayed on a visual display unit (VDU), or printed out on paper, on command.

3. Computer press. The advent of the computer has produced many specialised journals, *Computer Weekly* being the first in Britain in 1966. Today, there are some 330 British computer journals, ranging from those read by the professional data processors to those enjoyed by domestic microcomputer enthusiasts. Reed Business Publishing have the largest list of titles including international journals such as *Middle East Computing* and *Systems International.* There are also several exhibitions devoted to computers and aimed specifically at professionals, office users and home users.

Some typical applications

4. Advertising. Statistics can be recorded and printed out, such as daily records of the booking, usage and cost of media against budget, something which the larger advertising agencies have used for many years. It is also possible to calculate the most cost-effective media combinations and schedules by feeding in all the data variables on rates, circulation, readership and other available figures.

Computers can be used to get results from media. For instance, in the direct response field, TV commercials can be used to produce telephoned enquiries or orders (with credit card payment), the television programme company sending the advertiser a computer print-out within twenty-four hours.

Computer graphics i.e. colours, typography, shapes, rules and symbols, can be applied to TV commercials, including titles, exploded diagrams, skeletal views of products, and also cartoons. Advertisements can be drawn on a computer. In fact, a freelance artist can work at home, using a computer and visual display terminal (VDT) and transmitting the design to the client's computer where it can be simultaneously considered, or stored and retrieved as required.

5. Printing and publishing. Newspapers and magazine pages can be laid out by computer, and standard information such as headings (e.g. names of stations for radio/TV programmes) can be stored and retrieved whenever required. The contents of membership lists and entire trade and telephone directories can be stored (usually on floppy disc no bigger than a singles record) and updated for new editions, thus saving laborious and costly resetting.

Computerised photo-typesetting to produce camera-ready copy has been in use for many years, but has spread more widely with the setting up of new lithographic print shops and contract newspaper printers. Many Third World countries have enjoyed these technologies in advance of Britain with its old-fashioned letterpress printing, although this is mostly allied to computerised photo-typesetting.

The merits of filmsetting and lithographic printing combine with the simplicity of correcting stored and retrieved copy, while the old hot, dirty and noisy foundry has given way to a composing room that looks like a laboratory.

Datasetting permits the writer to compose on a word processor and send the copy direct by telephone to the printer who can process the data into type without re-keyboarding. Typesetting errors are minimised, time is saved, and proofs can usually be submitted the same day or overnight (*see* **21**).

With the exodus of the national press from Fleet Street, computerised paperless newsrooms may be located at a distance from the printing plant. The best example is *The Independent*, a national daily first published in 1986, which has a London editorial office from which made–up pages are transmitted by facsimile to contract printers strategically located in places like Portsmouth.

Laser printing of direct mail shots means that with suitably programmed computer software, each letter can be printed individually, character by character, and some 8,000–10,000 letters an hour can be produced. Colours, different typefaces and sizes, and other creative devices can be programmed to create a very original mailing shot. Laser printing is a system using a low power laser beam which scans the original artwork and produces each letter individually. As with some photocopiers, the image is coated with toner which is transferred on to the paper by a heated roller.

6. Sales audit. Given a reliable data base of customer and market information, a marketer can use a computer to conduct a sales audit, assessing his strengths and weaknesses against market trends. In this way, he can eliminate waste and concentrate on potentially profitable areas of business.

7. Mailing lists. The computer has largely replaced physical mailing lists, and categorised lists can be held on floppy disc or tape and used for addressing labels or envelopes. Databases are available to direct mail users, or can be created in-house, making use of existing customer information. Standardised letters can also be produced appropriate to information linked with names on the mailing list (e.g. yearly subscription reminders or follow-up letters to enquirers who have not yet ordered.) Computer lists can be used for the mailing of offers, catalogues, letters or accounts.

A problem with any system of mailing lists is duplication because opportunities arise to enter the same address again, or because names recur in independent lists. Various de-duplication systems have been evolved to search for and remove duplications, but this will be difficult if there are differences in the presentation of the address information (e.g. if initials are given in one version but first names are spelt out in another).

8. Monthly accounts. Management accounting systems exist for clients who submit daily records of sales so that within a few days of the end-of-month a set of books can be delivered showing the cash flow situation, while statements are despatched early so that accounts are paid quickly. Firms with large numbers of customers operate their own computerised account collection systems, e.g. gas and electricity undertakings, British Telecom, mail-order clubs and subscription publishers.

9. Telephone marketing. The Teledata (BHP) service allows the advertiser to use the Teledata telephone number (01-200-0-200) so that the customer can enquire or order by calling this number. The 24-hour personalised telephone marketing service saves the customer having to return a coupon, and saves the advertiser the trouble and cost of handling coupons and telephone calls. The transaction is quick. All the information is held on a computer, the advertiser buying an annual service. There are similar services such as Orderline (Aircall). The computer can provide detailed analyses such as a geographical breakdown of calls received. Orderline will print enquirers' names and addresses straight on to adhesive labels. Both have various ancillary services. Aircall is now a majority shareholder in Teledata.

Leisureline sells anything to do with hobbies and sports (whether skis, fishing tackle or climbing boots), while Telemart is a computerised exchange market which can bring buyers and sellers of anything together, the modern counterpart of *Exchange and*

Mart. Computerstamp is a Cameo stamp service. The buyer sends Cameo a wants list or area of interest for search, or the vendor sends a list of items for sale, and so buyers and sellers are brought together by computer. Homeline is a house selling service.

Computacar has proved to be a quick and effective way of bringing together buyers and sellers of second-hand motor cars. Details of the vehicle are put into the computer at a charge. Buyers ring up and state which car they want, specifying model, price, colour and area. The Computacar telephonist provides a short list of available cars. Sometimes, prices can be adjusted on both sides until a match is achieved, a matter of market price asserting itself.

10. Viewdata and teletext. Viewdata is the Prestel (British Telecom) system of transmitting information from a computer to a modified TV set, using the telephone link and with the customer usually paying pence per page for pages called up. Prestel can not only advertise products such as hotel accommodation, houses and transport (vacancies on hovercraft or aircraft can be updated hourly and called up by travel agencies anywhere), but the viewer can *interact* with the computer and actually buy the product. They do so by pressing buttons on the TV remote control unit in their armchair at home. They may also view their own bank statement (having given the correct code) and order a new cheque book.

Electronic correspondence is yet another use of Prestel, either using the Post Office Electronic Post direct mail service. A more personal form of electronic mail can be conducted in-house, messages being received on personal computer screens to which may be linked printers to provide hard copy print-outs.

Teletext is the alphanumeric TV information system provided free of charge by Oracle (ITV) and Ceefax (BBC). Oracle is a broadcast newspaper read on adapted TV sets, and includes advertisements, whereas there are none on the Ceefax information service.

11. Sales orders. Even the salesman on his journey cycle can use a small hand-held terminal such as those supplied by UCSL Microsystems. With his portable terminal the salesperson can feed orders direct to his or her central sales office computer. Various formats are available and, in addition to sales order entry, terminals can be programmed to include journey route plans, and the ability to display the product file specific to a customer. The latter is particularly useful when dealing with supermarket chains and large complicated orders are involved.

12. Warehouse stock control. Handlers of large volumes of merchandise (e.g. wholesalers, supermarket chains and multiples) use computers to control stock and advise on when to re-order, taking into account the lead time between submitting orders and getting delivery which may differ from one supplier to another. Nowadays many small shopkeepers such as newsagents are controlling stock on microcomputers.

13. Inventory control. Inventory control by computer permits a company to produce, buy or stock a minimum number of items against a changing daily forecast of stock requirements based on orders received. In this way capital is not unduly tied up in stock, and cash flow is controlled.

14. Distribution. Specialist contract distributors of merchandise such as beers provide an extension of the brewery marketing department by producing delivery documentation from computer terminals connected to the brewery computer.

15. Bar coding and till stock control. Many products bear bar codes on their packs. The check-out cashier reads the code by brushing it with a reader pen; this simultaneously gives the price to the till and informs the stockroom computer of the sale. Stock can also be controlled by other devices fitted to store tills which inform the central computer of sales.

These EPOS (electronic point-of-sale systems) were first introduced into British supermarkets in 1982, and they read EAN (European Article Number) bar codes.

Another system (often found at petrol stations) is EFTPS (electronic funds transfer at point-of-sale). When the motorist presents a Visa, American Express or other charge card the card is 'wiped' on an EFTPS terminal. This reads the logo on the card, checks its status with the charge-card company, records the transaction for payment, and the customer signs the till roll. The checking process takes only 15 seconds, and the customer is unaware of it.

16. Naming brands, renaming companies. The search for new names, whether for a new product or as part of a corporate identification programme, can be greatly aided by the speed of the computer. For instance, when the Weston Bancorporation of Los Angeles, a holding company for twenty-one banks operating as separate entities in eleven western states, sought a new single name, some 46,000 possible names were generated by computer. The chosen name was First Interstate. The name of the French petrol Elf was the product of a computer.

17. Marketing research. In marketing research, computers have been used for decades in the processing of information gained from surveys, especially quantitative ones. An interesting application of the computer is to use survey material as a data base for other purposes such as direct mail or salespeople's call lists.

Market Location, for instance, have carried out field research into the location of every factory and warehouse in 3 x 2 km sectors of Great Britain, discovering the characteristics and sales potential of each firm. Entered on a computer file, this information can be retrieved selectively for industrial market research purposes. It can also be used for direct mail, thus eliminating wasteful mailings, while area maps can be produced showing the locations of the best prospects.

Problems with computers

18. Garbage in, garbage out. Because computers are such powerful tools a wrongly thought out command or program can have disastrous consequences. A computer will do exactly what it is told to do at enormous speed. The saying 'put garbage in, get garbage out' is all too true. The user, if insufficiently skilled, may take a while to realise this.

19. Debugging. Although computers are excellent at rapidly repeating functions tailor-made for a particular task, it may take time to debug (remove errors from) a new program. Errors will occur when the computer hits a situation which the program writer did not envisage, and therefore failed to provide a solution for. That situation might only occur after the program had been run successfully for months.

20. Lack of familiarity. People unfamiliar with computers may be unsure of how best to use them. They often think that data is lost on magnetic tape, discs or floppy discs, and feel they can find data on paper more easily because it is visible. In fact, computers are used because data is easier to find, sort or quantify, and it can be seen on TV sets, VDUs, print-outs or ready-addressed labels so much more quickly than information buried in paper.

Such resistance to computers is being broken down by increasing use of computer newspapers such as Oracle and Ceefax; interactive databases such as Prestel; classified advertising data bases such as Computacar, Homeline, Telemart and Leisureline; banking databases such as Cash point machines outside banks; and point-of-sale bank debiting facilities and British Telecom's credit card telephones in shops to check out buyers' credit cards.

21. Typesetting problems. Computerised photo-typesetting has indisputable advantages, both in speed of production and in the quality of print that results from the repetition of identical characters. However, a common fault is that because corrections are so simple and inexpensive (compared with hot metal corrections) there can be a tendency for the operator to rely on his ability to replay a tape and type in corrections and so be careless about making mistakes. This can lead to a proof-reading nightmare. Word-processor typists also complain that because corrections can be made so easily authors tend to make more copy changes.

Another problem which may puzzle proof-readers is the style adopted regarding break words at the ends of lines. Some keyboard operators will use no break words, resulting in some lines being condensed and other lines having white spaces between words. Another keyboard operator will adopt hyphenated breakwords at the ends of lines, making for more uniform lines.

22. Cost of software. While the cost of computers falls the cost of software increases. *Firmware* is one answer to this problem, this being computer equipment which combines ready-to-use software (programs) with hardware.

23. Maintaining security. Finally, reliance should not be placed on the computer memory as the only record of information. Regular security copies should be kept of current discs. It is quicker to make copies of a computer memory than data held on paper. Precautions of this kind are necessary because it is possible for databases to suffer from power failures, erasure, loss or destruction.

Progress test 18

1. What are the two advantages of computers? (2)
2. How can the computer be used in advertising? (4)
3. What are computer graphics? (4)
4. What is a floppy disc? (5)
5. Describe laser printing and the special facilities it offers. (5)
6. What is meant by a sales audit? (6)
7. What is the value of de–duplication? (7)
8. Give some examples of telemarketing. (9)
9. How do Prestel, Oracle and Ceefax differ from one another? (10)
10. What is meant by the interactive nature of viewdata? (10)
11. How can a hand–held terminal help the salesperson? (11)
12. What problems occur with computers? (18–23)

Appendices

Appendix 1
Addresses of societies and educational organisations

Advertising Association, Abford House, 15 Wilton Road, London SW1V 1NJ. Federation of advertising organisations.

British Association of Industrial Editors, 3 Locks Yard, High Street, Sevenoaks, Kent TN13 1LT. Membership: editors of house journals. Entry by examination.

British Council, 10 Spring Gardens, London SW1A 2BH. Publishes a list of its offices throughout the world. Provides educational and library facilities overseas.

CAM Education Foundation, Abford House, 15 Wilton Road, London SW1V 1NJ. Examinations: CAM Certificate in Communication Studies and CAM Diplomas in Advertising and Public Relations. Facilities of the Advertising Association library at the same address.

Chartered Institute of Marketing, Moor Hall, Cookham, Berkshire SL6 9QH. Entry by examination or election. College of Marketing.

Incorporated Society of British Advertisers, 44 Hertford Street, London W1Y 8AE. Protects and advances advertising interests of member firms by organising representation, co–operation, action and exchange of information and experience.

Institute of Practitioners in Advertising, 44 Belgrave Square, London SW1X 8GS. Professional body of service advertising agencies.

Institute of Public Relations, Gate House, St John's Square, London EC1M 4DH. Members elected to grades by age and experience. Lunch–time meetings, annual conference, seminars, regional branches.

Institute of Sales Promotion, Arena House, 66–68 Pentonville

Road, Islington, London N1 9HS. Recognised professional body of that branch of marketing known as sales promotion. Services include standard rules for competitions and annual ISP awards. Works actively with ASA to prepare and monitor British Code of Sales Promotion Practice.

London Chamber of Commerce and Industry, Examinations Board, Marlowe House, Station Road, Sidcup, Kent DA15 7BJ. Third Level Certificate examinations in Advertising, Marketing, Public Relations, Selling and Sales Management, with Diploma for passes in three or four subjects taken at same time.

Market Research Society, 175 Oxford Street, London W1R 1TA. The professional body for those using survey techniques for market, social and economic research.

Public Relations Consultants Association, Premier House, 10 Greycoat Place, London SW1P 1SB. Corporate Membership.

Royal Society of Arts Examinations Board, Murray Road, Orpington, Kent BR5 3RB.

Appendix 2
Marketing, advertising and public relations services

Advertising Standards Authority, Brook House, Torrington Place, London WC1. Supervises British Code of Advertising Practice.

BBC External Services, Export Liaison Unit, Bush House, London WC2B 4PH. Broadcasts in many languages news about British products, events and achievements.

British Overseas Trade Board, Publicity Unit, 1 Victoria Street, London SW1H 0ET. Organises PR on behalf of British exporters in connection with Joint Ventures, All-British Exhibitions, overseas trade fairs. Publishes advice to exporters, export case studies.

Central Office of Information, Office of the Controller (Overseas), Hercules Road, London SE1 7DU. Distributes news, pictures, articles, documentary videos, radio tapes about British products, events and achievements.

EIBIS International Ltd, 3 Johnson's Court, Fleet Street, London EC4A 3EQ. Distributes translated articles to overseas press for clients. Meticulous translations.

Press Association, 85 Fleet Street, London EC4P 4BE. Distributes news to subscriber UK press. Supplies own transcripts of parliamentary speeches.

PNA, 13–19 Curtain Road, London EC2A 3LT. Press release distribution service with media and financial database. City News division. Media Town by Town geographic service.

Press cutting services. International services listed in *Hollis Annual* and *Benn's Media Directory*.

Universal News Services, Communication House, Gough Square, London EC4P 3DP. Distributes news for subscribers (e.g. PR clients) to UK and overseas press by own wire service and computerised news service of Press Association. Translation service. Taped interviews for radio.

Appendix 3
Further reading

Advertising, Frank Jefkins (M & E Handbooks, Pitman, London 1985)

Advertising Made Simple (fourth edition), Frank Jefkins (Heinemann Made Simple Books, London 1985)

Effective Marketing Strategy, Frank Jefkins (Frank Jefkins School of Public Relations, Croydon 1982)

Effective Press Relations and House Journal Editing (third edition), Frank Jefkins (Frank Jefkins School of Public Relations, Croydon 1985)

Fundamentals and Practice of Marketing, The (second edition), John Wilmshurst (Heinemann, London 1984)

Fundamentals of Advertising, John Wilmshurst (Heinemann, London 1985)

International Dictionary of Marketing and Communication, Frank Jefkins (Blackie, Glasgow 1987)

Introduction to Marketing, Advertising and Public Relations (third edition), Frank Jefkins (Macmillan, London 1989)

Marketing: An Introductory Text (fourth edition), Michael J. Baker (Macmillan, London 1985)

Marketing Made Simple, B. Howard Elvy (Heinemann Made Simple Books, London 1980)

Marketing Research for Managers, Sunny Crouch, (Pan, London 1985)

Marketing Theory & Practice (second edition), Ed. Michael J. Baker (Macmillan, London 1982)

Modern Marketing Communications, Frank Jefkins (Blackie, Glasgow 1989)

Planned Press and Public Relations (second edition), Frank Jefkins (Intertext, Glasgow 1986)
Practice of Public Relations, The (third edition), Ed. Wilfred Howard (Heinemann, London 1988)
Public Relations (third edition), Frank Jefkins (M & E Handbooks, Pitman, London 1988)
Public Relations Techniques, Frank Jefkins (Heinemann, London 1988)
Secrets of Successful Direct Response Marketing, Frank Jefkins (Heinemann, London 1988)
Selling: Management and Practice (second edition), P. Allen (M & E Handbooks, Pitman, London 1989)
The Third Wave, Alvin Toffler (Pan Books, London 1981)

Appendix 4

Syllabus for the London Chamber of Commerce certificate
Third Level examination in Marketing

MARKETING Third Level (3025)

Series 2 and 4

The aim of the examination is to test the candidate's knowledge and understanding of the concept of marketing and the techniques applied to the marketing of goods and services.

The nature of marketing

Definition of marketing. Marketing versus product orientated companies. The marketing concept and market theory. Role of the marketing department.

Market forces

Customer behaviour

How, why, when and where distributors and consumers buy. Decision making units and purchase behaviour. Consumer sovereignty. Consumerism.

Law and voluntary codes

Statutes, regulations and common law relating to marketing. Voluntary codes and self-regulatory procedures. The inter-relationship between legal and voluntary controls.

External forces

Political, economic, competitive, social and technological influences.

Elements of marketing.

The total strategy from concept of product or service to the after-market.

The product or service

(*i*)   **The product and new product development**
Product life cycle, and the re-cycled, leapfrog and staircase variations of the standard PLC; innovative behaviour; portfolio management; product screening.

(*ii*)   **Name and branding**
Choice of names for companies and products.

(*iii*)   **Packaging**
Materials and containers for packaging that are functional and legal and which aid promotion in order to provide customer satisfaction.

(*iv*)   **Pricing**
Policies and theories of pricing – economic, market, psychological, opportunity, penetration, creaming (or skimming) prices.

(*v*)   **Marketing research**
Quantitative and qualitative, primary and secondary research. Desk research. Product pretesting, test marketing, test houses and government research laboratories. Dealer audits, consumer panels, motivational research, discussion groups, opinion polls, hall testing, omnibus surveys, piggy-backing, media and advertising research. The sample, questionnaire, interviewing techniques, interpretation of research findings.

(*vi*)   **Sales forecasting**
Long, medium and short term forecasting as a tool for planning.

(*vii*)   **Distribution**
Channels of distribution. Factors, wholesalers, retailers, agents, markets, cash and carry warehouses, co-operatives, franchisers, vending, gift catalogues. Direct selling, mail-order trading/direct response marketing, telemarketing.

(*viii*)   **Selling**
Organisation of sales force and its role in marketing.

(*ix*)   **Advertising**
Place of trade and consumer advertising in marketing. The role of the advertising department and advertising agency.

(*x*)   **Sales promotion**
Techniques to stimulate sales at the point-of-sale.
Note: Candidates should be aware of current trends in this syllabus area.

(xi) **Sponsorship**
Various kinds of sponsorship to aid marketing.
(xii) **The after-market**
Guarantees, warranties, spare parts, after-sales servicing.

Special aspects of marketing
Public relations in relation to marketing.
Relevance of public relations to all aspects of marketing.
Relationships between marketing department and the public relations department or consultancy.
The marketing budget.
Integration of revenues and costs for effective control of marketing activities.

Special kinds of marketing
Industrial marketing.
Special techniques required when marketing industrial products and services.
Export and international marketing.
Special techniques required for marketing products and services overseas.

Examination requirements
A 3-hour examination. One question is compulsory; four other questions are to be answered from a choice of nine.

Appendix 5
Examination technique

1. Preliminaries.

(a) *Preparation*. Ample preparation, followed by thorough revision to consolidate the knowledge already gained, is necessary for any examination. Without it, a list of examination hints is virtually useless. Nevertheless, even a well-prepared candidate can fail through faulty presentation of their work, waste of valuable time and irrelevancy; it is for such a candidate that these hints have been compiled.

(b) *In the examination room*. Even before he or she comes to grips with the actual questions on the examination paper, the candidate can improve upon, or mar, his or her chances; therefore at this stage the following points ought to be borne in mind.

(i) *Read carefully* the instructions on the examination paper. Note that LCC papers will not be marked unless the compulsory question is answered.

(ii) *Supply the information required* on the outside cover of the answer book, e.g. date, subject, candidate's letter and number. (At the end of the examination enter the number of questions answered in the space provided.)

(iii) *Follow carefully the other instructions* as and when they become applicable; e.g. note the style of answer required such as 'explain briefly', 'discuss' or 'prepare a report'.

(iv) *Write answers legibly* on both sides of the paper provided, but commence each answer on a fresh sheet. An instruction to this effect is usually given on the outside cover. If you cross out mistakes in your answers do so neatly with one line.

(v) *Number the answers.* Be careful to number the answers so as to indicate the questions to which they refer and, where applicable, continue the numbering on to any additional sheet or sheets. Also, remember to number each page.

(vi) *Use the paper provided.* Usually the examining body provides headed paper, with spaces left for subject, and candidate's identification letter and number. This paper only must be used, and the spaces properly completed.

(c) *Planning the approach.* Having followed and/or memorised the procedural instructions, the candidate may now turn to the examination paper itself. *This is the crucial stage of the examination,* and the following suggestions for a planned approach are not to be regarded as wasteful of time; just the reverse, in fact, as an answer which has been planned (and is therefore logically arranged) saves time in the writing of it and, moreover, avoids much repetition. Another important advantage is that the finished answer will be less haphazard and easier to mark; therefore the examiner is less likely to miss the points you have attempted to make, and may even be sufficiently appreciative to award bonus marks for a well-planned answer.

(i) *Read carefully through the examination paper.* This enables the candidate to get a general impression of the nature and apparent difficulty (or relative simplicity) of the questions, from which he can plan his approach.

(ii) *Read the instructions.* Return to the beginning of the paper and read (or re-read) the instructions, e.g. number of questions to be attempted overall; compulsory questions, if any; and any other special instructions.

(iii) *Allot the available time* according to the number of questions to be answered. An allowance of, say, five to ten minutes ought to be made for the final reading through of the answers.

(iv) *Choose the first question* to be attempted. Obviously, it is not necessary to answer the questions in the same order as they appear in the paper, but the candidate must decide at this point whether to deal first with the compulsory question or answer one of the others. So long as the compulsory question is not overlooked, the choice is not vitally important, although it is usually advisable to deal first with a question that the candidate feels is well within his ability to handle. A good start engenders confidence, and may well boost his morale.

(v) *Plan the answer* to the first question. Having read the question again in order to understand clearly what is required, it will probably be found that it consists of two or more distinct parts. Underline the key word of each part and then make a note of the various key words on a separate rough working sheet. Alongside, or underneath, each key word jot down your ideas at random, leaving space for any after-thoughts. Rearrange the various points you have made and commit them to your examination script in a logical sequence. In this way the candidate will ensure that each part of the question is dealt with; moreover, he is less likely to omit important points which the examiner is looking for in the answer.

Be careful not to write an answer which you have previously written in class: exactly the same questions are not usually asked. Do not repeat what you have learned simply because you have learned it. Knowledge must be applied to questions, and questions are a test of intelligence, not memory.

Plan the answers to the remaining questions in the same way.

(d) *Rough notes on working paper*. If the candidate uses a separate sheet (or sheets) for his rough notes, it should be securely attached to his examination script, but he must be careful to cancel the sheet or mark it clearly as 'rough notes'. Failure to do this might cause some confusion for the examiner, and prove disastrous for the candidate.

2. Answering the questions. The foregoing hints might well be applied to practically any written examination, but it is now necessary to deal specifically with those examinations in preparation for which this HANDBOOK is primarily intended. In general, the questions might be divided into the following categories: (a) those requiring factual answers, (b) those calling for an outline of procedure, (c) the drafting of reports and memoranda and (d) discussion, comments or observations on quotations, statements, debatable points, etc.

The following suggestions might be helpful according to the type of question.

(*a*) *Questions requiring factual answers*, e.g. types of distribution outlet. Questions of this type demand concise but nevertheless *precise* answers. The examination candidate gains nothing by attempting to fill out his answer; in fact, most questions of this type can be answered in a short space; therefore, a half-page answer might well earn higher marks than a full-page answer which consists of a half-page preamble and a great deal of 'padding'. Such answers may be improved by the use of charts.

(*b*) *Procedures*, e.g. the procedure to be followed in carrying out a research survey. In outlining a procedure:

(*i*)   It must be arranged in *logical order* and each stage in the procedure should be numbered and (if appropriate) headed and sub-headed.

(*ii*)   It is not usually necessary to deal in detail with each stage of the procedure; a brief outline ought to be adequate in most cases, particularly if the procedure is a lengthy one.

NOTE: If the candidate is pressed for time, it is a good plan merely to list and number the stages of the procedure, leaving space between each stage. Subsequently, if time permits, a brief explanation can be added at each stage.

(*c*) *Drafting of reports, memoranda, etc.* e.g. the preparation of a report relating to a public relations programme. In handling this type of question, candidates must take great care in the drafting of the document required. If a report is called for, the candidate ought to regard it as a two-part question, i.e. the *form* of the report and the *subject* of the report, as it may be assumed that the examiner has allotted a specific number of marks for *each* of these aspects of the report.

(*d*) *Discussion, comment, observations, etc.* e.g. 'What is your opinion of the danger of 'recommended prices' leading to the abuse of 'double-pricing'?' Many questions of this type are *not* capable of a precise answer; if, however, the candidate presents a well-reasoned, imaginative answer he will, no doubt, merit high marks, even though the conclusion drawn does not exactly coincide with that of the examiner.

(*e*) *Defining lists of terms.* A typical question may ask for 10 terms to be defined, implying 2 marks per answer. So, if you cannot explain every term it will be worth answering such a question if you can describe at least 5 of the terms since this can earn 10 marks.

(f) *Length of answer*. Most LCC questions require an answer of about one-and-a-half to two pages. Shorter answers are unlikely to earn many marks.

Appendix 6
Specimen examination paper

Third level
The London Chamber of Commerce

Series 4 Examination 1988

Wednesday 23 December — 1800 to 2100

Marketing
Code No: 3025

Instructions to candidates

(a)   *Answer five questions — the compulsory question (Question 1) and four others.*

(b)   *Candidates must answer the compulsory question or they will not be eligible for the award of a Pass.*

(c)   *All questions carry equal marks.*

(d)   *All answers must be clearly and correctly numbered but need not be in numerical order.*

(e)   *Write legibly on both sides of the page. Rough work (if any) must be crossed through after use.*

(f)   *If supplementary sheets are used, candidate's number must be clearly shown and the sheets securely inserted inside the answer book. The question(s) to which they refer must be clearly numbered.*

Compulsory question

1. The consumer is said to be sovereign. Marketing is defined as producing at a profit goods that satisfy customers. Yet we have consumer protection laws and codes, which suggest that some manufacturers have failed to apply the marketing concept.

Discuss this contradiction, and suggest ways in which marketing tactics can be applied to satisfy customers.

2. (*i*)   What different services are supplied by advertising agencies and public relations consultancies?

(*ii*)   How can these organisations help in planning and executing a marketing strategy?

3. A food manufacturer is about to launch a new product but, before doing so, needs evidence that it could gain 25% of the national market. Plan a test-marketing exercise to discover whether this share of the market is feasible.

4. Describe four ways in which you could familiarise your national sales force with your forthcoming press and television advertising campaign.

5. (*i*) What type of goods are best distributed through wholesalers? Give your reasons.

(*ii*) What type of goods are best distributed direct to retailers, including buyers of large supermarket chains? Give your reasons.

6. Explain the following terms:

(*i*)   Mis-redemption
(*ii*)   Mal-redemption
(*iii*)   Buffer stock
(*iv*)   Cold calling
(*v*)   Fulfilment house
(*vi*)   Cross-couponing
(*vii*)   On-pack offer
(*viii*)Mail in
(*ix*)   Maildrop

    (*x*) High Street redemption scheme.

  7. Describe the following kinds of price:

    (*i*)   Skimming
    (*ii*) Economic
    (*iii*) Market
    (*iv*) Psychological.

  8. Describe four benefits that a marketing manager could enjoy or exploit by sponsoring a popular national sport.

  9. (*i*) Explain the conditions which make marketing research difficult to undertake in some countries.

    (*ii*) Describe any special research techniques which can be adopted to overcome these problems.

  10. In spite of extensive advertising, good distribution and good trade terms, your product is not achieving its sales target. A study has shown that retailers are not promoting the product with sufficient enthusiasm. You believe this is because they do not fully understand it.

  Using a product of your choice, plan a dealer education programme, so that they are better able to explain or demonstrate the product.

Index

Above-the line media, 57, 176, 185, 194–202, 212
  cinema, 57,202
  outdoor, 200–1
  press, 195–6
  radio, 55, 57, 185, 189, 197–8
  television, 55, 57, 58, 183, 185, 189, 198–200
Account executive, 182
ACORN, 134, 136, 137–9, 140, 181
Acronyms, 102, 103
Ad-mass, 19
Adopters, 29, 206
Advertisement manager, 186
Advertiser, the 175–7
Advertising, 23, 24, 33, 34, 40, 57–8, 135–7, 150, 165,
  171–90, 218
  agency, 177–185
  agency personnel, 182–4, 190
  co-operative, 122, 168
  costs, 57
  creativity, 191–4
  department, 176
  industrial, 243–5
  manager, 186
  overseas, 254–5
  reminder, 146
  three sides of, 175–86
  who pays for, 171
Advertising agencies, 179–182
  à la carte, 179, 180
  creative, 179
  direct response, 180
  financial, 181
  full-service, 179, 190
  hot shop, 179
  industrial, 180
  media independents, 179, 190
  overseas, 254
  overseas press, 181
  poster, 180
  product development, 180, 190
  radio, 181
  recruitment, 181
  sales promotion, 181
  sponsorship, 181
  studio, 180
  telephone selling, 181
  through-the-line, 191
Advertising Association, The, 75, 101, 172, 186, 187,
  191, 270
Advertising research, 58–9
Advertising Standards Authority, 26, 186–8, 190,
  220, 228, 229, 272
Advertising Standards Board of Finance, 187, 190
Aerosols, 91
After-market, 4, 35, 61–3, 141–9
After-sales service, 3, 23, 125, 141, 142, 167
After-use, 48
AGB Home Audit, 139
Ageing population, 6
Ages, 6, 10, 73
AIDCA formula, 192, 212
Aided recall, 83
Aircraft industry, 7
Airline marketing, 42–3, 114

Airships, 201
Alcock and Brown, 6
Alternative TV, 199–200, 212
American-English, 17–18
American Express, 49
Anticipating customer requirements, 2, 3, 4, 12
Appointed dealers, 129
Arena advertising, 201
Armchair shopping, 127, 134
ASA Case Report, 187, 188, 222
Ashcanning, 232
Ashtrays, 153
Aspro, 86, 93
Association of Independent Radio Contractors,
  184, 189
Association of Mail Order Publishers, 229
Attitude surveys, 75–6
Audi, 41, 98
Audio cassettes, 210
Audit Bureau of Circulations, 59, 210
Australia, 9
Automobile Association, The, 49
Availability of goods/services, 15

Bahrain, 205
Banded packs. 160, 164
Bangladesh, 4, 112, 48
Bar coding, Preface, 265
BARB, 60, 65, 102, 186, 210, 211, 212
Barbados, 29
Bazaars, 113, 128
BBC External Services, 258, 272
Below-the-line media, 57–8, 61, 176, 202–3, 212
  calendars, 207–8
  diaries, 208
  direct mail, 49, 57, 132, 135, 176, 203–4
  exhibitions, 57, 64, 146, 176
  point-of-sale material, 51, 55, 57, 149–55, 165, 206,
  207
  print, 207
  sponsorship, 42, 57, 181, 186, 1978, 208–9
Bemrose, 207
Bernstein, David, 58
Betting, Gaming and Lotteries Act 1976, 236
Bic pen, 41
Big Bang, 215
Billboards, 155
Bingo, 157
Bisto, 40
Black market, 61
Blind product test, 78
Blister packs, 86, 91
Blue Cross matches, 159
Borden, Neil, 33
Brand,
  image, 40
  loyalty, 28, 146, 164
  names, 34, 39, 40, 45, 221
Brand barometer survey, 77–8
Branding, 94103
British Code of Advertising Practice, 12, 26, 179,
  184, 187, 189, 232
British Direct Marketing Association, 229
British Overseas Trade Board, 252, 256–7, 272

British Rate and Data, 186
British Satellite Broadcasting, Preface, 136, 185, 200
British Telecom, 58, 135, 175, 199
Brokers, 42, 127–8, 247
Brooke Bond, PG Tips, 45, 94, 101
BSB, Preface, 136, 185, 200
Bubble packs, 90
Bucket shops, 114
Buffer stocks, 57, 65, 167
Building Societies Act 1987, 133
Bulk-buying purchases, 45, 124, 125
Buzby, 58
Buzz words, 193, 212
Buyer's market, 2
Buying patterns, 25, 29, 46
  process, 15
  purposes, 212
  stimuli, 22–5, 32

Cable TV, 190
CACI Market Analysis, 137–9, 140
  Monica, 139, 140
Cadbury Schweppes, Cadbury's, 39, 40, 41, 45, 93, 94
Cadillac, 44
Calendars, 207
CAM Education Foundation, 187, 270
Camera-ready copy, 261
Cannes Film Festival, 58
Canon, 208
Cans, 90
Caribbean, 20, 29–30, 202
Carrier bags, 153, 210
Carry packs, sacks, 91
Cartons, 89–90, 93
Cartoons, 62, 80, 143, 201
Cash-and carry warehouse, 124–5, 131
Cash awards, 159–60
Cash economy, Preface, 6, 10–11
Cash mats, 153
Cash refunds, 144
Cash tokens, 28
Cash vouchers, 157, 163–4
Catalogue selling, 49, 127, 133, 135, 136
Caveat emptor, 144
CCN Systems Ltd, 137
Ceefax, 64, 264
Census figures, 12, 75, 84, 137–9, 253
Central Office of Information, 258, 272
Chain stores, 40, 45, 253
Champagne, 41
Chapman, Russell, 187
Characteristics, sample, 69
Charge cards, 49, 117–18, 127
Charity marketing, 49, 135, 203
Charity schemes, 157
Chartered Institute of Marketing, Preface, 2, 3, 5, 14
Cherry-picker, 30
Cheskin, Louis, 79
Chevrolet Corvair, 27
Children's contests, 162
China, Chinese, 11, 29, 46, 94, 96, 111, 197, 201, 202, 250, 252, 255
Chocolate marketing, 45
Cigarette cards, 156–7
Cinema advertising, 57, 202
  mobile, 202
  overseas, 202

Circulation, 59, 72, 210
  international, 197
Clocks, advertising, 150, 152
Clutter Code 1962, 228
CLS, 139, 140
Coal, 36
Coca-Cola, 4, 11, 41, 87, 93, 94, 98, 126, 249
Codes of practice, 228–9
Cognitive dissonance, 30, 32
Cold calling, 51
Colour coding, 87
Colour schemes, 41, 235
Comet, 125
Commando salespeople, 168, 169
Commission, salespeople's, 51
Commission system, 184–5
Common law, 230, 239
Community radio, 185
Community viewing, 200
Company names, 40
Competitions, prize, 160–2, 236–7, 239
Computer graphics, 2
Computer in marketing, 260–8
Computerised photo-typesetting, 261–2, 267
Conferences, 246
Congeries, 31, 32, 130
Consonance, 30
Consumer behaviour, 25–6
Consumer Credit Act 1974, 230
Consumer durables, 32, 37, 141, 207
Consumer location system, 139, 140
Consumer panels, 77, 78, 79, 84
Consumer protection, 25, 119, 237
Consumer Protection Act 1987, 119, 237
Consumer sovereignty, 26
Consumerism, 26, 238
Consumers' Association, 26
Containers, 48
Contract, law of, 231–2, 239
Controlled circulation, 196, 212, 243, 248
Convenience goods, 30, 32
Co-operative stores, 128
Coppers, 36
Copy platform, 174, 183, 192
  techniques, 193–4
Copy testing, pre-testing, 58–9, 60, 65, 68
Copyright, Designs and Patents Act 1988, 230, 233–5
Copywriter, 176, 182, 183, 192, 204
Cornhill Insurance Company, 42
Corning Glass, 144, 147
Corporate and financial PR, 34, 53
Corporate identity, 41, 53, 147
Cost-per-conversion, 61
Cost-per-reply, 61
Cost-per-thousand, 186, 210
Coupon survey, 79
Coupons, 136
Cowrie shell, 20
CPC, 96–7
Credibility, 53, 165, 186, 218
Credit cards, 21, 117–18, 126, 133, 134, 136
Credit sales, 119
Credit traders, 129
Credit-worthiness, agency, 184
Cricket, test, 42
Crowners, 153, 169

Currys, 112
Customer behaviour, 15–32
Customer clubs, 64, 145
Customer interest and loyalty, 35, 63–4
Cycle of advertising development, 191, 212
Cyprus Airways, 100

Daily Times (Nigeria), 196
Dart mats, score boards, 154
Databases, 134, 135, 1379, 181, 203, 262–3
Datsun, 95, 96, 107, 252
Day-after recall tests, 59, 60
Dealer audit, 55, 60, 79, 84
Dealer contests, 162
Dealer loaders, 167
Dealer relations, 149, 162, 166–9, 222–3, 226
Debenhams, 40
Debugging, 266
Decision-making unit, 173, 190
Deduplication, 203
Defamation, law of, 232, 239
Definitions,
   above-the-line, 57
   advertising, 57, 172
   after-market, 141
   below-the-line, 57
Dealer relations, 149
Direct response marketing, 132
Distribution, 121
   market research, 66
   marketing, 1, 2
   marketing mix, 33
   marketing research, 66
   point-of-sale, 149
   public relations, 216, 217, 218
   sales promotion, 61, 149
   selling, 1
Demographic-geographic neighbourhood systems, 137–140
Department of Trade and Industry, 205
Department stores, 43, 128, 177
Desk research, 67, 68, 75, 219
Desk-top projectors, 51, 168
Diaries, research, 77
   as gifts, 208
Dichotomous questions, 82
Dichter, Dr. Ernst, 22, 79
Diner Club, 49
Direct mail, 49, 57, 132, 135, 176, 212, 243–4, 262
   timing of, 203
Direct response marketing, Preface, 21, 25, 49, 116–7, 121, 122, 126, 130, 132–40, 144, 176
   media of, 135–7
   reasons for, 133–4
   targeting, 133, 137–9
Direct selling, 121, 129, 131
Directories, 244
Discount stores, 25, 125
Discretionary income, 108–9
Discussion group, 60, 801, 252
Dispensers, (display), 153
Dispensers, ejectors, (packs), 91
Dispersion theory, 28–9
Display material, 51, 149
Display outers, 90, 153, 169
Display stands, 152–3
Dissonance reduction, 30

Distribution, 34, 48–9, 121–31
   adequate, 122–3, 165, 173
   channels of, 49, 65, 121, 247
   cycle, 121–2, 131
   industrial goods, 247–8
Distributors, 123–30
   overseas, 253
Door-to-door distribution, 136
Door transfers, 51
Doorstep selling, 121, 123, 129
Doorstoppers, 136
Draper, Gordon, 11
Dripmats, coasters, 153, 210
Dummy packs, 151
Dump bins, 151
Dumping, 12
Dunlop, 39
Dustbin audits, checks, 78

EAN, 265
Earhart, Amelia, 6
Economical products, 47
Economist Intelligence Unit, 252
EFTPS, 265–6
EIBIS International Ltd, 258, 272
Elf, 98, 99, 265
Emotions, 18–19
Employee-employer relations, 53–4, 214
Empty nesters, 80
EPOS, 265
Ethics, advertising, 186–8
   public relations, 228–9
Eurobrands, 99, 249
Eurotunnel, 216, 249
Eversheds, 207
Exchange process, 20, 32
Exhibitions, 57, 64, 146, 176
   kinds of, 205–6
   local, 55
   overseas, 256–7
   trade, 57, 204, 244
Export Credits Guarantee Department, 257
Export marketing, 143–4, 249–59

Facia boards, 154, 172
Factors, 128, 131
Fair dealing, 233
Fairy Snow, 163–4
Family, extended, 9
   nuclear, 9
Fast moving consumer goods, 24, 30, 37, 57, 72, 141, 146, 170, 173
Feature articles, 147, 226, 245
Festinger, Leon, 30
Financial services, marketing of, 20–1, 39, 133
Financial Services Act 1986, 133
Financial Times, 42, 72
First Bank of Nigeria, 40, 100
First Interstate, 266
Flags, 155
Flash packs, 119, 160, 164, 169
Fleet Street, Preface
Foil wrapping, 91
Folder technique, 58
Ford, Henry, 2
   Motor, 40, 94, 97, 98, 107
Four Ps, Preface, 33

Franchising, 126
Free gifts, samples, 158, 159, 207, 213
Free newspapers, 136, 178–9, 212
Freemans, 132
Friends of the Earth, 27
Fulfilment houses, 133
Fyffes banana label, 41

Gallup Poll, 2, 76
General Motors, 96
Generic names, 39–40, 97–8, 103
Germany, German products, 3, 6
Get-up, 41, 65, 235, 239
Gift catalogues, 49, 130
Gift coupons, 28, 156
Gillette, 38, 87, 94, 96
Glass containers, 88, 90
Global market, 2512
Gold Block tobacco, 41
Goodwill, 53, 62, 64, 87, 89, 141, 158
Goodyear, 208
Government Statistics, 75
Graf Zeppelin, 6
Grattan Warehouses, 132
Green Revolution, 29
Guarantees, 12, 23, 26, 62, 63, 141, 144
Guinness, 11, 36, 41, 93, 96, 97, 98, 111, 126
Gulf States, 200, 251

Habit buying, 27–8, 46, 61, 141
Halifax Building Society, 40
Halo effect, 99, 103,
Handbook of Consumer Motivation, 79
Harrods, 43
Heinz, H.J, 46
The Hidden Persuaders, 79
High Street redemptions, 157
Hire purchase terms, 119
Honda, 96, 97, 99
Hong Kong, 9, 29, 95–6, 97, 99, 111, 199, 201, 250, 251
Hot air balloons, 201
Hot line columns, 26
Hotelling, Harold, 312
House colour, 41
House journals, external, 64, 147, 196, 226, 246
Hunter, David Stewart, 191, 212
Hypermarket, 25, 85, 106, 124, 150, 165

IBM, 250
Identifying customer requirements, 2, 3, 4, 12
Ilford films, 93
Illuminated displays, 152
Image,
  brand, 40
  corporate, 23, 53, 99, 147
  current, 219
  mirror, 219
  multiple, 223
  product, 34, 65
  study, 767, 84, 218
Import duty, 44
Impulse buying, 44, 61
Incentive to buy, 15
Incentives for salesmen, 51
Independent, The, Preface, 72, 178
Independent Broadcasting Authority, 185, 197

Independent Television Association, 184, 189
Independent Television Authority, 230
Indesit, 250
Indonesia, 9, 11, 94, 200
Industrial marketing, 240–8
Industrial relations, 34, 53–4, 65
Inertia selling, 145
Inflationary spiral, 44
Infoplan, 174
Innovation, 34, 35
Innovator theory, 289, 32, 206
Inserts, 136
Instalment payments, 119
Instincts, 17, 1819, 32
Institute of Practitioners in Advertising, 172, 173, 179, 229, 258, 270
Institute of Public Relations, 216, 270
  Code of Professional Conduct, 228–9, 223, 258
Institute of Sales Promotion, 61, 160–1, 236, 270–1
Instructions, instruction manuals, 62, 143–4
Internal relations, 53–4
Interview,
  depth, 71
  structured, 71
Interviewee, 69
In-theatre testing, 59
ITT Europe, 246

Jaffa, 41
Japan, Japanese products, 3, 7, 9, 956, 143, 201, 238, 251, 252
JICNARS, 59, 72, 102, 186, 210, 211,
JICRAR, 59, 186, 211
Jingle, 192,
Joint ventures, 256,
Journey cycle, 501, 65
Jumbo packs, 160, 169

Kenya, 9, 20, 74, 202, 251
Knocking copy, 232
Kodak, 40, 41, 98
Korea, 9
Kotler, Philip, 33, 239

Laggards, 29
Languages, translations, 62, 143, 144, 201, 249, 254, 258
Laser-printing, 204, 262
Laws relating to advertising, 230
Layout-artist, 183
Lego, 40
Lever Brothers Ltd, 163
Library shots, 235
Life-styles, 5, 12, 26, 29
Lindbergh, 6
Linguaphone, 210
Linkage, 7
Lipman, Maureen, 58
List broker, 135
Littlewoods, 132
Livery, 53, 100
Living laboratory, 78
Lobby Lud, 157
Lockwood, 207
Logotype, 53, 87, 100
London Chamber of Commerce and Industry, Preface, 19, 57, 271, 279, 283

specimen exam paper, 284–6
syllabus, 276–8
London Underground, 201
Loss leaders, 119
Lost literacy, 13, 73
Lottery, 236
Lufthansa, 6
Lyons Quick Brew, 45
Mail drop, 55, 122, 136
Mail-ins, 159, 207
Mail-order, 49, 60, 132–40, 180
Mail Order Publishers Authority, 229
Mailing list, 135, 203, 262–3
Main distributor, 129
Malaysia, 9, 201, 251
Malredemption, 163–4
Market centrality, 8
Market education, 34, 52–3, 62, 145, 215, 225, 227
Market forces, 44
Market location, 266
Market research, 2, 66
Market Research Society, 66, 271
Market segments, Preface, 34, 42–4, 47, 65
Market theory, 7, 14
Market traders, 130
Marketing, 1, 2, 11, 13, 14
Marketing communications, Preface, 40, 221
Marketing concept, 3, 7
Marketing director, agency, 182
Marketing in developing countries, 9–3, 14, 29, 61, 71, 99, 101, 142, 143–4, 155, 196–7, 198, 200
Marketing mix, 3366
20 elements of, 34–5
Marketing Pocket Book, 75
Marketing research, Preface, 12, 34, 38, 66–84, 266
ad hoc, 67
continuous, 67, 68
desk, 67, 68, 75, 219
primary, 67, 84, 253, 259
secondary, 67, 84, 253, 259
Marketing research in developing countries, 71–4, 81, 253
Markets, street, Preface, 1, 25
Marks & Spencer, 40, 94, 125, 128, 144, 210, 223, 252
Marlboro, 208
Mars, 45
Maslow, A.M, 17, 32
Matching halves, 157
Mauritius, 250
Media,
buying, 183
export, 254–5
planning, 183, 212
research, 210–11
schedule, 174, 182, 183, 211–12
Media advertising, 58, 194
research, 58, 5960
Media owner, 178, 185–6, 210
Menu cards, 153
Merchandiser, 165, 169
Merchandising, 149
Metra Consultancy, 252
Metro, Austin, 3, 41
Mexican Statement, The, 218
Middlemen, 110, 122, 125, 127
Midland Bank, 64

Milk powder, 143–4, 155–6
Misleading advertisements, 26
Mobile cinema, 202
exhibitions, 206, 255
Mobiles, 150–1, 169
Models, figures, display, 152
Modern Marketing for Nigeria, 11, 73–4
Monetarist policies, 44
Money off offers, cash premiums, 149, 157, 163–4
Monica, 139, 140
Montgomery Ward, 132
MOSAIC, 137
Mosaic Cyprus Sherry, 57
Motivation and Personality, 17
Motivation research, 79, 81
Motor car marketing, 3, 43, 46, 100, 101, 104–5, 107
Multi-choice questions, 82–3
Multinationals, 250
Multiples, 128

McCarthy, E. Jerome, 33
McCormick, 29, 206
McDougall, William, 17, 18, 32
McIntyre Marketing, 137

Nader, Ralph, 26–7, 32, 238
Names,
acronyms, 102, 103
changing, 100–1
family, 94
generic, 97–8
initials, 101
internationally acceptable, 99, 103
Japanese, 95–6
made-up, 94
personal, 102–3
product, 95
registered, 98
rhythmic, 98
six essentials for new, 98–9, 103
vowels, 96, 98
Naming and branding, 34, 39–40, 48, 94–103, 266
National Opinion Polls, 68, 76
National Vigilance Committee, 186
Nationwide Building Society, 40
Necchi, 250
Needs, 3, 5, 14, 17, 19
Neighbourhood location systems, 133–4, 136, 137–9
Neighbourhood shops, 129
Nestlé, 93, 97
Net sales figures, 59, 210
New Internationalist, 27
New Smoking Mixture, 175
New Zealand, 9
News releases, 64
Newspaper Publishers Association, 180, 184
Newspaper Society, 180, 184
Nicholas Laboratories Ltd, 39
Nielsen, A.C, 2, 68
Nigeria, 1, 5, 9, 11, 25, 29, 40, 62, 73–4, 94, 97, 100, 143, 196, 200, 251, 253
Non-store retailing, 49, 65, 126–7
Notice boards, 54
Nwokoye, Nonyelu G, 11, 73
Nylon, 38

Obsolescence, 62, 142

Off-the-page, 133, 135–6
Office of Fair Trading, 26, 184, 229
Office of Population Censuses and Surveys, 74, 137
Olympus camera, 63
Omnibus surveys, 77
On approval, 144
One-piece mailers, 135, 203–4
One-stop shopping, 124, 131
Open-ended questions, 82, 83
Opinion polls, 68, 756, 84, 218
Opportunities to see, 186
Optrex, 41
Oracle, 64, 199, 264
Order of merit questions, 83
Outdoor advertising, 57, 200–1
Outspan, 41
Overseas marketing, 249–59
Own brand, label, 40–1, 125
Oxo, 40, 100

Pack recognition, 85, 202
Package tours marketing, 46, 57
Packaging, 4, 24, 34, 40, 41, 47, 48, 65, 85–93, 222
    cost of, 85–6, 87
    essentials of, 86–7, 93
    face-lifts for, 92, 93
    forms of, 89–91
    materials, 87–9
Packard, Vance, 79–80
Painted bus, 201
Paired comparison test, 78
Pantry check surveys, 77
Parker pen, 41
Party selling, 25, 126
Passing off, 41, 235
Paying for the name, 23, 96
Pelmets, 151
Performing Rights Society, 235
Periodical Publishers Associations, 180, 184
Persil Automatic, 163
Petrol prices, 119
Petrol Prices (Display) Order 1977, 119
Peugeot, 11, 98, 100
Pharmaceuticals, 86, 91
Philatelic Bureau, Post Office, 133
Philips, 96–7
Photographs, copyright of, 234
Picture cards, 28, 156–7
Piggy-backing, 77, 84
PIN, 137, 139
Pinpoint Identified Neighbourhoods, 137, 139
Placards, 153
Plans board, 182
Plastics, 86, 87, 88–9, 90, 91, 93
Play laboratory, 78
Player and Son, John, 206–7, 208
Point-of-sale material, 51, 55, 57, 149–55, 165, 206
    kinds of, 150–55
    value of, 149–50
Pollution, 27
Poor man's art gallery, 201
Pop rivets, 40
Population, 69, 75, 84
Population triangle, Preface, 6, 910, 14
Post Office, 133, 136
Postcodes, 137
Postal questionnaires, 79

Posters, 150, 151, 180, 186, 201, 212
PPM Radio Waves, 198
PR consultancy, 223–5, 227
    department, 223–4, 227
PR planning model, 219–221
PR transfer process, 215–16
Premium offers, 28, 61, 122, 149, 157, 158, 164–5
Press relations, 226
Prestel, 64
Price, 24, 44, 134
    bashing, 113
    bracket, 24
    competitive, 112
    controls, 44, 106, 114, 120
    creaming, 105
    discounted, 44–5, 113
    discrimination, 109–10
    distorted, 111, 120
    divisionary, 112
    double,. 113, 120
    dumping, 112–3, 120
    economic, 106–7
    geographic, 114
    guaranteed, 115, 120
    in relation to delivery, 109–11
    inelastic, 105
    last, 113
    legal aspects of, 118–9
    list, 109
    manufacturer's recommended retail price, 109, 118, 120
    market, 106, 107–8
    penetration, 112, 120
    plateau, 111
    presentation of, 117
    psychological, 106, 108
    reduced, 118, 119
    rings, 113
    skimming, 105
    stability, 111, 120
    subsidised, 114, 120
    twenty-one kinds of, 115–6
    wholesale, 45, 110, 125
Price Commission Act 1977, 113
Prices, researching of, 116–7
Pricing, 34, 44–5, 47, 65, 85, 104–115
Printed envelopes, 204
Printing processes, 178
    flexography, 178
    laser-printing, 204, 262
    letterpress, 178
    lithography, 178, 261–2
    photogravure, 178
    web-offset-litho, 178–9
Prizes, 160–1, 169
Proctor & Gamble Ltd, 164
Producer, TV, 183, 190
Product image, 34, 41–2
Product life cycle, 34, 35–9, 45
    continuous, 36–7,
    leapfrog effect, 37
    recycled, 37
    staircase effect, 38–9
    standard, 35–6, 65
Product mix, 33, 34, 45–6, 65
Product planning, 47
    pre-testing, 54, 78

recall, 147
Production manager, agency, 183
Profitability, Preface, 2, 5, 8, 12
Profits, maximising, 8, 14
Proliferation, 46–7, 65
Promises, 63, 144
Propaganda, 218
Psychodrawing, 80
Psychographic types, 80
Public relations, 33–4, 42, 57, 63–4, 147, 174–5,
    214–227
    areas of communication, 214–15
    assessment of results, 220
    budget, 220
    corporate and financial, 34
    industrial, 245–7, 248
Public Relations Consultants Association, 229, 272
    Code of Consultancy Practice, 229
publicity, Preface, 33
publics, 217, 220
purchasing power, 15, 20

quadrant journey cycle, 51
qualitative research, 81, 84, 253
quantitative research, 81, 84
questionnaire, 68, 78, 79, 80, 81–3
    checking, tabulation, 83
    style, 81
    types of question, 812
quota sample, 69, 70, 71, 77, 84

Radio, local, 55, 57, 185, 197–8
Radio Authority, 197, 230
Radio Times, 147, 208
Random numbers, 70
Random sample. 69–70, 77, 84
Rank, Hovis, McDougall, 101
Rantzen, Esther, 26, 235
Rate card, 186
Rationalisation, 34, 47, 65
Reader's Digest, 210
Readership, 59, 210
    in Kenya, 74
    of British press, class, 72
Reading and noting tests, 60
Recall test, 59, 60, 83
Reckitt Colman, 176
Recognition, agency, 179, 184–5, 190
Recommendation, 234
Refunds, cash, 63
Registered names, 40
Remuneration, salesmen, 51, 65
Rentokil, 98, 101, 104, 144, 221, 246
Reputation, 23, 53
Resale Prices Act 1976, 119
Research and development, 35
Respondent, 69, 77, 80, 81
Restrictive Trade Practices Act 1976, 230
Retail price maintenance, 113
Robotics, 8
Role-playing, 16–17, 19, 23
Roll-on sticks, 91
Rolls-Royce, 41, 44, 95, 99, 175
Rowntree, 45, 94, 99
Royal Mail, 139
Royal Mint, 133
Royal Society of Arts, Preface

Russia, 7, 201, 252

Saab, 250
Saatchi and Saatchi, 180, 192
Sachets, 90
Sainsbury's, 40, 94, 123, 124
Sales force, 34, 502
    industrial, 2412
    relations, 223
Sales letter, 204
Sales literature, 154, 207
Sales organisation, 50
    bulletings, 52
    contests, 51
    literature, 57
    manager, 50, 52
    manual, 52
    meetings, 52
    presenter, 51
    reports, 52
    trainer, 50
sales promotion, 28, 34, 55, 57, 122, 145, 149, 176,
    206–7
    gifts, 158, 159, 207
    overseas, 155
    problems with, 162–5, 169
    reasons for, 61
schemes, 156–65
sales staff training, 166–7
sample, free, 158
    interval, 69
    probability, 69
    quota, 69, 70, 71, 77, 84, 253
    random, 69–70, 77, 84, 253
    random walk, location, 71
    research, 69
    size, 70, 80
    stratified random, 71
Sampling,
    area, 70
    cluster, 70
    frame, 69
    multi-stage, 70
    points, 70
Satellite television, Preface, 13, 99, 108, 136,
    199–200, 211, 249
Satisficing, 89
Satisfying customer requirements, Preface, 2, 3, 4,
    12, 26, 856
Scandinavia, 250
Schick razors, 38
Scottish Widows Fund, 99
Sears Roebuck, 132
Self-liquidating premium offers, 158, 1645
Self-regulatory controls, 18688, 2289
Self-service, 123
Selfridge, Gordon, 26
Seller's market, 1, 13
Selling, 1, 11, 13, 14, 502, 66
Selling-in, 123
Semantic differential questions, 82, 83
Seminars, 246
Servicing, 623
Share of voice, 60
Shareholder lists, 135
Shelf-edging strips, 51, 153
Shift surveys, 756

Shopping, 38
Shoppers, 112
Shopping characteristics, 30
Shopping goods, 30
Shopping habits, changes in, 123
Shopping malls, plazas, precincts, Preface, 25, 124
Shopping without shops, 132, 136, 140
Shops, location of, 31–2
Showcards, 51, 150
Signs, 154, 155
Silver market, 80
Simon, H.A, 8
Sinclair C3, 175
Singapore, 9, 29, 94, 124, 251
Single European Market, 207, 250
Sky Channel, Preface, 185, 200
Slander of goods, 232, 239
Slide presentations, 145, 147, 246
Slip editions, 55
Slogans, 96, 102
Social grades, 69, 71, 84
Socio-economic groups, 71, 72, 73, 84
  in developing countries, 73, 74
Sole traders, 130
Sotheby's, 25, 108
South Africa, 9
Space-broker, 178
Spare parts, 62, 142
Speciality goods, 30, 31, 32
Spillers, 45
Spitting Image, 175
Sponsorship, 42, 57, 181, 197–8, 213, 246
St. Ivel Gold, 57, 102, 105, 221
Standard error, 70
Standardisation, 34, 47, 65
Statute law, 231, 239
Stork margarine, 40, 98
Storyboard, TV, 183
Strapline, 193, 212
Stuffer, 62
Sun, The , 42, 72, 147, 196
Super Profiles, 137, 139
Supply of Goods (Implied Terms Act) 1973, 145
Supranationals, 250
Swan Vestas, 41, 93, 97
Swarfega, 102
symbol groups, 125

Taiwan, 9, 250
Tallymen, 129
Target Group Index, 139, 212
Tea marketing, 45
research, 74
Teledata, 263
Telemarketing, 25, 49, 126, 130, 136–7, 181
Telephone questionnaires, 78
Telephone selling, 127, 136–7, 181, 263–4
Teletext, 199, 264
Television, commercial, 55, 57, 58, 183, 185, 189, 198–200
Tesco, 41, 123
Test-marketing, 34, 54–6, 65
Thailand, 25
That's Life, 26
Thoresen car ferries, 174
Toblerone, 45
Tracking studies, 60

Trade, technical;, professional magazines, 57, 195–6, 243
Trade characters, 159
Trade Descriptions Act 1968, 118, 237, 239
Trade marks, 39
Trade Marks Act, 97
Trade names, 39, 978, 235
Trade terms, 445, 122, 166
Traffic-free shopping areas, Preface, 25, 124
Transportation advertising, 2001
Trinidad, 9, 11, 74, 100, 124, 251
Tubes, 91
TV Times, 55, 147, 157, 208, 220
TVUS, 211
Twenty-eight day clause, 118, 120
Typhoo, 45
Typographers, 183
Typography, 53, 204

UK Press Gazette, 40, 187
Understanding, 215, 216
Universal News Services, 2589, 272
Universe, 69
USA, 2, 7, 26, 29, 132, 147, 155

Value added tax, 44, 111
Van den Bergh, 40
Variety stores, 128
Vending machines, 25, 1256, 131
Video magazines, 54
Videotapes, cassettes, 64, 145, 147, 166, 189, 199, 200, 210, 226, 246
Viewdata, 121, 199, 264
Visual literacy, 202
Visualiser, 183
Voluntary controls, 1868, 2289
Volvo, 250
Voter's lists, 12
Vowels, 96, 98

Wants, 3, 4, 14
War On Want, 27
Weekend magazines, Preface, 55
Weston Bancorporation, 266
Which? reports, 26
Wholesalers, 122, 125, 127
Wholesale prices, 45, 110, 125
Wilkinson razors, 38
Window bills, 52
Window stickers, transfers, 153
Wine, origin of, 237–8
Wire stands, 151
Woolworth, 40, 94, 128
Women's magazines, 178
Woopies, 80
Working models, 152, 166
Works visits, 167, 245
World In Action, 26
Wrapping paper, 154

Yuppies, 80

Zambia, 101, 196
Zenith media agency, 180
Zimbabwe, 9, 94
Zoned launches, 567